101 Labs
CompTIA Network+

Hands-on Practical Labs for the
CompTIA Network+ Exam (N10-007)

Paul Browning
(LLB Hons), CCNP, MCSE, Net+, A+

https://www.101labs.net

ISBN-13: 9781726841290

Published by:
Reality Press Ltd.
15 Triumph Gardens
UK
NN56YH

LEGAL NOTICE
The advice in this book is designed to help you achieve the standard of the CompTIA Network+ engineer. A Network+ engineer is able to carry out basic network installations and troubleshooting. Before you carry out more complex operations, it is advisable to seek the advice of experts or your equipment vendor.

The practical scenarios in this book are meant to illustrate only a technical point and should be used only on your privately owned equipment, never on a live network. They are not to be taken as installation instructions, network design templates, or configuration guidelines.

About the Author

Paul Browning

Paul Browning worked as a police officer in the UK for 12 years before changing careers and becoming a helpdesk technician. He passed several IT certifications and began working for Cisco Systems doing WAN support for large enterprise customers.

He started an IT consulting company in 2002 and helped to design, install, configure, and troubleshoot global networks for small to large companies. He started teaching IT courses soon after that and through his classroom courses, online training, and study guides has helped tens of thousands of people pass their IT exams and enjoy successful careers in the IT industry.

In 2006 Paul started the online IT training portal www.howtonetwork.com, which has grown to become one of the leading IT certification websites.

In 2013 Paul moved to Brisbane with his family. In his spare time he plays the guitar, reads, drinks coffee, and practices Brazilian jiu-jitsu.

Table of Contents

Introduction–101 Labs

Welcome to your 101 Labs book.

When I started teaching IT courses back in 2002, I was shocked to discover that most training manuals were almost exclusively dedicated to theoretical knowledge. Apart from a few examples of commands to use or configuration guidelines, you were left to plow through without ever knowing how to apply what you learned to live equipment or to the real world.

Fast forward 16 years and little has changed. I still wonder how, when around 50% of your exam marks are based on hands-on skills and knowledge, most books give little or no regard to equipping you with the skills you need to both pass the exam and then make money in your chosen career as a network, security, or cloud engineer (or whichever career path you choose).

101 Labs is NOT a theory book: it's here to transform what you have learned in your study guides into valuable skills you will be using from day one on your job as a network engineer. I don't teach DHCP, for example; instead, I show you how to configure a DHCP server, which addresses you shouldn't use, and which parameters you can allocate to hosts. If the protocol isn't working, I show you what the probable cause is. Sound useful? I certainly hope so.

I choose the most relevant parts of the exam syllabus and use free software or free trials to walk you through configuration and troubleshooting commands step by step. As your confidence grows, I increase the difficulty level. If you want to be an exceptional IT engineer, you can make your own labs up, add other technologies, try to break them, fix them, and do it all over again.

101 COMPTIA NETWORK+ LABS

The Network+ exam is probably the most useful exam in the IT industry. When I started out studying for IT exams in 2001, the only exams available to equip myself with a strong foundation for an IT career were Microsoft Networking Essentials (now expired) and a new exam called CompTIA Network+.

The Network+ exam equips you with all the necessary knowledge you need in order to work with other IT professionals and work in the IT industry. You learn TCP/IP, security, networking protocols and standards, best practices, subnetting and IP addressing, IPv6, troubleshooting tools and software, security, wireless, routing protocol basics, and much more.

CompTIA presumes around 9–12 months of on-the-job experience for all of its exams, but of course, most of the students who take the exam don't have this. Even if they are working in IT roles, such as in helpdesk or server support, they will have been exposed to only a tiny number of the skills tested in the exam.

Performance-based questions (PBQs) were added to the exam recently. These questions test your configuration and troubleshooting skills and add a new level of complexity to the exam. The only way to answer these types of questions is to have hands-on experience with the protocols and technology listed in the exam syllabus.

My team of experts has carefully reviewed the Network+ (N10-007) exam syllabus and created 101 hands-on labs to prepare you for the exam and give you a head start when you come to work on a live network. By the end of the book, you will have configured more services, protocols, and equipment than most network engineers get to do in five years.

We have tried our best to map to the current syllabus but have also grouped the subjects into the most relevant categories. According to the exam syllabus, many of the topics require only a theoretical understanding (such as NIC teaming), but we show you how to configure them. It's next to impossible to really understand a technology until you configure it. This is the entire concept of the 101 Labs book series.

INSTRUCTIONS

1. Please follow the labs from start to finish. If you get stuck, do the next lab and come back to the problem lab later. There is a good chance you will work out the solution as you gain confidence and experience in configuring the software and using the commands.

2. Before you attempt these labs, please use the free resources for software installation, Packet Tracer advice, and other tips at www.101labs.net/resources

3. Please DO NOT configure these labs on a live network or on equipment belonging to private companies or individuals.

4. You MUST be reading or have read a Network+ study guide. I don't explain any theory in this book; it's all hands-on labs. I presume you know (for example) when you need to use a crossover cable (router to router or PC to router or switch to switch) or a straight-through (PC to switch or router to switch). I don't point this out in most of the network diagrams.

5. For all of the labs on Cisco equipment using Packet Tracer any model of switch and router should work fine. I typically used an 1841 router and 2960 switch. Feel free to try other models which support different interface types. Do this after going through the lab a few times first.

6. In the instructions I enclose commands you need to issue in single quotes (e.g., 'ping 192.168.1.1'), but please don't use them when issuing commands on network equipment.

7. It's impossible for me to give individual support to the thousands of readers of this book (sorry!), so please don't contact me for tech support. Each lab has been tested by several tech editors from beginner to expert.

VIDEO TRAINING

Each 101 Labs book has an associated video training course. You can watch the instructor configure each lab and talk you through the entire process step by step as well as share helpful tips for the real world of IT. Each course also has 200 exam-style questions to prepare you for the real thing. It's certainly not necessary to take use this resource, but if you do, please use the coupon code '101book' at the checkout page to get a big discount as a thank you for buying this book.

https://www.101labs.net

ALSO FROM REALITY PRESS LTD.

Cisco CCNA Simplified
Cisco CCDA Simplified
Cisco CCDP Simplified
Cisco CCNA in 60 Days
IP Subnetting—Zero to Guru

101 Labs—CompTIA A+ (due 2019)
101 Labs—IP Subnetting
101 Labs—Cisco CCNA
101 Labs—Cisco CCNP (due 2019)
101 Labs—Wireshark WCNA (due 2019)

TECH EDITORS

Thanks to all the tech editors who donated their time to check all the labs and give feedback.

Arvinder Singh	Thierry Merle	Terry Buckingham
Steve Quan	John S. Galliano	Ivan Rajic
David Gonzales	Harvey Collman	Sam Gonzales
Beverly Simpson	Gemoh Mal. Tihfon	Jair J. Bolivar
Elmarine Jimenez	James Gross	Sven Claassen
Desmond Rooplal	Ron Myers	Zoran Vujovic
Chris Kaiser	Jeff Echano	Arnold Palmares
Charles Pacheco	Pedro Indio	Bryant Schaper
Iresh Ekanayake	Troy Clayton	Miroslav Milisavljevic
Mohammed Al-Jarrash	Daniel Downs	Tim Peel
Georgia E Jaeger	Sean Smith	Mark Musciano
Ellsworth Wilson	Mark Lehmann	Glen Millard
Samuel N. Taylor	Clyde Hause	Dolan Hoffman
Dante Alarcón	Lee Freeman	James Hill
Tariq Khan	Rodrigo B. Calderon	Frank Faith
Carol Wood	Charlie Burkholder	Erik Stoddard
Mario Rodriguez	Brian Mayle	James T. Marsh
Roy Thelin	Timothy A. Clark	Ian Edwin Armstrong
Ger Juhel	Marcus Herstik	Nic Conroy
John DeGennaro	Paul Willis	Joshua James Prom
Eric Fields	Alexandru Stefan Marinescu	Greg Lord
Desmond Rooplal	Michael A. Sisson	David Gonzales
David Parris	Jim Myers	Faruk Mamaniat
Thomas Roach	Michael J. Moeller	Jasmine Campbell
Simon Shtipelman	Jurijs Scerbinskis	

1.0 Networking Concepts

LAB 1

SSH

Lab Objective:
The objective of this lab exercise is for you to learn and understand how to enable SSH access to a device—in this case, a Cisco router.

Lab Purpose:
It's never a good idea to permit Telnet access to network devices, especially in corporate settings. SSH is a secure way to connect to network devices. In order to configure SSH you need to:

1. Create a hostname.
2. Create a domain name.
3. Generate a crypto key.

Lab Tool:
Packet Tracer

Lab Topology:
Please use the following topology to complete this lab exercise:

192.168.1.0/24

Lab Walkthrough:

Task 1:

Drag two routers onto the canvas. I don't point this out in the labs because I presume you know this from reading your theory books, but connecting routers together requires a crossover cable (because we aren't using a switch). I used 1941 models for this lab, but for most of the others I used 1841 models (which have Fast Ethernet interfaces).

Configure the hostnames on routers Router0 and Router1 as illustrated in the topology. You must always answer no at the start because the routers will drop into a question-and-answer mode in an attempt to self-configure. I'll use R0 and R1 as hostnames. Here is how you do it on Router0: repeat the tasks on the other router, but give the hostname as R1.

```
--- System Configuration Dialog ---

Continue with configuration dialog? [yes/no]: no

Press RETURN to get started!
Router>enable
Router#config t
Enter configuration commands, one per line. End with CNTL/Z.
Router(config)#hostname R0
R0(config)#
```

Task 2:

Add an IP address to each Ethernet interface and 'no shut' them in order to bring them up.

```
R0(config)#interface g0/0
R0(config-if)#ip address 192.168.1.1 255.255.255.0
R0(config-if)#no shut
%LINK-5-CHANGED: Interface GigabitEthernet0/0, changed state to up
```

Over to Router1:

```
R1(config)#interface g0/0
R1(config-if)#ip address 192.168.1.2 255.255.255.0
R1(config-if)#no shut
%LINK-5-CHANGED: Interface GigabitEthernet0/0, changed state to up
R1(config-if)#end
```

Make sure you can ping across the link.

```
R1#ping 192.168.1.1
Type escape sequence to abort.
Sending 5, 100-byte ICMP Echos to 192.168.1.1, timeout is 2 seconds:
```

```
.!!!!
Success rate is 80 percent (4/5), round-trip min/avg/max = 0/0/0 ms
```

Task 3:

Secure Router1 so that it accepts SSH incoming connections. We need to set a domain name and generate keys. As options, we have set retries for the password to 2 attempts and a timeout of 60 seconds if there is no activity.

```
R1#conf t
Enter configuration commands, one per line.  End with CNTL/Z.
R1(config)#ip domain-name 101labs.net
R1(config)#crypto key generate rsa
The name for the keys will be: R1.101labs.net
Choose the size of the key modulus in the range of 360 to 2048 for your
General Purpose Keys. Choosing a key modulus greater than 512 may take
a few minutes.

How many bits in the modulus [512]: 1024
% Generating 1024 bit RSA keys, keys will be non-exportable...[OK]
R1(config)#ip ssh time-out 60
R1(config)#ip ssh authentication-retries 2
R1(config)#line vty 0 15
R1(config-line)#transport input ssh
R1(config-line)#password cisco
R1(config-line)#end
```

Next you can go to the router Telnet lines. There are 16 available lines on most Cisco devices, numbered 0 to 15 inclusive. You need to permit incoming SSH connections on these and 'transport input ssh' above does this.

```
R1#show ip ssh
SSH Enabled - version 1.99
Authentication timeout: 60 secs; Authentication retries: 2
R1#
```

Task 4:

Connect to Router1 from Router0 using SSH. You should be prompted for the password, which, as you can see above, is 'cisco'. You can add a username for the connection, which I've done here. Use the letter 'l' below after 'ssh' not the number 1.

```
R0#ssh -l paul 192.168.1.2
Open
Password:

R1>
```

You can quit the session by holding down the Ctrl + Shift + 6 keys at the same time, then letting go and pressing the X key.

Task 5:

Attempt to telnet from Router0 to Router1 to check that the connection is refused.

```
R0#telnet 192.168.1.2
Trying 192.168.1.2 ...Open

[Connection to 192.168.1.2 closed by foreign host]
R0#
```

Notes:

Almost any model of router will do for this lab. Just make sure you connect the routers with a crossover cable because we aren't using a switch in this lab. Ensure you have watched the video on how Packet Tracer works at **www.101labs.net/resources**.

DNS

Lab Objective:

The objective of this lab exercise is for you to learn and understand how to configure a DNS entry on a generic server and then test it from a host device.

Lab Purpose:

As I'm sure you've learned in your Network+ study guide or video course, DNS allows you to use hostnames in the browser address bar instead of an IP address. You can see how to do this in this lab.

Lab Tool:

Packet Tracer

Lab Topology:

Please use the following topology to complete this lab exercise:

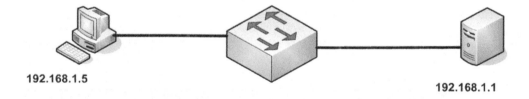

192.168.1.5

192.168.1.1

Lab Walkthrough:

Task 1:

Drag your generic host PC and server onto the canvas and connect the Ethernet ports to any ports on any generic or Cisco switch. You can then add IP addresses via the IP configuration utility. On the PC add the IP address 192.168.1.5. The subnet mask should auto-complete, and the DNS server IP address should be 192.168.1.1.

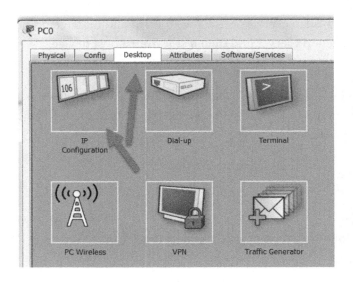

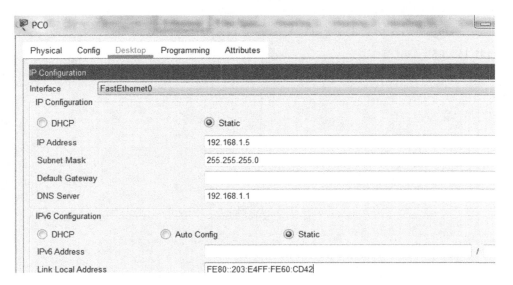

Task 2:

On the server configure the IP address 192.168.1.1 255.255.255.0.

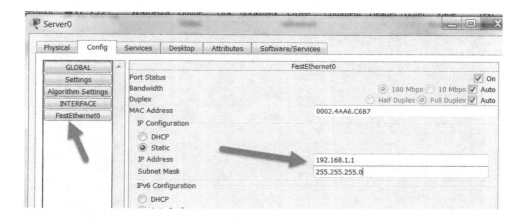

Task 3:

Ensure you can ping the server from the PC.

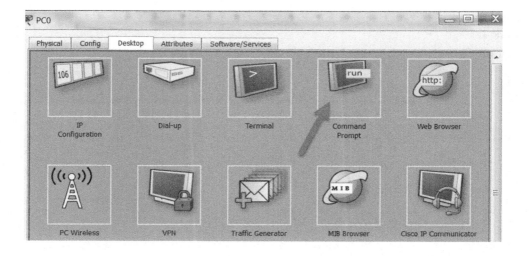

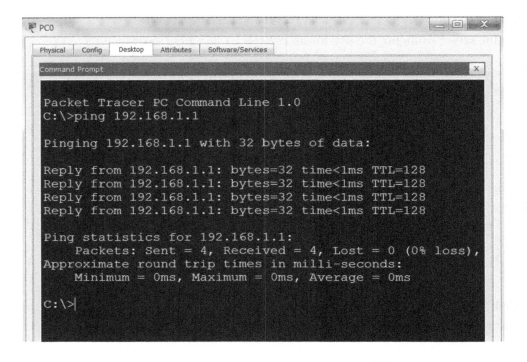

Task 4:

Test on the PC if you can reach the web URL **www.mypage.com**.

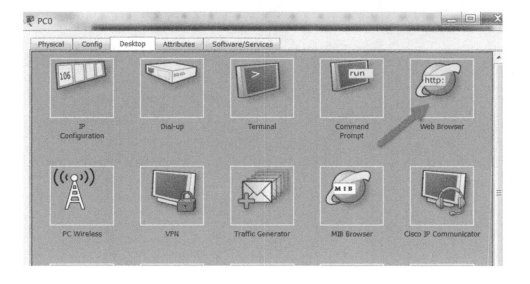

The PC can't resolve this name because there is no DNS entry.

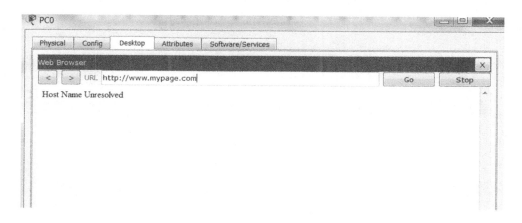

Task 5:

Create a DNS record on the server for this URL and associate it with the server's own IP address. Use the 'DNS' service, add the URL **www.mypage.com**, and hit the 'Add' button. Ensure DNS is turned on. The default record type is 'A Record'.

You have now created an A record for the domain.

Task 6:

Using the web browser on the PC, enter the domain name **www.mypage.com**. It should resolve this time.

Note:

Remember to input the DNS server IP address on the host as per step 1.

LAB 3

Telnet

Lab Objective:

The objective of this lab exercise is for you to learn and understand how to enable Telnet access to a device—in this case, a Cisco router.

Lab Purpose:

Telnet is one protocol you can use to remotely connect to network devices. It's not recommended for use in commercial environments due to the fact that the session information is not encrypted.

Lab Tool:

Packet Tracer

Lab Topology:

Please use the following topology to complete this lab exercise:

192.168.1.0/24

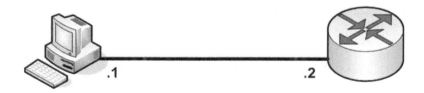

Lab Walkthrough:

Task 1:

Connect a generic PC to a Cisco router. Any model with an Ethernet interface will do fine. Then configure IP addresses on either side and ping across the link.

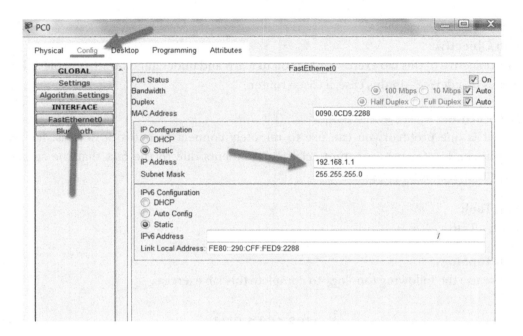

```
Press RETURN to get started!
Router>enable
Router#config t
Router(config)#interface g0/0
Router(config-if)#ip address 192.168.1.2 255.255.255.0
Router(config-if)#no shut
Router(config-if)#end
Router#
%SYS-5-CONFIG_I: Configured from console by console

Router#ping 192.168.1.1

Type escape sequence to abort.
Sending 5, 100-byte ICMP Echos to 192.168.1.1, timeout is 2 seconds:
.!!!!
Success rate is 80 percent (4/5), round-trip min/avg/max = 0/0/0 ms
```

Task 2:

Configure the router to permit incoming Telnet sessions. Routers use virtual terminal lines for these; they are referred to as VTY, and there are usually 16, numbered 0 to 15.

```
Router#conf t
Enter configuration commands, one per line. End with CNTL/Z.
Router(config)#line vty 0 15
Router(config-line)#transport input ?
all All protocols
none No protocols
ssh TCP/IP SSH protocol
telnet TCP/IP Telnet protocol
Router(config-line)#transport input telnet
Router(config-line)#password cisco
Router(config-line)#end
```

Task 3:

Test your connection by telnetting from the PC to the router. You should be challenged for the password. We don't have an enable password, so don't worry about going into that mode.

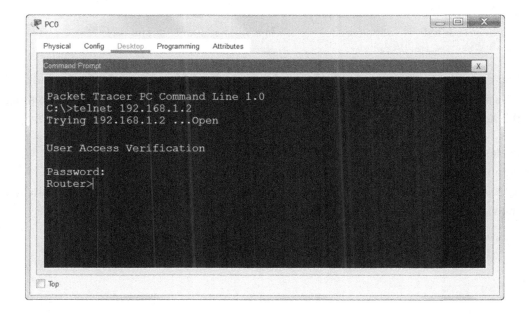

Task 4:

As an option, you can issue the 'show line' command on the router to see which Telnet line the incoming connection was allocated to.

```
Router#show line
Tty Line Typ Tx/Rx A Roty AccO AccI Uses Noise Overruns Int
*  0  0  CTY  -  -  -  -  0 0 0/0  -
1  1  AUX 9600/9600  -  -  -  -  0 0 0/0  -
*  132 132 VTY  -  -  -  -  2 0 0/0  -
133 133 VTY  -  -  -  -  0 0 0/0  -
134 134 VTY  -  -  -  -  0 0 0/0  -
135 135 VTY  -  -  -  -  0 0 0/0  -
136 136 VTY  -  -  -  -  0 0 0/0  -
137 137 VTY  -  -  -  -  0 0 0/0  -
138 138 VTY  -  -  -  -  0 0 0/0  -
139 139 VTY  -  -  -  -  0 0 0/0  -
140 140 VTY  -  -  -  -  0 0 0/0  -
141 141 VTY  -  -  -  -  0 0 0/0  -
142 142 VTY  -  -  -  -  0 0 0/0  -
143 143 VTY  -  -  -  -  0 0 0/0  -
144 144 VTY  -  -  -  -  0 0 0/0  -
145 145 VTY  -  -  -  -  0 0 0/0  -
146 146 VTY  -  -  -  -  0 0 0/0  -
147 147 VTY  -  -  -  -  0 0 0/0  -
Line(s) not in async mode -or- with no hardware support:
3-131
```

You can quit the session from the PC to the router by holding down the Ctrl + Shift + 6 keys at the same time (in your PC console session window), then letting go and pressing the X key.

Notes:

Almost any model of router will do for this lab. Just make sure you connect the PC with a crossover cable because we aren't using a switch in this lab. Ensure you have watched the video on how Packet Tracer works at **www.101labs.net/resources**.

Network Time Protocol

Lab Objective:

The objective of this lab exercise is for you to learn and understand how to enable an NTP server and configure a device to obtain its clock time from the server. In this case, a Cisco router gets its clock from the server.

Lab Purpose:

NTP servers allow the internet as we know it to function. The NTP master servers receive more hits per day than Google (although of course all those hits are asking, 'What time is it?').

Note that for this lab I used an 1841 model router, which automatically boots with the below IOS image. If you have issues with any commands, please use the same model. A 'show version' command displays your IOS version. We cover changing the IOS version in the TFTP lab.

"flash:c1841-advipservicesk9-mz.124-15.T1.bin"

Lab Tool:

Packet Tracer

Lab Topology:

Please use the following topology to complete this lab exercise:

192.168.1.0/24

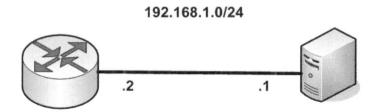

.2   .1

Lab Walkthrough:

Task 1:

Connect a generic server to a Cisco router using a crossover cable. Any model with an Ethernet interface will do fine. Then configure IP addresses on either side and ping across the link.

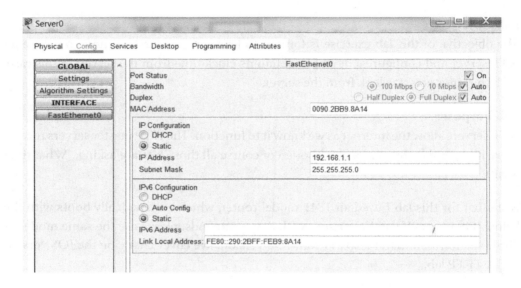

```
Press RETURN to get started!
Router>enable
Router#config t
Router(config)#interface g0/0
Router(config-if)#ip address 192.168.1.2 255.255.255.0
Router(config-if)#no shut
Router(config-if)#end
Router#
%SYS-5-CONFIG_I: Configured from console by console

Router#ping 192.168.1.1

Type escape sequence to abort.
Sending 5, 100-byte ICMP Echos to 192.168.1.1, timeout is 2 seconds:
.!!!!
Success rate is 80 percent (4/5), round-trip min/avg/max = 0/0/0 ms
```

Task 2:

Check the clock time on the router. You will see that it's set to an internal time and is out-of-date.

```
Router#show clock
*0:1:32.502 UTC Mon Mar 1 1993
```

Task 3:

Configure the router to obtain its clock time from the server.

```
Router#config t
Router(config)#ntp server 192.168.1.1
Router(config)#end
Router#
```

Task 4:

Configure the server to give the time via NTP. It should take the time and date from your system clock.

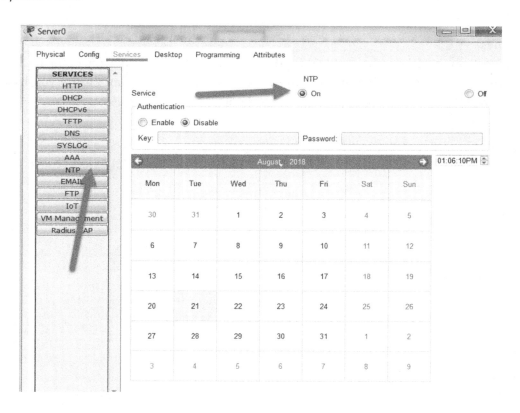

Task 5:

It may take a minute for the router clock to be updated. You can then input two NTP show commands. You can see the server IP address is used for the NTP source.

```
Router#show ntp associations

address ref clock st when poll reach delay offset disp
~192.168.1.1 127.127.1.1 1 10 16 1 1.00 803912199172.00 0.00
* sys.peer, # selected, + candidate, - outlyer, x falseticker, ~
configured
Router#show ntp status
Clock is synchronized, stratum 16, reference is 192.168.1.1
nominal freq is 250.0000 Hz, actual freq is 249.9990 Hz, precision is
2**24
reference time is 0EE1CFA7.0000007B (1:57:59.123 UTC Thu Feb 11 2044)
clock offset is 1.00 msec, root delay is 0.00 msec
root dispersion is 14.13 msec, peer dispersion is 0.00 msec.
loopfilter state is 'CTRL' (Normal Controlled Loop), drift is -
0.000001193 s/s system poll interval is 4, last update was 10 sec ago.
Router#show clock
13:1:39.866 UTC Tue Aug 21 2018
```

Notes:

Almost any model of router will do for this lab. Just make sure you connect the routers with a crossover cable because we aren't using a switch in this lab. Ensure you have watched the video on how Packet Tracer works at www.101labs.net/resources.

DHCP

Lab Objective:

Learn how DHCP servers allocate IP information.

Lab Purpose:

The vast majority of IP networks use DHCP to allocate IP information to hosts. Here we'll configure a scope of addresses and other IP information to be allocated.

Lab Tool:

Packet Tracer

Lab Topology:

Please use the following topology to complete this lab exercise:

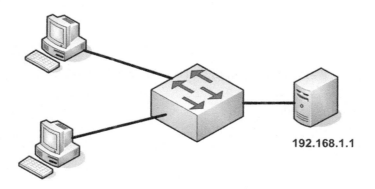

192.168.1.1

Lab Walkthrough:

Task 1:

Connect a generic server to a Cisco switch using straight-through cables. You will add an IP address to the server but not to the host PCs, which will be using DHCP.

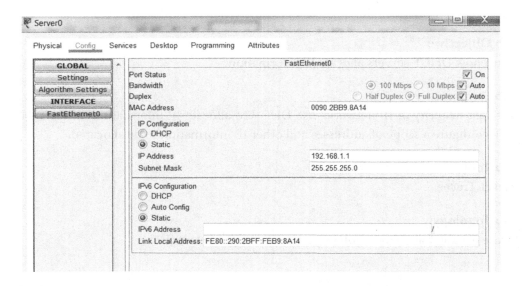

Task 2:

Configure the DHCP information on the server. Allocate the following:

Address start—192.168.1.2
Subnet mask—255.255.255.0
Pool name—101Pool

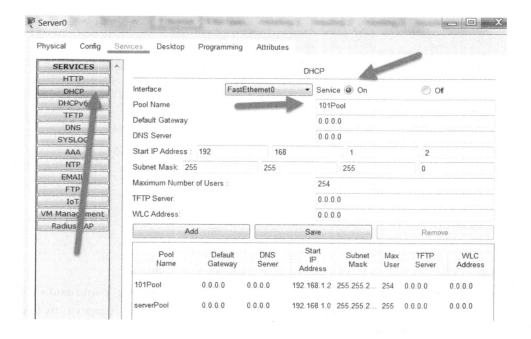

Task 3:

Configure the hosts to obtain information via DHCP. Here is how to do it on one of the hosts.

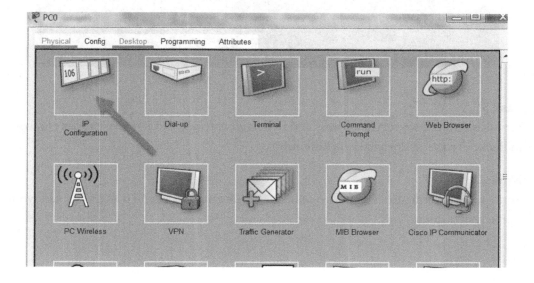

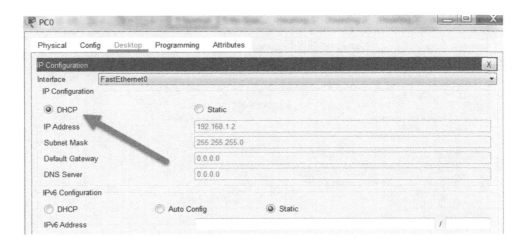

Task 4:

Check the configuration has been applied by issuing the 'ipconfig' command on the hosts. Here it is on one of the hosts. If you hover your mouse over the image of any device in Packet Tracer, you will also see the IP configuration settings.

```
C:\>ipconfig

FastEthernet0 Connection:(default port)

    Link-local IPv6 Address..........: FE80::200:CFF:FE11:C9A8
    IP Address.....................: 192.168.1.3
    Subnet Mask....................: 255.255.255.0
    Default Gateway................: 0.0.0.0
```

Task 5:

I tried adding a DNS server address and IP default gateway, but it doesn't appear to work in Packet Tracer. It does have its limitations.

Note:

You can also configure a router to allocate IP information via DHCP as I'm sure your home router does.

LAB 6

TCP

Lab Objective:
Learn how to recognize a TCP packet.

Lab Purpose:
TCP is the first part of the naming convention for the entire TCP/IP suite. It enables all connection-oriented services and protocols to run over networks such as Telnet, FTP, and some routing protocols, such as BGP.

Lab Tool:
VirtualBox and Wireshark/Putty—or your home PC / Putty

Lab Topology:
You can run Wireshark on your home PC just as easily, so feel free to do that. I've installed it on a VM Windows 10 machine and installed Putty, which is a Telnet/SSH client. You can download Putty from https://putty.org/. It will make using Telnet much easier because most client software disables it by default.

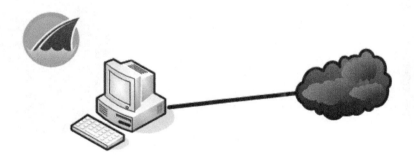

Lab Walkthrough:

Task 1:
Install Putty onto your device.

Task 2:

You may find using Telnet to access other devices on your network a bit tricky, so I checked on Google for hosts that permit Telnet. I found **https://www.telnet.org/htm/places.htm** and tried some of the suggestions there. The list may change, so your first attempt may fail.

Task 3:

Boot Wireshark on your main PC (the one you will be doing the testing from) and check the correct interface is the one being monitored. Click on the interface name to open the capture window.

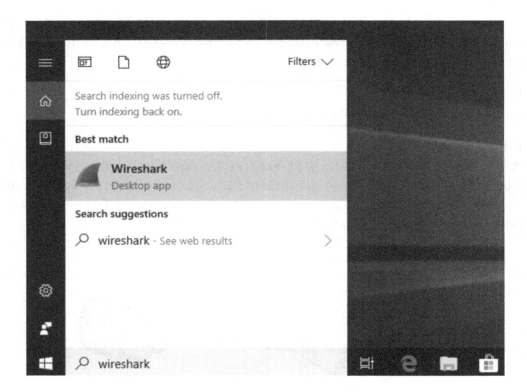

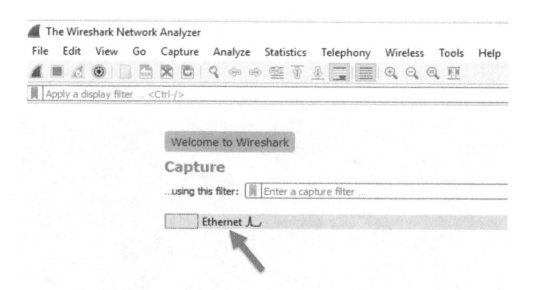

Task 4:

Open the Putty utility and enter the URL you wish to telnet to. I found telehack.com worked well. You need to change from the default SSH to Telnet.

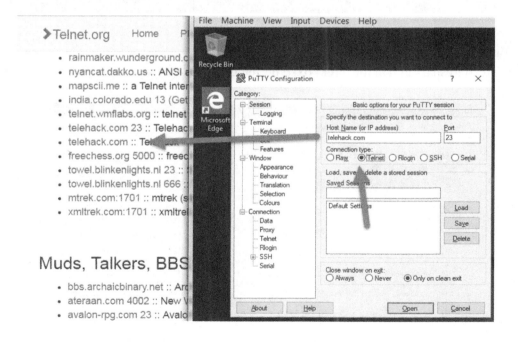

Task 5:

Your Telnet session should work. Below is the window I was taken to for the Telehack website.

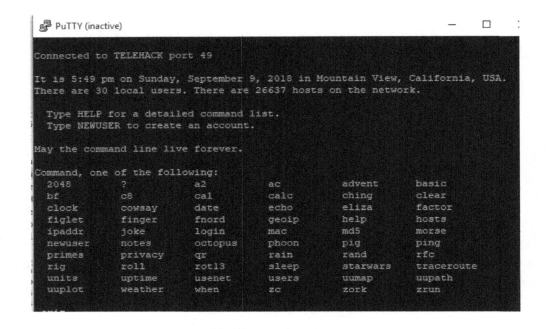

Task 6:

Go to Wireshark and in the filter box, type 'telnet' so you can see only the relevant traffic.

Task 7:

If you click on one of the packets, you can drill down to more detail. Please note that it says 'TCP', which is what Telnet uses. Compare the fields to the image of the TCP packet below. See how many of the fields you can view. You can see the source port is 23, which of course is Telnet. The bottom frame shows the actual text sent, which is in clear text, demonstrating the fact that there is no encryption involved.

```
224 29.980176      64.13.139.230        10.0.2.15            TELNET    1151 Telnet Data ...
225 29.980322      10.0.2.15            64.13.139.230        TELNET      63 Telnet Data ...
226 29.980406      10.0.2.15            64.13.139.230        TELNET      65 Telnet Data ...
227 29.980480      10.0.2.15            64.13.139.230        ELNET       57 Telnet Data ...
231 30.461964      64.13.139.230        10.0.2.15            TE  ET      60 Telnet Data ...
233 35.802277      10.0.2.15            64.13.139.230        TELN        55 Telnet Data ...
235 36.024466      64.13.139.230        10.0.2.15            TELNET      60 Telnet Data ...
236 36.025971      10.0.2.15            64.13.139.230        TELNET      55 Telnet Data ...
```

```
∨ Transmission Control Protocol, Src Port: 23, Dst Port: 49822, Seq: 4, Ack: 22, Len: 1097
    Source Port: 23
    Destination Port: 49822
    [Stream index: 16]
    [TCP Segment Len: 1097]
    Sequence number: 4      (relative sequence number)
    [Next sequence number: 1101      (relative sequence number)]
    Acknowledgment number: 22      (relative ack number)
    0101 .... = Header Length: 20 bytes (5)
  > Flags: 0x018 (PSH, ACK)
    Window size value: 65535
    [Calculated window size: 65535]
```

```
0020   02 0f 00 17 c2 9e 4a 07   2c 05 2e 3b 79 e3 50 18   ······J· ,·.;y·P·
0030   ff ff e2 61 00 00 ff fb   01 ff fd 18 ff fd 1f 0d   ···a···· ········
0040   0a 43 6f 6e 6e 65 63 74   65 64 20 74 6f 20 54 45   ·Connect ed to TE
0050   4c 45 48 41 43 4b 20 70   6f 72 74 20 34 39 0d 0a   LEHACK p ort 49··
0060   ff fe 20 ff fa 18 01 ff   f0 ff fe 27 0d 0a 49 74   ·· ····· ···'··It
0070   20 69 73 20 35 3a 34 39   20 70 6d 20 6f 6e 20 53    is 5:49  pm on S
0080   75 6e 64 61 79 2c 20 53   65 70 74 65 6d 62 65 72   unday, S eptember
0090   20 39 2c 20 32 30 31 38   20 69 6e 20 4d 6f 75 6e    9, 2018  in Moun
00a0   74 61 69 6e 20 56 69 65   77 2c 20 43 61 6c 69 66   tain Vie w, Calif
00b0   6f 72 6e 69 61 2c 20 55   53 41 2e 0d 0a 54 68 65   ornia, U SA.··The
00c0   72 65 20 61 72 65 20 33   30 20 6c 6f 63 61 6c 20   re are 3 0 local
00d0   75 73 65 72 73 2e 20 54   68 65 72 65 20 61 72 65   users. T here are
00e0   20 32 36 36 33 37 20 68   6f 73 74 73 20 6f 6e       26637 h osts on
```

Task 8:

You can use the below image as a reference to check the TCP fields.

TCP Segment Header Format						
Bit #	0	7	8	15	16	23	24	31
0	Source Port				Destination Port			
32	Sequence Number							
64	Acknowledgment Number							
96	Data Offset	Res		Flags		Window Size		
128	Header and Data Checksum				Urgent Pointer			
160...	Options							

Copyright - http://microchipdeveloper.com

Task 9:

Lastly, note that Telnet does not encrypt the contents of the session, so you can easily see in the data stream what is being sent. This would include any passwords. You will find the actual data sent on the wire in the bottom window of Wireshark.

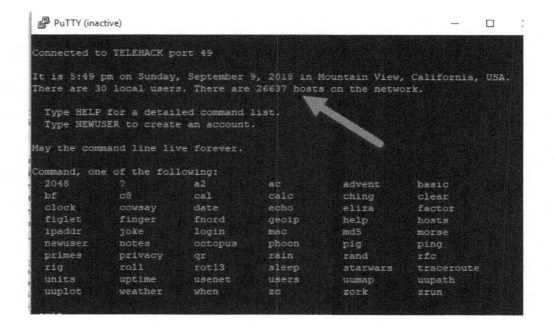

```
02 0f 00 17 c2 9e 4a 07   2c 05 2e 3b 79 e3 50 18    ······J· ,·.;y·P·
ff ff e2 61 00 00 ff fb   01 ff fd 18 ff fd 1f 0d    ···a···· ········
0a 43 6f 6e 6e 65 63 74   65 64 20 74 6f 20 54 45    ·Connect ed to TE
4c 45 48 41 43 4b 20 70   6f 72 74 20 34 39 0d 0a    LEHACK p ort 49··
ff fe 20 ff fa 18 01 ff   f0 ff fe 27 0d 0a 49 74    ·· ····· ···'··It
20 69 73 20 35 3a 34 39   20 70 6d 20 6f 6e 20 53    is 5:49  pm on S
75 6e 64 61 79 2c 20 53   65 70 74 65 6d 62 65 72    unday, S eptember
20 39 2c 20 32 30 31 38   20 69 6e 20 4d 6f 75 6e     9, 2018  in Moun
74 61 69 6e 20 56 69 65   77 2c 20 43 61 6c 69 66    tain Vie w, Calif
6f 72 6e 69 61 2c 20 55   53 41 2e 0d 0a 54 68 65    ornia, U SA.··The
72 65 20 61 72 65 20 33   30 20 6c 6f 63 61 6c 20    re are 3 0 local
75 73 65 72 73 2e 20 54   68 65 72 65 20 61 72 65    users. T here are
20 32 36 36 33 37 20 68   6f 73 74 73 20 6f 6e 20     26637 h osts on
```

Note:

Please have fun with this lab and refer to your study guides to see what you would expect to see in this type of packet.

LAB 7

UDP

Lab Objective:
Learn how to recognize a UDP packet.

Lab Purpose:
UDP is used by many services and protocols, such as RIP, DNS, SNMP, and DHCP, and routing protocols, such as RIP. It offers low overhead but with no guarantee of delivery. There are no acknowledgments: the packets are numbered and sent, but that's it.

Lab Tool:
VirtualBox and Wireshark—or your home PC

Lab Topology:
You can run Wireshark on your home PC just as easily, so feel free to do that. I've installed it on a VM Windows 10 machine. You need to be able to get out to the internet because we will be checking for a DNS lookup for a website.

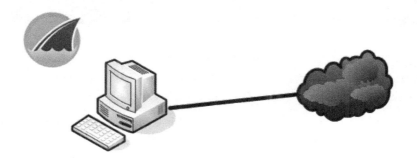

Lab Walkthrough:

Task 1:
Install Wireshark or another packet sniffer onto your device.

Task 2:
Open a web browser, but don't input any URL yet.

Task 3:

Boot Wireshark on your main PC (the one you will be doing the testing from) and check the correct interface is the one being monitored. Click on the interface name to open the capture window. Note that mine says 'Ethernet', but your device configuration and hardware will differ and so you may see 'En0', 'WiFi', or something else.

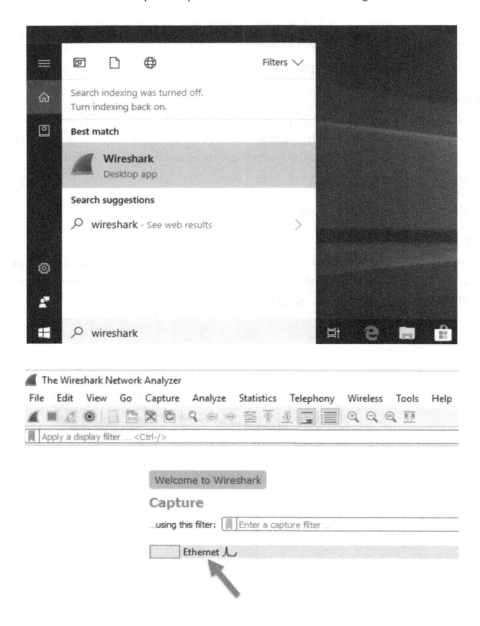

Task 4:

Browse to a website which isn't in your local cache. You want to prompt a DNS lookup (because it uses UDP). I've never used this virtual machine, so any URL will work for me because my DNS cache is empty—there will have to be a name lookup performed (generating traffic on Wireshark).

Task 5:

Go to Wireshark. Stop the captures by pressing the red square. Then use the filter bar to search for DNS. For some reason you have to use lowercase for the search!

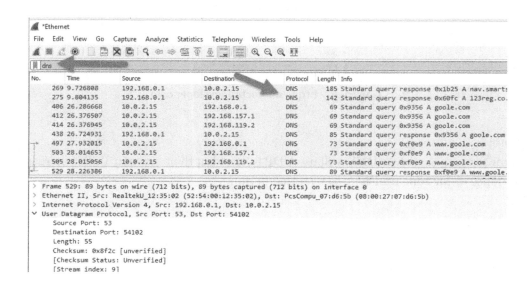

Task 6:

Click on one of the DNS entries and drill into the packet capture. Check the entries against the UDP image below. Note that we are missing many of the TCP fields, such as sequence number and flags.

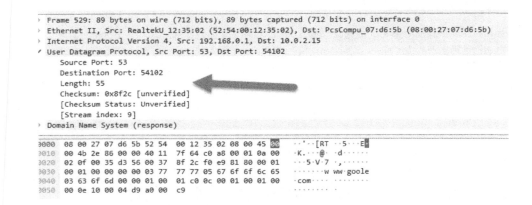

Task 7:

UDP does have a checksum for error checking, but that's about it. Check the above packet capture for the checksum fields.

Task 8:

You can use the below image as a reference to check the UDP fields.

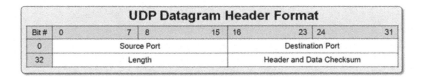

Bit #	0		7	8		15	16		23	24		31
0		Source Port						Destination Port				
32		Length						Header and Data Checksum				

UDP Datagram Header Format

Copyright - http://microchipdeveloper.com

Note:

Some protocols, such as DNS, will use UDP to start but then move to TCP if there is no response or for zone transfers, so bear that in mind.

ICMP

Lab Objective:
Learn how to recognize an ICMP packet.

Lab Purpose:
The Internet Control Message Protocol is used by network devices to report on reliability and send error messages. It is different from most of the other protocols within TCP/IP inasmuch as it isn't used to transport data. You will use ICMP when you ping other devices.

Lab Tool:
VirtualBox and Wireshark—or your home PC

Lab Topology:
You can run Wireshark on your home PC just as easily, so feel free to do that. I've installed it on a VM Windows 10 machine. You need to be able to get out to the internet because we will be pinging a website name.

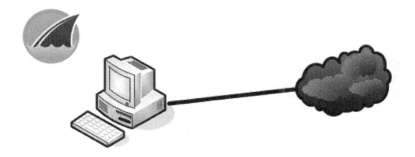

Lab Walkthrough:

Task 1:
Install Wireshark or another packet sniffer onto your device.

Task 2:

Boot Wireshark on your PC (or your virtual PC if you are using one) and check the correct interface is the one being monitored. Click on the interface name to open the capture window.

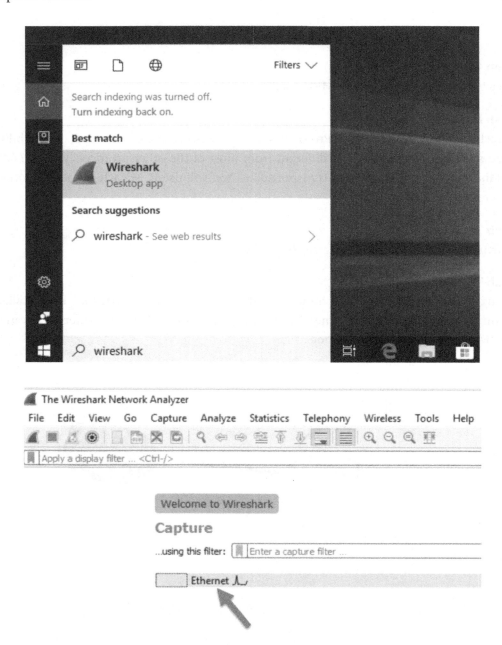

Task 4:

Ensure Wireshark is capturing general network traffic.

No.	Time	Source	Destination	Protocol	Length	Info
3	17.365843	192.168.0.1	10.0.2.15	DNS	151	Standard query response 0x1f64 No such name A wpad.localdomain SOA a.root
4	21.240380	10.0.2.15	10.0.2.255	BROWSER	258	Domain/Workgroup Announcement WORKGROUP, NT Workstation, Domain Enum
5	23.614756	10.0.2.15	52.230.84.217	TLSv1	107	Application Data
6	23.615004	52.230.84.217	10.0.2.15	TCP	60	443 → 49726 [ACK] Seq=1 Ack=54 Win=65535 Len=0
7	23.811821	52.230.84.217	10.0.2.15	TLSv1	224	Application Data, Application Data
8	23.865095	10.0.2.15	52.230.84.217	TCP	54	49726 → 443 [ACK] Seq=54 Ack=171 Win=62880 Len=0
9	35.366279	165.254.191.195	10.0.2.15	TLSv1.2	247	Application Data
10	35.366716	10.0.2.15	165.254.191.195	TLSv1.2	877	Application Data
11	35.366874	165.254.191.195	10.0.2.15	TCP	60	443 → 49674 [ACK] Seq=194 Ack=824 Win=65535 Len=0

> Frame 1: 157 bytes on wire (1256 bits), 157 bytes captured (1256 bits) on interface 0
> Ethernet II, Src: PcsCompu_07:d6:5b (08:00:27:07:d6:5b), Dst: IPv6mcast_01:00:02 (33:33:00:01:00:02)
> Internet Protocol Version 6, Src: fe80::54b2:5b3e:5de2:fb13, Dst: ff02::1:2
> User Datagram Protocol, Src Port: 546, Dst Port: 547
> DHCPv6

Task 5:

Open a command line window by typing 'cmd' in the search bar.

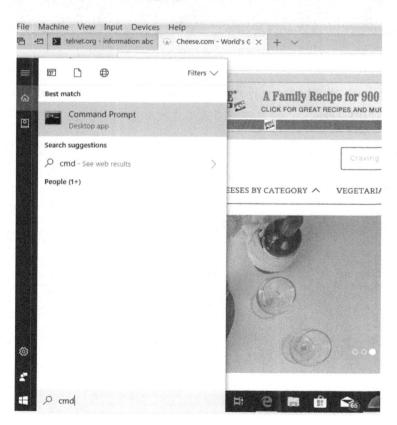

Task 6:

Ping a common URL, such as cisco.com. Many sites will block ICMP, so find one which doesn't (or ping an internal machine on your network).

```
Command Prompt

Microsoft Windows [Version 10.0.17134.228]
(c) 2018 Microsoft Corporation. All rights reserved.

C:\Users\paulw>ping cisco.com

Pinging cisco.com [72.163.4.185] with 32 bytes of data:
Reply from 72.163.4.185: bytes=32 time=221ms TTL=237
Reply from 72.163.4.185: bytes=32 time=224ms TTL=237
Reply from 72.163.4.185: bytes=32 time=227ms TTL=237
Reply from 72.163.4.185: bytes=32 time=229ms TTL=237

Ping statistics for 72.163.4.185:
    Packets: Sent = 4, Received = 4, Lost = 0 (0% loss),
Approximate round trip times in milli-seconds:
    Minimum = 221ms, Maximum = 229ms, Average = 225ms

C:\Users\paulw>
```

Task 7:

Use the Wireshark filter bar to narrow down results and use ICMP traffic. It only works if you type in lowercase!

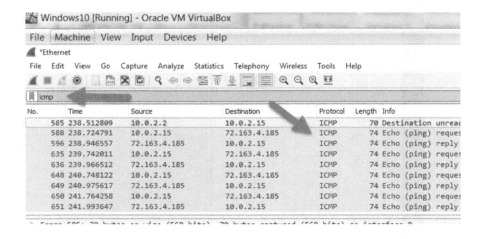

Task 8:

Note that ping uses ICMP echo request and echo reply packets. Compare the other fields with the command line output. You should be able to identify the response time, length, etc.

```
> Internet Protocol Version 4, Src: 72.163.4.185, Dst: 10.0.2.15
∨ Internet Control Message Protocol
      Type: 0 (Echo (ping) reply)
      Code: 0
      Checksum: 0x555a [correct]
      [Checksum Status: Good]
      Identifier (BE): 1 (0x0001)
      Identifier (LE): 256 (0x0100)
      Sequence number (BE): 1 (0x0001)
      Sequence number (LE): 256 (0x0100)
      [Request frame: 588]
      [Response time: 221.766 ms]
   ∨ Data (32 bytes)
         Data: 6162636465666768696a6b6c6d6e6f707172737475767761...
         [Length: 32]
```

Task 9:

You will find the time to live (TTL) field in the IP header.

```
∨ Internet Protocol Version 4, Src: 72.163.4.185, Dst: 10.0.2.15
      0100 .... = Version: 4
      .... 0101 = Header Length: 20 bytes (5)
   > Differentiated Services Field: 0x00 (DSCP: CS0, ECN: Not-ECT)
      Total Length: 60
      Identification: 0x4dc4 (19908)
   > Flags: 0x0000
      Time to live: 237          ◄──────
      Protocol: ICMP (1)
      Header checksum: 0x2692 [validation disabled]
      [Header checksum status: Unverified]
      Source: 72.163.4.185
```

Note:

You can use sniffers to really dig into the packet contents to understand the protocols and services in great detail.

VLANs

Lab Objective:
Learn how to configure VLANs and see why you need a Layer 3 device to communicate between them.

Lab Purpose:
VLANs help you segment your network for easier administration and added security. It's important you understand how they work because they will form part of your daily routine as a network engineer.

Lab Tool:
Packet Tracer

Lab Topology:
Please use the following topology to complete this lab exercise:

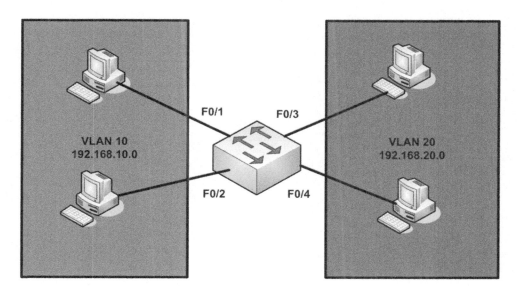

Lab Walkthrough:

Task 1:

Connect four hosts to a Cisco switch (I always used a 2960 in these labs) using straight-through cables. Note which devices you connect to which switch interfaces because you will be putting these interfaces into their respective VLANs shortly.

Task 2:

Allocate IP addresses to the hosts from within the subnets they are assigned to:

VLAN 10—192.168.10.0
VLAN 20—192.168.20.0

I suggest you use 192.168.10.1 and 192.168.10.2 for VLAN 10 and 192.168.20.1 and 192.168.20.2 for VLAN 20, but feel free to use any IP address within the subnet.

Here is an example from a host on VLAN 10:

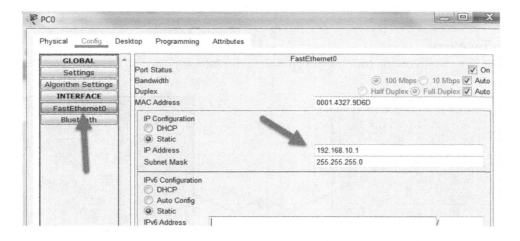

Task 3:

Configure interfaces F0/1 and F0/2 into VLAN 10 and F0/3 and F0/4 into VLAN 20. Force the ports to be access-only (to never become a trunk), which you do with the 'switchport mode access' command.

```
Switch#conf t
Enter configuration commands, one per line. End with CNTL/Z.
Switch(config)#vlan 10
Switch(config-vlan)#interface f0/1
Switch(config-if)#switchport mode access
Switch(config-if)#switchport access vlan 10
Switch(config-if)#interface f0/2
Switch(config-if)#switchport mode access
Switch(config-if)#switchport access vlan 10
Switch(config-if)#vlan 20
Switch(config-vlan)#interface f0/3
Switch(config-if)#switchport mode access
Switch(config-if)#switchport access vlan 20
Switch(config-if)#int f0/4
Switch(config-if)#switchport mode access
Switch(config-if)#switchport access vlan 20
Switch(config-if)#end
Switch#
```

Task 4:

Check the VLANs on the switch and which ports are in which VLANs. By default, all ports are in the native VLAN named 'default'. Use the 'show vlan brief' command.

```
Switch#show vlan brief

VLAN Name                             Status    Ports
---- -------------------------------- --------- -------------------------------
1    default                          active    Fa0/5, Fa0/6, Fa0/7, Fa0/8
                                                Fa0/9, Fa0/10, Fa0/11, Fa0/12
                                                Fa0/13, Fa0/14, Fa0/15, Fa0/16
                                                Fa0/17, Fa0/18, Fa0/19, Fa0/20
                                                Fa0/21, Fa0/22, Fa0/23, Fa0/24
                                                Gig0/1, Gig0/2
10   VLAN0010                         active    Fa0/1, Fa0/2
20   VLAN0020                         active    Fa0/3, Fa0/4
1002 fddi-default                     active
1003 token-ring-default               active
1004 fddinet-default                  active
1005 trnet-default                    active
```

Task 5:

Now test some pings. You should be able to ping between hosts in the same VLAN but not to the other VLAN (you would need a router to be able to do this). Here is a test from 192.168.10.1, which sits on VLAN 10.

```
Command Prompt                                                      X

Packet Tracer PC Command Line 1.0
C:\>ping 192.168.10.2

Pinging 192.168.10.2 with 32 bytes of data:

Reply from 192.168.10.2: bytes=32 time=2ms TTL=128
Reply from 192.168.10.2: bytes=32 time=3ms TTL=128
Reply from 192.168.10.2: bytes=32 time<1ms TTL=128
Reply from 192.168.10.2: bytes=32 time=2ms TTL=128

Ping statistics for 192.168.10.2:
    Packets: Sent = 4, Received = 4, Lost = 0 (0% loss),
Approximate round trip times in milli-seconds:
    Minimum = 0ms, Maximum = 3ms, Average = 1ms

C:\>ping 192.168.20.1

Pinging 192.168.20.1 with 32 bytes of data:

Request timed out.
```

Notes:

You will need a Layer 3 device to ping between VLANs. We will do this in another lab.

You can make recognizing each VLAN easier by naming it ADMIN or SALES, for example.

```
Switch>en
Switch#conf t
Enter configuration commands, one per line. End with CNTL/Z.
Switch(config)#vlan 10
Switch(config-vlan)#name SALES
Switch(config-vlan)#end
Switch#show vlan brief
[output truncated]
10 SALES active
1002 fddi-default active
```

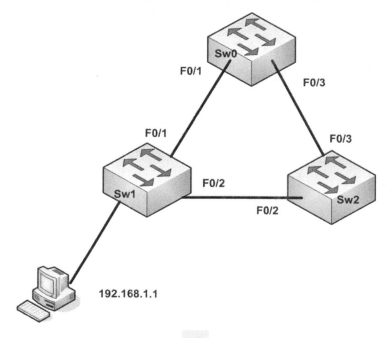

LAB 10

Switching Loops

Lab Objective:
Learn how to spot a switching loop on your layer 2 networks.

Lab Purpose:
My first consulting customer called me in a panic. Their multimillion-dollar network kept crashing every few minutes, even after a complete reboot. I immediately suspected a switching (spanning tree) loop. Most network engineers have never seen one and don't know how to fix it, usually because the Spanning Tree Protocol works so well.

WARNING—Never try this lab on a production network!

Lab Tool:
Packet Tracer

Lab Topology:
Please use the following topology to complete this lab exercise:

Lab Walkthrough:

Task 1:

Connect three switches and one PC onto the canvas. Connect them up as per the diagram. Add the IP address to the PC and default gateway of 192.168.1.2 (which doesn't exist on the network).

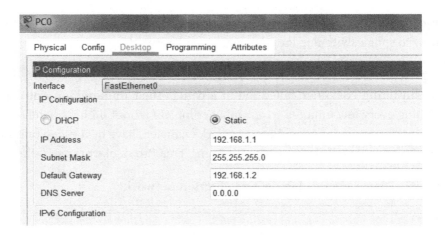

Task 2:

Name the switches and then turn off STP in order to create a switching loop. Here is how to do it on Switch0. Do the same on the other two switches, but name them Switch1 and Switch2.

```
Switch>en
Switch#conf t
Enter configuration commands, one per line.  End with CNTL/Z.
Switch(config)#hostname Sw0
Sw0(config)#interface range f0/1-3
Sw0(config-if-range)#no spanning-tree vlan 1
Sw0(config)#end
Sw0#
```

Task 3:

Set Packet Tracer to simulation mode so you can see the packets moving across the network. Set 'Edit Filters' to show only ARP and ICMP. (Please ensure you have watched all of our training videos at www.101labs.net/resources if you are stuck on this step.)

Click on 'Show All/None' and then tick the two you want.

Task 4:

From the PC, ping host 192.168.1.2. You can press the play button in the simulation mode. Keep pressing play and watch the packet travel around the network endlessly, never resolving the ARP request for the host.

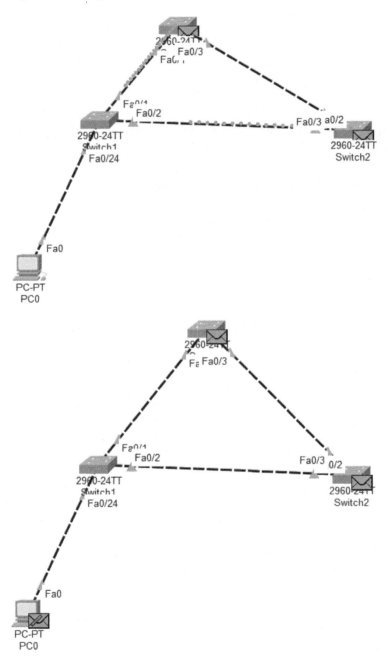

Task 5:

The packet capture window quickly fills with ARP requests. This will slow your network to a crawl and eventually lead to a crash.

Vis.	Time(sec)	Last Device	At Device		Type
	0.002	Switch0	Switch2		ARP
	0.002	Switch2	Switch0		ARP
	0.003	Switch2	Switch1		ARP
	0.003	Switch0	Switch1		ARP
	0.004	--	Switch1		ARP
	0.004	--	Switch1		ARP
	0.004	--	Switch1		ARP
	0.005	Switch1	PC0		ARP
	0.005	Switch1	Switch0		ARP
	0.005	Switch1	Switch2		ARP
	0.006	Switch0	Switch2		ARP
	0.006	Switch2	Switch0		ARP
	0.007	Switch2	Switch1		ARP
	0.007	Switch0	Switch1		ARP
	0.008	--	Switch1		ARP
	0.008	--	Switch1		ARP
	0.008	--	Switch1		ARP
Visible	0.009	Switch1	PC0		ARP
Visible	0.009	Switch1	Switch0		ARP
Visible	0.009	Switch1	Switch2		ARP

Simulation Panel — Event List. Reset Simulation / Constant Delay. Captured to: 0.009 s. Play Controls. Event List Filters - Visible Events: ARP, ICMP. Edit Filters / Show All/None.

Task 6:

You can fix this particular issue by reenabling STP on the switches for VLAN1. Here is how to do it on Switch0. Repeat the steps on the other switches.

```
Sw0#conf t
Sw0(config)#interface range f0/1-3
Sw0(config-if-range)#spanning-tree vlan 1
Sw0(config-if-range)#end
```

Task 7:

You can redo the test, however, from the canvas; you can see one of the switchports has been shut down by STP and so will not forward traffic. You may well have a different port to mine shutdown. This time around the ARP lookup will fail, and ICMP will inform the PC of the timeout. Only five ping packets will be sent.

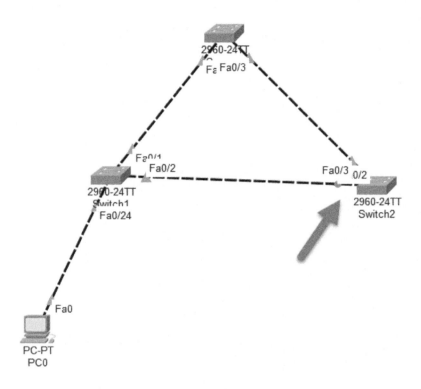

Note:

STP loops are very serious, so make sure you study this protocol in your study guide and in the later lab we have on it.

LAB 11

MAC Address Table

Lab Objective:
Learn how a switch populates its MAC table in order to quickly forward frames out of the correct interface.

Lab Purpose:
When switches boot, they have no directory of which MAC addresses are connected to which interface. As traffic enters the port, the switch adds the source MAC address to a MAC address table so it doesn't have to broadcast for the address next time.

Lab Tool:
Packet Tracer

Lab Topology:
Please use the following topology to complete this lab exercise:

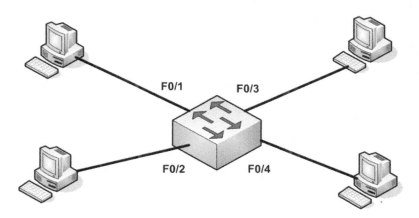

Lab Walkthrough:

Task 1:
Connect four hosts to a Cisco switch using straight-through cables.

Task 2:

Check the MAC address table on the switch. It should be empty at the moment.

```
Switch#show mac-address-table
Mac Address Table
-------------------------------------------

Vlan Mac Address Type Ports
---- ----------- -------- -----

Switch#
```

Task 3:

Allocate IP addresses to the hosts from within the subnet 192.168.1.0. Here is how I did it on the first PC. You can use 192.168.1.1, then 192.168.1.2, and so on.

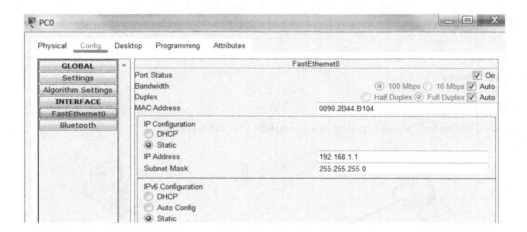

Task 4:

From one of the PCs ping the other three. Below, I'm on host 192.168.1.1, and I ping hosts .2, .3, and then .4.

```
Physical    Config    Desktop    Programming    Attributes

Command Prompt

C:\>ping 192.168.1.2

Pinging 192.168.1.2 with 32 bytes of data:

Reply from 192.168.1.2: bytes=32 time<1ms TTL=128
Reply from 192.168.1.2: bytes=32 time=1ms TTL=128
Reply from 192.168.1.2: bytes=32 time<1ms TTL=128
Reply from 192.168.1.2: bytes=32 time=1ms TTL=128

Ping statistics for 192.168.1.2:
    Packets: Sent = 4, Received = 4, Lost = 0 (0% loss),
Approximate round trip times in milli-seconds:
    Minimum = 0ms, Maximum = 1ms, Average = 0ms

C:\>ping 192.168.1.3

Pinging 192.168.1.3 with 32 bytes of data:

Reply from 192.168.1.3: bytes=32 time=1ms TTL=128
Reply from 192.168.1.3: bytes=32 time<1ms TTL=128
Reply from 192.168.1.3: bytes=32 time<1ms TTL=128
Reply from 192.168.1.3: bytes=32 time=1ms TTL=128

Ping statistics for 192.168.1.3:
    Packets: Sent = 4, Received = 4, Lost = 0 (0% loss),
Approximate round trip times in milli-seconds:
    Minimum = 0ms, Maximum = 1ms, Average = 0ms

C:\>ping 192.168.1.4

Pinging 192.168.1.4 with 32 bytes of data:

Reply from 192.168.1.4: bytes=32 time=1ms TTL=128
Reply from 192.168.1.4: bytes=32 time<1ms TTL=128
Reply from 192.168.1.4: bytes=32 time<1ms TTL=128
Reply from 192.168.1.4: bytes=32 time=1ms TTL=128

Ping statistics for 192.168.1.4:
```

Task 5:

Check the MAC address table on the switch once more.

```
Switch#show mac-address-table
Mac Address Table
-------------------------------------------

Vlan Mac Address Type Ports
---- ----------- -------- -----

1 0001.641d.579c DYNAMIC Fa0/3
1 0050.0fd5.d238 DYNAMIC Fa0/4
1 0060.5c7b.6cbd DYNAMIC Fa0/2
1 0090.2b44.b104 DYNAMIC Fa0/1
Switch#
```

Note:

Feel free to check the MAC address on your host to ensure the one in the switch MAC address table is correct.

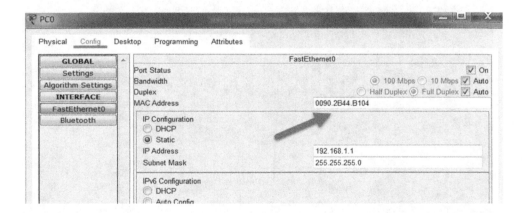

LAB 12

ARP Table

Lab Objective:

Learn how to interrogate a router ARP table.

Lab Purpose:

ARP maps a known IP address to an unknown MAC address. It allows a router to encapsulate a packet correctly before forwarding.

Lab Tool:

Packet Tracer

Lab Topology:

Please use the following topology to complete this lab exercise:

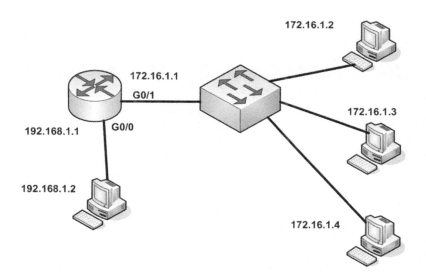

Lab Walkthrough:

Task 1:

Connect a router to a switch. Add hosts as indicated in the diagram. You will need a crossover cable for the one directly connected to the router. Check the router ARP table (which will be empty) and then configure IP addresses as per the diagram. I'm sure you know how to change the router hostname by now.

```
R0#show arp
R0#config t
R0(config)#int g0/0
R0(config-if)#ip add 192.168.1.1 255.255.255.0
R0(config-if)#no shut
R0(config-if)#int g0/1
R0(config-if)#ip add 172.16.1.1 255.255.0.0
R0(config-if)#no shut
```

Task 2:

Configure the hosts with an IP address and the default gateway, which should be the router interface it connects to. Here is the configuration for one PC. Remember that there are two networks, so choose the correct gateway IP address.

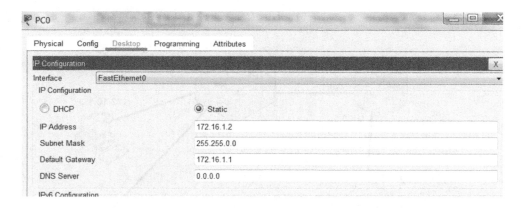

Task 3:

Ping each of the four hosts. The first ping packet will fail as the ARP request-and-response process takes place.

```
R0#ping 192.168.1.2

Type escape sequence to abort.
Sending 5, 100-byte ICMP Echos to 192.168.1.2, timeout is 2 seconds:
.!!!!
```

```
Success rate is 80 percent (4/5), round-trip min/avg/max = 0/0/0 ms

R0#ping 172.16.1.2

Type escape sequence to abort.
Sending 5, 100-byte ICMP Echos to 172.16.1.2, timeout is 2 seconds:
.!!!!
Success rate is 80 percent (4/5), round-trip min/avg/max = 0/0/1 ms

R0#ping 172.16.1.3

Type escape sequence to abort.
Sending 5, 100-byte ICMP Echos to 172.16.1.3, timeout is 2 seconds:
.!!!!
Success rate is 80 percent (4/5), round-trip min/avg/max = 0/0/0 ms

R0#ping 172.16.1.4

Type escape sequence to abort.
Sending 5, 100-byte ICMP Echos to 172.16.1.4, timeout is 2 seconds:
.!!!!
Success rate is 80 percent (4/5), round-trip min/avg/max = 0/0/1 ms
```

Task 4:

Check the ARP table. A dash (–) indicates that the entry is directly connected and will never time out. Other entries will eventually time out.

```
R0#show arp
Protocol  Address        Age (min)  Hardware Addr   Type    Interface
Internet  172.16.1.1     -          0004.9AE0.1E02  ARPA    GigabitEthernet0/1
Internet  172.16.1.2     0          0005.5EAA.50BD  ARPA    GigabitEthernet0/1
Internet  172.16.1.3     0          000D.BD1B.81C4  ARPA    GigabitEthernet0/1
Internet  172.16.1.4     0          00D0.5833.253B  ARPA    GigabitEthernet0/1
Internet  192.168.1.1    -          0004.9AE0.1E01  ARPA    GigabitEthernet0/0
Internet  192.168.1.2    0          00E0.B01A.8E89  ARPA    GigabitEthernet0/0
```

Task 5:

After a minute or so issue the command again and check the age column.

```
R0#show arp
Protocol  Address        Age (min)  Hardware Addr   Type    Interface
Internet  172.16.1.1     -          0004.9AE0.1E02  ARPA    GigabitEthernet0/1
Internet  172.16.1.2     1          0005.5EAA.50BD  ARPA    GigabitEthernet0/1
Internet  172.16.1.3     1          000D.BD1B.81C4  ARPA    GigabitEthernet0/1
Internet  172.16.1.4     1          00D0.5833.253B  ARPA    GigabitEthernet0/1
Internet  192.168.1.1    -          0004.9AE0.1E01  ARPA    GigabitEthernet0/0
Internet  192.168.1.2    1          00E0.B01A.8E89  ARPA    GigabitEthernet0/0
```

Notes:

As a packet travels across the network, the IP source and destination addresses never change. The MAC address source and destination change between hops.

LAB 13

Static IP Routes

Lab Objective:
Learn how to configure static IP routing.

Lab Purpose:
Small networks have no need of running dynamic routing protocols, which take up router CPU cycles and reserve bandwidth for routing updates. Static routes are easy to configure, and you need to know how to configure them as a network engineer.

Lab Tool:
Packet Tracer

Lab Topology:
Please use the following topology to complete this lab exercise:

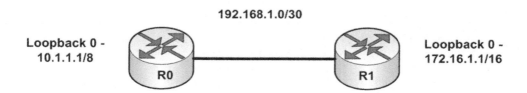

Lab Walkthrough:

Task 1:
Connect two routers together using a crossover cable.

Task 2:
Add the IP addresses to the routers connecting the interfaces and then the loopback interfaces. Loopback interfaces exist in software only but let you test all your routing before installing into a customers network.

```
Router>en
Router#conf t
Router(config)#hostname R0
```

```
R0(config)#
Enter configuration commands, one per line.  End with CNTL/Z.
R0(config)#int lo0
R0(config-if)#ip add 10.1.1.1 255.0.0.0
R0(config-if)#int g0/0
R0(config-if)#ip add 192.168.1.1 255.255.255.252
R0(config-if)#no shut
%LINK-5-CHANGED: Interface GigabitEthernet0/0, changed state to up
```

Then onto Router 1.

```
Router>en
Router#conf t
Router(config)#hostname R1
R1(config)#
Enter configuration commands, one per line.  End with CNTL/Z.
R1(config)#int lo0
R1(config-if)#ip add 172.16.1.1 255.255.0.0
R1(config-if)#int g0/0
R1(config-if)#ip add 192.168.1.2 255.255.255.252
R1(config-if)#no shut
%LINK-5-CHANGED: Interface GigabitEthernet0/0, changed state to up
```

Task 3:

Ping from R0 to R1 to check the connection works.

```
R0#ping 192.168.1.2

Type escape sequence to abort.
Sending 5, 100-byte ICMP Echos to 192.168.1.2, timeout is 2 seconds:
.!!!!
Success rate is 80 percent (4/5), round-trip min/avg/max = 0/0/0 ms
```

Task 4:

Ping from the loopback interface on R0 to the loopback on R1. Because the routers have no route to these networks, the ping packet will fail. You need to use an extended ping command which lets you specify the source interface.

```
R0#ping
Protocol [ip]:
Target IP address: 172.16.1.1
Repeat count [5]:
Datagram size [100]:
Timeout in seconds [2]:
Extended commands [n]: yes
Source address or interface: 10.1.1.1
Type of service [0]:
Set DF bit in IP header? [no]:
```

```
Validate reply data? [no]:
Data pattern [0xABCD]:
Loose, Strict, Record, Timestamp, Verbose[none]:
Sweep range of sizes [n]:
Type escape sequence to abort.
Sending 5, 100-byte ICMP Echos to 172.16.1.1, timeout is 2 seconds:
Packet sent with a source address of 10.1.1.1
.....
Success rate is 0 percent (0/5)
```

Task 5:

Add static routes. You can choose a next hop address or an exit interface. Bear in mind that R0 needs to know how to get to 172.16.0.0, but R1 also needs to know how to get to the 10.0.0.0 network.

```
R0(config)#ip route 172.16.0.0 255.255.0.0 192.168.1.2

R1(config)#ip route 10.0.0.0 255.0.0.0 g0/0
%Default route without gateway, if not a point-to-point interface, may
impact performance
```

Task 6:

Test your static routes by pinging each loopback interface from the opposite router. Make sure you type 'yes' or 'y' at the 'Extended commands' prompt. This feature lets you change the source interface of the ping, the ping number and size, etc.

```
R0#ping
Protocol [ip]:
Target IP address: 172.16.1.1
Repeat count [5]:
Datagram size [100]:
Timeout in seconds [2]:
Extended commands [n]: y
Source address or interface: 10.1.1.1
Type of service [0]:
Set DF bit in IP header? [no]:
Validate reply data? [no]:
Data pattern [0xABCD]:
Loose, Strict, Record, Timestamp, Verbose[none]:
Sweep range of sizes [n]:
Type escape sequence to abort.
Sending 5, 100-byte ICMP Echos to 172.16.1.1, timeout is 2 seconds:
Packet sent with a source address of 10.1.1.1
!!!!!
Success rate is 100 percent (5/5), round-trip min/avg/max = 0/0/1 ms

R1#ping
Protocol [ip]:
```

```
Target IP address: 10.1.1.1
Repeat count [5]:
Datagram size [100]:
Timeout in seconds [2]:
Extended commands [n]: y
Source address or interface: 172.16.1.1
Type of service [0]:
Set DF bit in IP header? [no]:
Validate reply data? [no]:
Data pattern [0xABCD]:
Loose, Strict, Record, Timestamp, Verbose[none]:
Sweep range of sizes [n]:
Type escape sequence to abort.
Sending 5, 100-byte ICMP Echos to 10.1.1.1, timeout is 2 seconds:
Packet sent with a source address of 172.16.1.1
!!!!!
Success rate is 100 percent (5/5), round-trip min/avg/max = 0/0/1 ms
```

Notes:

We used a /30 mask for the link between the two routers. This subnet mask would be used on point-to-point links because only two addresses are required.

Loopback interfaces stay up and do not require the 'no shutdown' command. They are very useful for testing and use in home labs where you have limited space and equipment.

LAB 14

RIP

Lab Objective:

Learn how to configure the routing protocol RIP.

Lab Purpose:

RIP was created to allow dynamic routing for small networks. It doesn't understand VLSM because RIP predates this facility. RIPv2 addresses this shortcoming by recognizing VLSM.

Lab Tool:

Packet Tracer

Lab Topology:

Please use the following topology to complete this lab exercise:

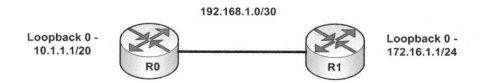

Lab Walkthrough:

Task 1:

Connect two routers together using a crossover cable.

Task 2:

Add the IP addresses to the routers connecting the interfaces and then the loopback interfaces.

```
Router>en
Router#conf t
Router(config)#hostname R0
R0(config)#
Enter configuration commands, one per line.  End with CNTL/Z.
```

```
RO(config)#int lo0
RO(config-if)#ip add 10.1.1.1 255.255.240.0
RO(config-if)#int g0/0
RO(config-if)#ip add 192.168.1.1 255.255.255.252
RO(config-if)#no shut
%LINK-5-CHANGED: Interface GigabitEthernet0/0, changed state to up
```

Then Router1.

```
Router>en
Router#conf t
Router(config)#hostname R1
R1(config)#
Enter configuration commands, one per line.  End with CNTL/Z.
R1(config)#int lo0
R1(config-if)#ip add 172.16.1.1 255.255.255.0
R1(config-if)#int g0/0
R1(config-if)#ip add 192.168.1.2 255.255.255.252
R1(config-if)#no shut
%LINK-5-CHANGED: Interface GigabitEthernet0/0, changed state to up
```

Task 3:

Ping from R0 to R1 to check the connection works.

```
RO#ping 192.168.1.2

Type escape sequence to abort.
Sending 5, 100-byte ICMP Echos to 192.168.1.2, timeout is 2 seconds:
.!!!!
Success rate is 80 percent (4/5), round-trip min/avg/max = 0/0/0 ms
```

Task 4:

Configure RIP on both R0 and R1 to advertise the connected networks.

```
RO(config)#router rip
RO(config-router)#network 10.0.0.0
RO(config-router)#network 192.168.1.0

R1(config)#router rip
R1(config-router)#network 192.168.1.0
R1(config-router)#network 172.16.0.0
```

Task 5:

Check the routing table with the 'show ip route' command and the routing configurations with the 'show ip protocols' command. Note that the network has been registered with its default subnet mask and that the version of RIP is 1. [120/1] means that the administrative distance, which is the believability of the route, is 120 for RIP and 1 is how many hops away the network is.

```
R0#show ip route
Codes: L - local, C - connected, S - static, R - RIP, M - mobile, B
- BGP
D - EIGRP, EX - EIGRP external, O - OSPF, IA - OSPF inter area
N1 - OSPF NSSA external type 1, N2 - OSPF NSSA external type 2
E1 - OSPF external type 1, E2 - OSPF external type 2, E - EGP
i - IS-IS, L1 - IS-IS level-1, L2 - IS-IS level-2, ia - IS-IS inter
area
* - candidate default, U - per-user static route, o - ODR
P - periodic downloaded static route

Gateway of last resort is not set

10.0.0.0/8 is variably subnetted, 2 subnets, 2 masks
C 10.1.0.0/20 is directly connected, Loopback0
L 10.1.1.1/32 is directly connected, Loopback0
R 172.16.0.0/16 [120/1] via 192.168.1.2, 00:00:30, GigabitEthernet0/0
192.168.1.0/24 is variably subnetted, 2 subnets, 2 masks
C 192.168.1.0/30 is directly connected, GigabitEthernet0/0
L 192.168.1.1/32 is directly connected, GigabitEthernet0/0

R0#show ip protocols
Routing Protocol is "rip"
Sending updates every 30 seconds, next due in 21 seconds
Invalid after 180 seconds, hold down 180, flushed after 240
Outgoing update filter list for all interfaces is not set
Incoming update filter list for all interfaces is not set
Redistributing: rip
Default version control: send version 1, receive any version
Interface Send Recv Triggered RIP Key-chain
Loopback0 1 2 1
GigabitEthernet0/0 1 2 1
Automatic network summarization is in effect
Maximum path: 4
Routing for Networks:
10.0.0.0
192.168.1.0
Passive Interface(s):
Routing Information Sources:
Gateway Distance Last Update
192.168.1.2 120 00:00:07
Distance: (default is 120)
```

Task 6:

Ping the remote network IP address.

```
R0#ping 172.16.1.1

Type escape sequence to abort.
Sending 5, 100-byte ICMP Echos to 172.16.1.1, timeout is 2 seconds:
!!!!!
Success rate is 100 percent (5/5), round-trip min/avg/max = 0/0/1 ms
```

Task 7:

Change the version of RIP to 2 and check the routing table again. You may need to clear it first with the 'clear ip route *' command. It will take a few moments for the new routes to be advertised. RIP will still auto-summarize networks, so you need to add the 'no auto-summary' command.

```
R0#conf t
Enter configuration commands, one per line. End with CNTL/Z.
R0(config)#router rip
R0(config-router)#version 2
R0(config-router)#no auto-summary
R0(config-router)#end

R1#conf t
Enter configuration commands, one per line. End with CNTL/Z.
R1(config)#router rip
R1(config-router)#version 2
R1(config-router)#no auto-summary
R1(config-router)#end
R1#clear ip route *

R0#show ip protocols
Routing Protocol is "rip"
Sending updates every 30 seconds, next due in 7 seconds
Invalid after 180 seconds, hold down 180, flushed after 240
Outgoing update filter list for all interfaces is not set
Incoming update filter list for all interfaces is not set
Redistributing: rip
Default version control: send version 2, receive 2
Interface Send Recv Triggered RIP Key-chain
Loopback0 2 2
GigabitEthernet0/0 2 2
Automatic network summarization is not in effect
Maximum path: 4
Routing for Networks:
10.0.0.0
192.168.1.0
Passive Interface(s):
```

```
Routing Information Sources:
Gateway Distance Last Update
192.168.1.2 120 00:00:04
Distance: (default is 120)
R0#

R0#show ip route
Codes: L - local, C - connected, S - static, R - RIP, M - mobile, B
- BGP
D - EIGRP, EX - EIGRP external, O - OSPF, IA - OSPF inter area
N1 - OSPF NSSA external type 1, N2 - OSPF NSSA external type 2
E1 - OSPF external type 1, E2 - OSPF external type 2, E - EGP
i - IS-IS, L1 - IS-IS level-1, L2 - IS-IS level-2, ia - IS-IS inter
area
* - candidate default, U - per-user static route, o - ODR
P - periodic downloaded static route

Gateway of last resort is not set

10.0.0.0/8 is variably subnetted, 2 subnets, 2 masks
C 10.1.0.0/20 is directly connected, Loopback0
L 10.1.1.1/32 is directly connected, Loopback0
172.16.0.0/24 is subnetted, 1 subnets
R 172.16.1.0/24 [120/1] via 192.168.1.2, 00:00:09, GigabitEthernet0/0
192.168.1.0/24 is variably subnetted, 2 subnets, 2 masks
C 192.168.1.0/30 is directly connected, GigabitEthernet0/0
L 192.168.1.1/32 is directly connected, GigabitEthernet0/0
```

Notes:

Don't worry too much about the commands because the Network+ command is vendor-neutral. You need learn the specific commands only when you take a vendor exam, such as Cisco CCNA.

LAB 15

EIGRP

Lab Objective:
Learn how to configure the EIGRP routing protocol.

Lab Purpose:
EIGRP was developed by Cisco Systems as an advanced distance vector routing protocol. It shares periodic routing updates with neighbors in the same autonomous system. In this lab you will learn some configuration basics.

Lab Tool:
Packet Tracer

Lab Topology:
Please use the following topology to complete this lab exercise:

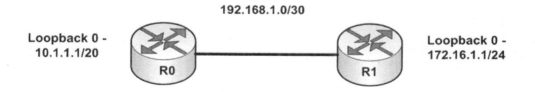

Lab Walkthrough:

Task 1:
Connect two routers together using a crossover cable.

Task 2:
Add the IP addresses to the routers connecting the interfaces and then the loopback interfaces. Hopefully you are getting familiar with this process now, so I'll just walk you through R0 configuration.

```
Router>en
Router#conf t
Router(config)#hostname R0
```

```
R0(config)#
Enter configuration commands, one per line.  End with CNTL/Z.
R0(config)#int lo0
R0(config-if)#ip add 10.1.1.1 255.255.240.0
R0(config-if)#int g0/0
R0(config-if)#ip add 192.168.1.1 255.255.255.252
R0(config-if)#no shut
%LINK-5-CHANGED: Interface GigabitEthernet0/0, changed state to up
```

Task 3:

Ping from R0 to R1 to check the connection works.

```
R0#ping 192.168.1.2

Type escape sequence to abort.
Sending 5, 100-byte ICMP Echos to 192.168.1.2, timeout is 2 seconds:
.!!!!
Success rate is 80 percent (4/5), round-trip min/avg/max = 0/0/0 ms
```

Task 4:

Configure EIGRP on both R0 and R1 to advertise the connected networks. The number 10 below refers to the autonomous system the networks will be placed into. This number must match on both routers if they are to exchange routes.

```
R0(config)#router eigrp 10
R0(config-router)#network 10.0.0.0
R0(config-router)#network 192.168.1.0

R1(config)#router eigrp 10
R1(config-router)#network 192.168.1.0
R1(config-router)#network 172.16.0.0
```

You should see the below information message appear when the neighbor relationship is established.

```
%DUAL-5-NBRCHANGE: IP-EIGRP 10: Neighbor 192.168.1.1
(GigabitEthernet0/0) is up: new adjacency
```

Task 5:

Check the routing table with the 'show ip route' command and the routing configurations with the 'show ip protocols' command. Note that the network has been registered with its default subnet mask. [90/130816] means that the administrative distance, which is the believability of the route, is 90 for EIGRP and 130816 is the metric calculated to the remote network.

EIGRP uses a router ID to identify its routing updates. You can see the networks being advertised from the below 'show ip protocols' output.

```
R0#show ip route
Codes: L - local, C - connected, S - static, R - RIP, M - mobile, B
- BGP
D - EIGRP, EX - EIGRP external, O - OSPF, IA - OSPF inter area
N1 - OSPF NSSA external type 1, N2 - OSPF NSSA external type 2
E1 - OSPF external type 1, E2 - OSPF external type 2, E - EGP
i - IS-IS, L1 - IS-IS level-1, L2 - IS-IS level-2, ia - IS-IS inter
area
* - candidate default, U - per-user static route, o - ODR
P - periodic downloaded static route

Gateway of last resort is not set

10.0.0.0/8 is variably subnetted, 2 subnets, 2 masks
C 10.1.0.0/20 is directly connected, Loopback0
L 10.1.1.1/32 is directly connected, Loopback0
172.16.0.0/24 is subnetted, 1 subnets
D 172.16.1.0/24 [90/130816] via 192.168.1.2, 00:00:52,
GigabitEthernet0/0
192.168.1.0/24 is variably subnetted, 2 subnets, 2 masks
C 192.168.1.0/30 is directly connected, GigabitEthernet0/0
L 192.168.1.1/32 is directly connected, GigabitEthernet0/0

R0#show ip protocols

Routing Protocol is "eigrp 10 "
Outgoing update filter list for all interfaces is not set
Incoming update filter list for all interfaces is not set
Default networks flagged in outgoing updates
Default networks accepted from incoming updates
Redistributing: eigrp 10
EIGRP-IPv4 Protocol for AS(10)
Metric weight K1=1, K2=0, K3=1, K4=0, K5=0
NSF-aware route hold timer is 240
Router-ID: 10.1.1.1
Topology : 0 (base)
Active Timer: 3 min
Distance: internal 90 external 170
Maximum path: 4
Maximum hopcount 100
Maximum metric variance 1

Automatic Summarization: disabled
Automatic address summarization:
Maximum path: 4
Routing for Networks:
192.168.1.0
10.0.0.0
```

```
Routing Information Sources:
Gateway Distance Last Update
192.168.1.2 90 319551
Distance: internal 90 external 170
```

Task 6:

Ping the remote network IP address.

```
R0#ping 172.16.1.1

Type escape sequence to abort.
Sending 5, 100-byte ICMP Echos to 172.16.1.1, timeout is 2 seconds:
!!!!!
Success rate is 100 percent (5/5), round-trip min/avg/max = 0/0/1 ms
```

Task 7:

There are many other commands you can use with every routing protocol, but they're well outside the syllabus requirements. Try these if you wish:

```
R0#show ip eigrp ?
interfaces IP-EIGRP interfaces
neighbors IP-EIGRP neighbors
topology IP-EIGRP Topology Table
traffic IP-EIGRP Traffic Statistics
```

Notes:

EIGRP scales from small to large networks. There are many configuration parameters you can add and tweak, but you won't need to know about these for the Network+ exam.

OSPF

Lab Objective:

Learn how to configure the OSPF routing protocol.

Lab Purpose:

OSPF is a link state routing protocol which scales very well for large to very large networks. It uses a link state algorithm to determine the best (shortest) path to take to a particular network. OSPF uses the concept of areas in order to determine which type of routing update to send. We will stick to area 0 in this lab for simplicity.

Lab Tool:

Packet Tracer

Lab Topology:

Please use the following topology to complete this lab exercise:

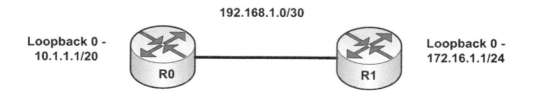

Lab Walkthrough:

Task 1:

Connect two routers together using a crossover cable.

Task 2:

Add the IP addresses to the routers connecting the interfaces and then the loopback interfaces. Hopefully you are getting familiar with this process now, so I'll just walk you through R0 configuration.

```
Router>en
Router#conf t
```

```
Router(config)#hostname R0
R0(config)#
Enter configuration commands, one per line.  End with CNTL/Z.
R0(config)#int lo0
R0(config-if)#ip add 10.1.1.1 255.255.240.0
R0(config-if)#int g0/0
R0(config-if)#ip add 192.168.1.1 255.255.255.252
R0(config-if)#no shut
%LINK-5-CHANGED: Interface GigabitEthernet0/0, changed state to up
```

Task 3:

Ping from R0 to R1 to check the connection works.

```
R0#ping 192.168.1.2

Type escape sequence to abort.
Sending 5, 100-byte ICMP Echos to 192.168.1.2, timeout is 2 seconds:
.!!!!
Success rate is 80 percent (4/5), round-trip min/avg/max = 0/0/0 ms
```

Task 4:

Configure OSPF on both R0 and R1 to advertise the connected networks. OSPF requires you add an area as well as a wildcard mask instead of a subnet mask. This tells the router exactly which subnet you wish to advertise. As a quick cheat, you take whatever the subnet value is in each octet and take it away from 255, so:

```
255.255.240.0 gives you
0.0.15.255
255.255.255.252 gives you
0.0.0.3
```

The number following OSPF is only locally significant, so you need not match it on a neighbor router.

```
R0(config)#router ospf 10
R0(config-router)#network 10.1.1.0 0.0.15.255 area 0
R0(config-router)#network 192.168.1.0 0.0.0.3 area 0

R1(config)#router ospf 20
R1(config-router)#network 192.168.1.0 0.0.0.3 area 0
R1(config-router)#network 172.16.1.0 0.0.0.255 area 0
```

You should see the below information message appear when the link comes up.

```
00:48:11: %OSPF-5-ADJCHG: Process 20, Nbr 10.1.1.1 on
GigabitEthernet0/0 from LOADING to FULL, Loading Done
```

Task 5:

Check the routing table with the 'show ip route' command and the routing configurations with the 'show ip protocols' command. Because we are using loopback interfaces, OSPF will advertise /32 as the subnet. You can google what to do about this, but it's well outside the syllabus.

You can see that OSPF has 110 as its administrative distance and the metric is 2, which for OSPF is the cost to get to the remote link.

```
R0#show ip route
Codes: L - local, C - connected, S - static, R - RIP, M - mobile, B
 - BGP
D - EIGRP, EX - EIGRP external, O - OSPF, IA - OSPF inter area
N1 - OSPF NSSA external type 1, N2 - OSPF NSSA external type 2
E1 - OSPF external type 1, E2 - OSPF external type 2, E - EGP
i - IS-IS, L1 - IS-IS level-1, L2 - IS-IS level-2, ia - IS-IS inter
area
* - candidate default, U - per-user static route, o - ODR
P - periodic downloaded static route

Gateway of last resort is not set

10.0.0.0/8 is variably subnetted, 2 subnets, 2 masks
C 10.1.0.0/20 is directly connected, Loopback0
L 10.1.1.1/32 is directly connected, Loopback0
172.16.0.0/32 is subnetted, 1 subnets
O 172.16.1.1/32 [110/2] via 192.168.1.2, 00:01:19, GigabitEthernet0/0
192.168.1.0/24 is variably subnetted, 2 subnets, 2 masks
C 192.168.1.0/30 is directly connected, GigabitEthernet0/0
L 192.168.1.1/32 is directly connected, GigabitEthernet0/0

R0#show ip protocols

Routing Protocol is "ospf 10"
Outgoing update filter list for all interfaces is not set
Incoming update filter list for all interfaces is not set
Router ID 10.1.1.1
Number of areas in this router is 1. 1 normal 0 stub 0 nssa
Maximum path: 4
Routing for Networks:
192.168.1.0 0.0.0.3 area 0
10.1.0.0 0.0.15.255 area 0
Routing Information Sources:
Gateway Distance Last Update
10.1.1.1 110 00:06:44
172.16.1.1 110 00:06:44
Distance: (default is 110)
```

Task 6:

Ping the remote network IP address. Feel free to try this on the R1 to R0 loopback also.

```
R0#ping 172.16.1.1

Type escape sequence to abort.
Sending 5, 100-byte ICMP Echos to 172.16.1.1, timeout is 2 seconds:
!!!!!
Success rate is 100 percent (5/5), round-trip min/avg/max = 0/0/1 ms
```

Task 7:

There are many other commands you can use with every routing protocol, but they're well outside the syllabus requirements. Try these if you wish:

```
R0#show ip ospf ?
<1-65535> Process ID number
border-routers Border and Boundary Router Information
database Database summary
interface Interface information
neighbor Neighbor list
virtual-links Virtual link information
<cr>
```

Notes:

We have just dipped our toes into OSPF here. It's extensively covered in Cisco CCNP and partially in Cisco CCNA.

BGP

Lab Objective:

Learn how to configure BGP.

Lab Purpose:

BGP is the protocol which allows the internet to function. It is an exterior gateway routing protocol and concerns itself with autonomous systems rather than networks. You can see R0 below is in AS1 and R1 is in AS2. BGP makes its forwarding decisions based on paths and rules. In order to understand it fully we would need to spend several weeks studying it, but today we'll just cover some very basic commands.

Lab Tool:

Packet Tracer

Lab Topology:

Please use the following topology to complete this lab exercise:

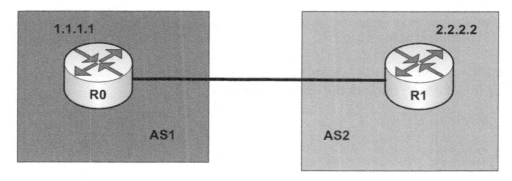

Lab Walkthrough:

Task 1:

Connect two routers together using a crossover cable.

Task 2:

Add the IP addresses to the routers connecting the interfaces and then the loopback interfaces. BGP will use the loopback interfaces as the BGP identifier (inserted into the routing updates). The identifier allows the source of the packets to be recorded by all other routers as well as establishes the best path to take.

```
Router>en
Router#conf t
Router(config)#hostname R0
R0(config)#
Enter configuration commands, one per line.  End with CNTL/Z.
R0(config)#int loopback 0
R0(config-if)#ip add 1.1.1.1 255.255.255.0
R0(config-if)#int g0/0
R0(config-if)#ip add 192.168.1.1 255.255.255.252
R0(config-if)#no shut

Router>en
Router#conf t
Router(config)#hostname R1
R1(config)#
Enter configuration commands, one per line.  End with CNTL/Z.
R1(config)#int lo0
R1(config-if)#ip add 2.2.2.2 255.255.255.0
R1(config-if)#int g0/0
R1(config-if)#ip add 192.168.1.2 255.255.255.252
R1(config-if)#no shut
```

Task 3:

Ping from R0 to R1 to check the connection works.

```
R0#ping 192.168.1.2

Type escape sequence to abort.
Sending 5, 100-byte ICMP Echos to 192.168.1.2, timeout is 2 seconds:
.!!!!
Success rate is 80 percent (4/5), round-trip min/avg/max = 0/0/0 ms

R0#
```

Task 4:

Configure BGP on both routers. You need to specify the neighbor details you want the Router to communicate with and the network you wish to advertise.

```
R0(config)#router bgp 1
R0(config-router)#neighbor 192.168.1.2 remote-as 2
R0(config-router)#network 1.1.1.0 mask 255.255.255.0

R1(config)#router bgp 2
R1(config-router)#neighbor 192.168.1.1 remote-as 1
%BGP-5-ADJCHANGE: neighbor 192.168.1.1 Up
R1(config-router)#network 2.2.2.0 mask 255.255.255.0
```

You should see the below information message appear when the link comes up.

```
BGP-5-ADJCHANGE: neighbor 192.168.1.1 Up
```

Task 5:

Check the routing table with the 'show ip route' command and the routing configurations with the 'show ip protocols' command. We'll also look at some other BGP commands.

```
R0#show ip route
Codes: L - local, C - connected, S - static, R - RIP, M - mobile, B
 - BGP
D - EIGRP, EX - EIGRP external, O - OSPF, IA - OSPF inter area
N1 - OSPF NSSA external type 1, N2 - OSPF NSSA external type 2
E1 - OSPF external type 1, E2 - OSPF external type 2, E - EGP
i - IS-IS, L1 - IS-IS level-1, L2 - IS-IS level-2, ia - IS-IS inter
area
* - candidate default, U - per-user static route, o - ODR
P - periodic downloaded static route

Gateway of last resort is not set

1.0.0.0/8 is variably subnetted, 2 subnets, 2 masks
C 1.1.1.0/24 is directly connected, Loopback0
L 1.1.1.1/32 is directly connected, Loopback0
2.0.0.0/24 is subnetted, 1 subnets
B 2.2.2.0/24 [20/0] via 192.168.1.2, 00:00:00
192.168.1.0/24 is variably subnetted, 2 subnets, 2 masks
C 192.168.1.0/30 is directly connected, GigabitEthernet0/0
L 192.168.1.1/32 is directly connected, GigabitEthernet0/0

R0#show ip protocols
Routing Protocol is "bgp 1"
Outgoing update filter list for all interfaces is not set
Incoming update filter list for all interfaces is not set
IGP synchronization is disabled
```

```
Automatic route summarization is disabled
Neighbor(s):
Address FiltIn FiltOut DistIn DistOut Weight RouteMap
192.168.1.2
Maximum path: 1
Routing Information Sources:
Gateway Distance Last Update
192.168.1.2 20 00:00:00
Distance: external 20 internal 200 local 200
```

Task 6:

Issue the 'show tcp brief' and 'show ip bgp neighbors' commands. Keep an eye out for the BGP TCP port, which is 179.

```
R0#show tcp brief
TCB Local Address Foreign Address (state)
517164B0 192.168.1.1.179 192.168.1.2.1025 ESTABLISHED

R0#show ip bgp neighbors
BGP neighbor is 192.168.1.2, remote AS 2, external link
BGP version 4, remote router ID 2.2.2.2
BGP state = Established, up for 00:23:01
Last read 00:23:01, last write 00:23:01, hold time is 180, keepalive
interval is 60 seconds
Neighbor capabilities:
Route refresh: advertised and received(new)
Address family IPv4 Unicast: advertised and received
[output truncated]
```

Note:

BGP is an advanced topic and is usually studied for Cisco CCNP or other advanced routing exams.

IPv6 Addressing

Lab Objective:
Learn how to configure IPv6 addressing on an interface.

Lab Purpose:
Most networks are in the process of transitioning from IPv4 to IPv6. If you can't configure and troubleshoot IPv6, you will find yourself unemployable in the near future. This lab will cover basic interface addressing as well as the auto-address configuration facility.

Lab Tool:
Packet Tracer

Lab Topology:
Please use the following topology to complete this lab exercise:

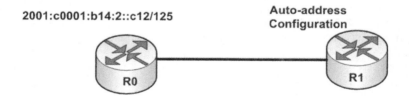

Lab Walkthrough:

Task 1:
Connect two routers together using a crossover cable.

Task 2:
Add the IPv6 addresses to the routers' interfaces. Note that, at least on Cisco routers, you need to enable IPv6 first.

```
Router>en
Router#conf t
Router(config)#hostname R0
R0(config)#ipv6 unicast-routing
```

```
Enter configuration commands, one per line.  End with CNTL/Z.
R0(config-if)#int g0/0
R0(config-if)#ipv6 address 2001:c001:b14:2::c12/125
R0(config-if)#no shut
R0(config-if)#end
```

Task 3:

Use the auto-address facility for Router1.

```
Router>en
Router#conf t
Router(config)#hostname R1
R1(config)#ipv6 unicast-routing
Enter configuration commands, one per line.  End with CNTL/Z.
R1(config-if)#int g0/0
R1(config-if)#ipv6 address autoconfig
R1(config-if)#no shut
R1(config-if)#end
```

Task 4:

Check the interfaces are up.

```
R0#show ipv6 interface g0/0
GigabitEthernet0/0 is up, line protocol is up
IPv6 is enabled, link-local address is FE80::230:A3FF:FE6A:2301
No Virtual link-local address(es):
Global unicast address(es):
2001:C001:B14:2::C12, subnet is 2001:C001:B14:2::C10/125
Joined group address(es):
FF02::1
FF02::2
FF02::1:FF00:C12
FF02::1:FF6A:2301
```

The R1 interface should have self-configured an IPv6 address.

```
R1#show ipv6 interface g0/0
GigabitEthernet0/0 is up, line protocol is up
IPv6 is enabled, link-local address is FE80::2E0:F9FF:FED7:3401
No Virtual link-local address(es):
No global unicast address is configured
Joined group address(es):
FF02::1
FF02::2
FF02::1:FFD7:3401
```

Task 5:

Ping from R0 to R1. The process is slightly different for IPv6. You need to specify an exit interface on Ethernet links. You might want to cut-and-paste the address from R1 into the command in order to save time and avoid mistakes.

```
R0#ping ipv6 FE80::2E0:F9FF:FED7:3401
Output Interface: GigabitEthernet0/0
Type escape sequence to abort.
Sending 5, 100-byte ICMP Echos to FE80::2E0:F9FF:FED7:3401, timeout is
2 seconds:
!!!!!
Success rate is 100 percent (5/5), round-trip min/avg/max = 0/0/1 ms
```

Note:

Make sure you repeat this lab a few times because we will be using IPv6 for associated routing protocols and EUI64 addressing.

LAB 19

RIPng

Lab Objective:

Learn how to configure RIPng.

Lab Purpose:

RIPng (next generation) was created to support IPv6 over RIP networks. It requires you to enable RIP under each interface you want to advertise, and to create a tag to identify different RIPng processes.

Lab Tool:

Packet Tracer

Lab Topology:

Please use the following topology to complete this lab exercise:

2001::/64

LO0
2000::1/64
.1
.2
LO0
2002::1/64

Lab Walkthrough:

Task 1:

Connect two routers together using a crossover cable. Note that my routers have f0/0 as their interface (see below), but yours may differ, so check with the 'show ip interface brief' command. Remember the note at the start at the book telling you that I used 1841 models mostly and by default mine ran image flash:c1841-advipservicesk9-mz.124-15. T1.bin. This allowed me to run all the routing protocols, security commands and services in these labs.

Task 2:

Enable IPv6 and then add the IPv6 addresses to the routers connecting the interfaces and then the loopback interfaces. Here is the configuration for R0. R1 will be .2 on the Ethernet link, and the loopback network is 2002.

```
Router>en
Router#conf t
Enter configuration commands, one per line. End with CNTL/Z.
Router(config)#host R0
R0(config)#ipv6 unicast-routing
R0(config)#int f0/0
R0(config-if)#ipv6 add 2001::1/64
R0(config-if)#no shut
R0(config-if)#int lo0
R0(config-if)#ipv6 add 2000::1/64
R0(config-if)#exit
```

Task 3:

Enable RIPng on all interfaces. Add the tag '101labs' so they all identify as belonging to the same RIP process. Here is the configuration for R0; please issue the same commands on R1.

```
R0(config)#int f0/0
R0(config-if)#ipv6 rip 101labs enable
R0(config-if)#int lo0
R0(config-if)#ipv6 rip 101labs enable
```

Task 4:

Check the RIPng database.

```
R1#show ipv6 rip database
RIP process "101labs" local RIB
2000::/64, metric 2, installed
FastEthernet0/0/FE80::201:97FF:FE3D:EE01, expires in 155 sec
2001::/64, metric 2
FastEthernet0/0/FE80::201:97FF:FE3D:EE01, expires in 155 sec
```

Task 5:

Check the IPv6 routing table. You should see the remote network listed.

```
R1#show ipv6 route
IPv6 Routing Table - 6 entries
Codes: C - Connected, L - Local, S - Static, R - RIP, B - BGP
U - Per-user Static route, M - MIPv6
I1 - ISIS L1, I2 - ISIS L2, IA - ISIS interarea, IS - ISIS summary
O - OSPF intra, OI - OSPF inter, OE1 - OSPF ext 1, OE2 - OSPF ext 2
ON1 - OSPF NSSA ext 1, ON2 - OSPF NSSA ext 2
```

```
D - EIGRP, EX - EIGRP external
R 2000::/64 [120/2]
via FE80::201:97FF:FE3D:EE01, FastEthernet0/0
C 2001::/64 [0/0]
via ::, FastEthernet0/0
L 2001::2/128 [0/0]
via ::, FastEthernet0/0
C 2002::/64 [0/0]
via ::, Loopback0
L 2002::1/128 [0/0]
via ::, Loopback0
L FF00::/8 [0/0]
via ::, Null0
```

Task 6:

Issue the 'show ipv6 protocols' command.

```
R1#show ipv6 protocols
IPv6 Routing Protocol is "connected"
IPv6 Routing Protocol is "static"
IPv6 Routing Protocol is "rip 101labs"
Interfaces:
FastEthernet0/0
Loopback0
Redistribution:
None
```

Notes:

Don't worry too much about the commands because the Network+ command is vendor-neutral. You need learn the specific commands only when you take a vendor exam, such as Cisco CCNA.

LAB 20

EIGRP for IPv6

Lab Objective:
Learn how to configure EIGRP for IPv6.

Lab Purpose:
EIGRP for IPv6 was created to address the requirements of running EIGRP over IPv6 networks. There are some configuration differences from IPv4, including having to configure it under the interface.

Lab Tool:
Packet Tracer

Lab Topology:
Please use the following topology to complete this lab exercise:

2001::/64

LO0
2000::1/64

.1   .2

LO0
2002::1/64

Lab Walkthrough:

Task 1:
Connect two routers together using a crossover cable.

Task 2:
Enable IPv6 and then add the IPv6 addresses to the routers connecting the interfaces and then the loopback interfaces. Here is the configuration for R0. R1 will be .2 on the Ethernet link, and the loopback network is 2002.

```
Router>en
Router#conf t
```

```
Enter configuration commands, one per line. End with CNTL/Z.
Router(config)#host R0
R0(config)#ipv6 unicast-routing
R0(config)#int f0/0
R0(config-if)#ipv6 add 2001::1/64
R0(config-if)#no shut
R0(config-if)#int lo0
R0(config-if)#ipv6 add 2000::1/64
R0(config-if)#exit
```

Task 3:

Enable EIGRP for IPv6 on the interfaces and set the identifier for the router, which will be an IPv4 address. Here is the config for R0; set the ID for R1 as 2.2.2.2. In order to enable EIGRP for IPv6 you must issue the 'no shutdown' command.

```
R0(config)#ipv6 router eigrp 1
R0(config-rtr)#no shutdown
R0(config-rtr)#eigrp router-id 1.1.1.1
R0(config-rtr)#exit
R0(config)#int f0/0
R0(config-if)#ipv6 eigrp 1
R0(config-if)#int lo0
R0(config-if)#ipv6 eigrp 1
```

Task 4:

There are four show commands we can check for EIGRP. Here is the output for one of them:

```
R1#show ipv6 eigrp ?
interfaces EIGRP interfaces
neighbors EIGRP neighbors
topology EIGRP Topology Table
traffic EIGRP Traffic Statistics

R1#show ipv6 eigrp topology
IPv6-EIGRP Topology Table for AS 1/ID(2.2.2.2)

Codes: P - Passive, A - Active, U - Update, Q - Query, R - Reply,
r - Reply status

P 2000::/64, 1 successors, FD is 156160
via FE80::2D0:97FF:FE43:AA01 (156160/128256), FastEthernet0/0
P 2001::/64, 1 successors, FD is 28160
via Connected, FastEthernet0/0
P 2002::/64, 1 successors, FD is 128256
via Connected, Loopback0
```

Task 5:

Check the EIGRP for IPv6 routing table.

```
R1#show ipv6 route
IPv6 Routing Table - 6 entries
Codes: C - Connected, L - Local, S - Static, R - RIP, B - BGP
U - Per-user Static route, M - MIPv6
I1 - ISIS L1, I2 - ISIS L2, IA - ISIS interarea, IS - ISIS summary
O - OSPF intra, OI - OSPF inter, OE1 - OSPF ext 1, OE2 - OSPF ext 2
ON1 - OSPF NSSA ext 1, ON2 - OSPF NSSA ext 2
D - EIGRP, EX - EIGRP external
D 2000::/64 [90/156160]
via FE80::2D0:97FF:FE43:AA01, FastEthernet0/0
C 2001::/64 [0/0]
via ::, FastEthernet0/0
L 2001::2/128 [0/0]
via ::, FastEthernet0/0
C 2002::/64 [0/0]
via ::, Loopback0
L 2002::1/128 [0/0]
via ::, Loopback0
L FF00::/8 [0/0]
via ::, Null0
```

Task 6:

Issue the 'show ipv6 protocols' command.

```
R1#show ipv6 protocols
IPv6 Routing Protocol is "connected"
IPv6 Routing Protocol is "static"
IPv6 Routing Protocol is "eigrp 1"
EIGRP metric weight K1=1, K2=0, K3=1, K4=0, K5=0
EIGRP maximum hopcount 100
EIGRP maximum metric variance 1
Interfaces:
FastEthernet0/0
Loopback0
Redistributing: eigrp 1
Maximum path: 16
Distance: internal 90 external 170
```

Notes:

Don't worry too much about the commands because the Network+ command is vendor-neutral. You need learn the specific commands only when you take a vendor exam, such as Cisco CCNA.

LAB 21

OSPFv3

Lab Objective:

Learn how to configure OSPFv3.

Lab Purpose:

OSPF for IPv6 works in a very similar way to OSPF. There are some configuration differences as well as small changes to authentication processes and the way adjacencies form.

Lab Tool:

Packet Tracer

Lab Topology:

Please use the following topology to complete this lab exercise:

2001::/64

LO0
2000::1/64   .1   .2   LO0
2002::1/64

Lab Walkthrough:

Task 1:

Connect two routers together using a crossover cable.

Task 2:

Enable IPv6 and then add the IPv6 addresses to the routers connecting the interfaces and then the loopback interfaces. Here is the configuration for R0. R1 will be .2 on the Ethernet link, and the loopback network is 2002.

```
Router>en
Router#conf t
```

```
Enter configuration commands, one per line. End with CNTL/Z.
Router(config)#host R0
R0(config)#ipv6 unicast-routing
R0(config)#int f0/0
R0(config-if)#ipv6 add 2001::1/64
R0(config-if)#no shut
R0(config-if)#int lo0
R0(config-if)#ipv6 add 2000::1/64
R0(config-if)#exit
```

Task 3:

Enable OSPFv3 on R0. Set the router ID as 1.1.1.1 and the process on the router as 1, and put all interfaces into area 0. For R1 set the ID as 2.2.2.2.

```
R0(config)#ipv6 router ospf 1
R0(config)#int f0/0
R0(config-if)#ipv6 ospf 1 area 0
%OSPFv3-4-NORTRID: OSPFv3 process 1 could not pick a router-id,please
configure manually
R0(config-if)#int lo0
R0(config-if)#ipv6 ospf 1 area 0
R0(config-if)#exit
R0(config)#router ospf 1
R0(config-rtr)#router-id 1.1.1.1
```

Task 4:

Check the OSPF IPv6 routing table.

```
R1#show ipv6 route ospf
IPv6 Routing Table - 6 entries
Codes: C - Connected, L - Local, S - Static, R - RIP, B - BGP
U - Per-user Static route, M - MIPv6
I1 - ISIS L1, I2 - ISIS L2, IA - ISIS interarea, IS - ISIS summary
O - OSPF intra, OI - OSPF inter, OE1 - OSPF ext 1, OE2 - OSPF ext 2
ON1 - OSPF NSSA ext 1, ON2 - OSPF NSSA ext 2
D - EIGRP, EX - EIGRP external
O 2000::1/128 [110/1]
via FE80::201:C9FF:FEAC:2701, FastEthernet0/0
```

Task 5:

Enter some IPv6 OSPF show commands. Here is one:

```
R1#show ipv6 ospf ?
<1-65535> Process ID number
border-routers Border and Boundary Router Information
database Database summary
interface Interface information
neighbor Neighbor list
```

```
virtual-links Virtual link information
<cr>

R1#show ipv6 ospf 1
Routing Process "ospfv3 1" with ID 2.2.2.2
SPF schedule delay 5 secs, Hold time between two SPFs 10 secs
Minimum LSA interval 5 secs. Minimum LSA arrival 1 secs
LSA group pacing timer 240 secs
Interface flood pacing timer 33 msecs
Retransmission pacing timer 66 msecs
Number of external LSA 0. Checksum Sum 0x000000
Number of areas in this router is 1. 1 normal 0 stub 0 nssa
Reference bandwidth unit is 100 mbps
Area BACKBONE(0)
Number of interfaces in this area is 2
SPF algorithm executed 4 times
Number of LSA 6. Checksum Sum 0x037c88
Number of DCbitless LSA 0
Number of indication LSA 0
Number of DoNotAge LSA 0
Flood list length 0
```

Notes:

Don't worry too much about the commands because the Network+ command is vendor-neutral. You need learn the specific commands only when you take a vendor exam, such as Cisco CCNA.

LAB 22

IPv6 EUI-64 Addressing

Lab Objective:
Learn how to configure IPv6 EUI-64 addressing on an interface.

Lab Purpose:
EUI-64 addressing is a convenient way of configuring IPv6 addresses on your interface. You can choose the host portion of your address to be autoconfigured by using the MAC address plus some padding. Please refer to your study guide for the theory behind this process.

Lab Tool:
Packet Tracer

Lab Topology:
Please use the following topology to complete this lab exercise:

2001:aa::/64 EUI

RO

Lab Walkthrough:

Task 1:
Use any Cisco router.

Task 2:
Check the MAC address on the interface. EUI-64 will use this for the host portion of the address. Please note that your MAC address will differ from mine because each one is unique. Even Packet Tracer interface MAC addresses differ.

```
Router>en
Router#conf t
```

```
Router(config)#hostname R0
Router(config)#exit
R0#show interface g0/0
GigabitEthernet0/0 is administratively down, line protocol is down
(disabled)
Hardware is CN Gigabit Ethernet, address is 0001.9669.ec01 (bia
0001.9669.ec01)
```

Task 3:

Configure IPv6 on the router and then add the network portion of the IPv6, leaving EUI-64 to take care of the host portion.

```
R0#conf t
R0(config)#ipv6 unicast-routing
Enter configuration commands, one per line.  End with CNTL/Z.
R0(config)#int g0/0
R0(config-if)#ipv6 address 2001:aa::/64 eui-64
R0(config-if)#no shut
R0(config-if)#end
```

Task 4:

Check the interface has been configured and is using the EUI-64 address.

```
R0#show ipv6 interface g0/0
GigabitEthernet0/0 is administratively down, line protocol is down
IPv6 is tentative, link-local address is FE80::201:96FF:FE69:EC01 [TEN]
No Virtual link-local address(es):
Global unicast address(es):
2001:AA::201:96FF:FE69:EC01, subnet is 2001:AA::/64 [EUI/TEN]
Joined group address(es):
FF02::1

Compare your MAC and IPv6 addresses side by side.
0001.9669.ec01
2001:AA::201:96FF:FE69:EC01
```

Notes:

Your study guide should cover how EUI-64 addressing manipulates the MAC address and inverts the seventh bit. Above you can see 0001 has been changed to 0201. It has been compressed to 201 in the output as per IPv6 addressing conventions. Check your study guide for details.

LAB 23

Static NAT

Lab Objective:
Learn how to configure static network address translation (NAT).

Lab Purpose:
NAT is used by routers and firewalls to swap one address for another. Many manuals tell you that it's used to allow private IP addresses (non-routable RFC 1918) to access the internet. This is true, but actually you can NAT routable addresses to different routable addresses. You would do this if you wanted to keep your address masked from hosts outside your network.

Lab Tool:
Packet Tracer

Lab Topology:
Please use the following topology to complete this lab exercise:

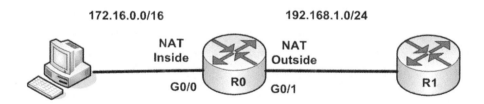

Lab Walkthrough:

Task 1:
Connect a host to a router via a crossover cable. Add another router, which will be the IP address the host pings.

Task 2:

Set the IP configuration for the host. The Ethernet interface should be 172.16.1.2 and the default gateway 172.16.1.1, which will be the closest IP address of R0.

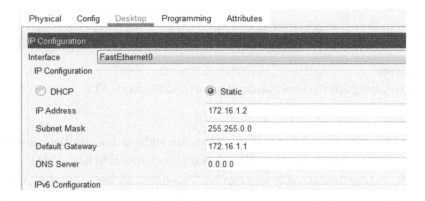

Task 3:

Configure IP addressing on R0 and R1. The routers are connected via G0/1.

```
Router(config)#host R0
R0(config)#int g0/0
R0(config-if)#ip add 172.16.1.1 255.255.0.0
R0(config-if)#no shut
%LINK-5-CHANGED: Interface GigabitEthernet0/0, changed state to up
R0(config-if)#int g0/1
R0(config-if)#ip add 192.168.1.1 255.255.255.0
R0(config-if)#no shut

R1(config)#int g0/1
R1(config-if)#ip add 192.168.1.2 255.255.255.0
R1(config-if)#no shut
R1(config-if)#exit
```

Task 4:

Add a static route on R1 to send all traffic to R0. We do this because the NAT address won't be in any routing tables and will otherwise be dropped by the router.

```
R1(config)#ip route 0.0.0.0 0.0.0.0 192.168.1.1
```

Task 5:

Add your NAT configuration to R0. The address 172.16.1.2 should be NAT-ted to 10.0.0.1. We would usually use a routable address, but I don't want to take the risk here, so we'll stick to private IP addressing. Note also that you must tell the router which is the inside/outside of your network for the purposes of NAT.

```
R0(config)#ip nat inside source static 172.16.1.2 10.0.0.1
R0(config)#int g0/0
R0(config-if)#ip nat inside
R0(config-if)#int g0/1
R0(config-if)#ip nat outside
R0(config-if)#end
```

Task 6:

Test your configuration by pinging 192.168.1.2 from your host. R0 should swap (NAT) this address for 10.0.0.1.

```
Physical   Config   Desktop   Programming   Attributes

Command Prompt

Packet Tracer PC Command Line 1.0
C:\>ping 192.168.1.2

Pinging 192.168.1.2 with 32 bytes of data:

Request timed out.
Reply from 192.168.1.2: bytes=32 time<1ms TTL=254
Reply from 192.168.1.2: bytes=32 time<1ms TTL=254
Reply from 192.168.1.2: bytes=32 time<1ms TTL=254

Ping statistics for 192.168.1.2:
    Packets: Sent = 4, Received = 3, Lost = 1 (25% loss),
Approximate round trip times in milli-seconds:
    Minimum = 0ms, Maximum = 0ms, Average = 0ms

C:\>
```

Check the NAT table on R0. The inside global address is the NAT address. The inside local is your host, and the outside local is the destination address.

```
R0#show ip nat translations
Pro Inside global Inside local Outside local Outside global
icmp 10.0.0.1:1 172.16.1.2:1 192.168.1.2:1 192.168.1.2:1
icmp 10.0.0.1:2 172.16.1.2:2 192.168.1.2:2 192.168.1.2:2
```

```
icmp 10.0.0.1:3 172.16.1.2:3 192.168.1.2:3 192.168.1.2:3
icmp 10.0.0.1:4 172.16.1.2:4 192.168.1.2:4 192.168.1.2:4
--- 10.0.0.1 172.16.1.2 --- ---

RO#show ip nat statistics
Total translations: 5 (1 static, 4 dynamic, 4 extended)
Outside Interfaces: GigabitEthernet0/1
Inside Interfaces: GigabitEthernet0/0
Hits: 3 Misses: 4
Expired translations: 0
Dynamic mappings:
RO#
```

Note:

NAT is used on every network running IPv4, including your home network.

LAB 24

NAT Pool

Lab Objective:
Learn how to configure a pool of network address translation (NAT) addresses.

Lab Purpose:
As you know, even your home router uses NAT to reach the internet. Chances are you have several devices that use your router, which means that a pool of addresses might be used instead of that in our last lab (i.e., static NAT). In this lab we will configure a pool of addresses to be available for NAT.

Lab Tool:
Packet Tracer

Lab Topology:
Please use the following topology to complete this lab exercise:

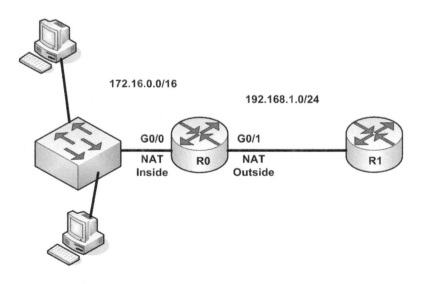

Lab Walkthrough:

Task 1:

Connect a couple of hosts to a switch. Connect two routers via a crossover cable.

Task 2:

Set the IP configuration for the hosts. The Ethernet interfaces should be 172.16.1.2 and .3 and the default gateway 172.16.1.1, which will be the closest IP address of R0. Here it is on one host device:

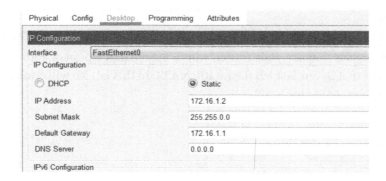

Task 3:

Configure IP addressing on R0 and R1. The routers are connected via G0/1.

```
Router(config)#host R0
R0(config)#int g0/0
R0(config-if)#ip add 172.16.1.1 255.255.0.0
R0(config-if)#no shut
%LINK-5-CHANGED: Interface GigabitEthernet0/0, changed state to up
R0(config-if)#int g0/1
R0(config-if)#ip add 192.168.1.1 255.255.255.0
R0(config-if)#no shut
R0(config-if)#exit

R1(config)#int g0/1
R1(config-if)#ip add 192.168.1.2 255.255.255.0
R1(config-if)#no shut
R1(config-if)#exit
```

Task 4:

Add a static route on R1 to send all traffic to R0. We do this because the NAT address won't be in any routing tables and will otherwise be dropped by the router.

```
R1(config)#ip route 0.0.0.0 0.0.0.0 192.168.1.1
```

Task 5:

Add your NAT configuration to R0. The address 172.16.1.0 should be NAT-ted to a pool of addresses from the 10.0.0.0/8 network. We would usually use a routable address, but I don't want to take the risk here, so we'll stick to private IP addressing. Note also that you must tell the router which is the inside/outside of your network for the purposes of NAT.

For a NAT pool we must add a bit more configuration. We create a NAT pool, a source list which tells the router which pool to use, and then an access list. This access list is used by NAT to decide which subnets or networks to NAT.

```
R0(config)#ip nat pool 101labs 10.0.0.0 10.0.0.254 netmask 255.0.0.0
R0(config)#ip nat inside source list 1 pool 101labs
R0(config)#access-list 1 permit 172.16.0.0 0.0.255.255
R0(config)#int g0/0
R0(config-if)#ip nat inside
R0(config-if)#int g0/1
R0(config-if)#ip nat outside
R0(config-if)#end
```

Task 6:

Test your configuration by pinging 192.168.1.2 from your host. R0 should swap (NAT) this address for an address from the pool. Quickly do the same from the second host machine. We want to be fairly brisk because routers will time out NATs to keep the pool from running out of addresses.

```
PC2

Physical   Config   Desktop   Programming   Attributes

Command Prompt

Packet Tracer PC Command Line 1.0
C:\>ping 192.168.1.2

Pinging 192.168.1.2 with 32 bytes of data:

Reply from 192.168.1.2: bytes=32 time=1ms TTL=254
Reply from 192.168.1.2: bytes=32 time=1ms TTL=254
Reply from 192.168.1.2: bytes=32 time<1ms TTL=254
Reply from 192.168.1.2: bytes=32 time=1ms TTL=254

Ping statistics for 192.168.1.2:
    Packets: Sent = 4, Received = 4, Lost = 0 (0% loss),
Approximate round trip times in milli-seconds:
    Minimum = 0ms, Maximum = 1ms, Average = 0ms

C:\>
```

Check the NAT table on R0. The inside global address is the NAT address. The inside local is your host, and the outside local is the destination address. You should see your 172.16.1.2 and .3 hosts using addresses from the NAT pool.

```
R0#show ip nat translations
Pro Inside global Inside local Outside local Outside global
icmp 10.0.0.1:29 172.16.1.2:29 192.168.1.2:29 192.168.1.2:29
icmp 10.0.0.1:30 172.16.1.2:30 192.168.1.2:30 192.168.1.2:30
icmp 10.0.0.1:31 172.16.1.2:31 192.168.1.2:31 192.168.1.2:31
icmp 10.0.0.1:32 172.16.1.2:32 192.168.1.2:32 192.168.1.2:32
icmp 10.0.0.2:5 172.16.1.3:5 192.168.1.2:5 192.168.1.2:5
icmp 10.0.0.2:6 172.16.1.3:6 192.168.1.2:6 192.168.1.2:6
icmp 10.0.0.2:7 172.16.1.3:7 192.168.1.2:7 192.168.1.2:7
icmp 10.0.0.2:8 172.16.1.3:8 192.168.1.2:8 192.168.1.2:8

R0#show ip nat statistics
Total translations: 4 (0 static, 4 dynamic, 4 extended)
Outside Interfaces: GigabitEthernet0/1
Inside Interfaces: GigabitEthernet0/0
Hits: 15 Misses: 63
Expired translations: 12
Dynamic mappings:
-- Inside Source
access-list 1 pool 101labs refCount 4
pool 101labs: netmask 255.0.0.0
start 10.0.0.0 end 10.0.0.254
type generic, total addresses 255 , allocated 1 (0%), misses 0
```

Note:

NAT is used on every network running IPv4, including your home network.

LAB 25

Port Address Translation (PAT)/NAT Overload

Lab Objective:

Learn how to configure port address translation (PAT).

Lab Purpose:

Many businesses and homes can afford only one IP address but still have several hosts which need to access the internet. PAT allows one IP address to be used by thousands of hosts. They all use the same IP address but add a port number to the translation and keep a log of which host uses which port.

Lab Tool:

Packet Tracer

Lab Topology:

Please use the following topology to complete this lab exercise:

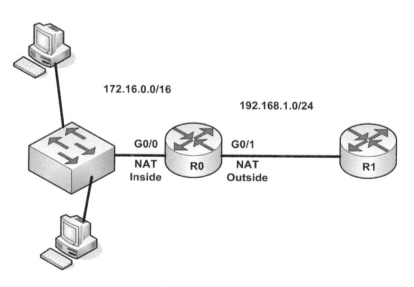

Lab Walkthrough:

Task 1:

Connect a couple of hosts to a switch. Connect two routers via a crossover cable.

Task 2:

Set the IP configuration for the hosts. The Ethernet interfaces should be 172.16.1.2 and .3 and the default gateway 172.16.1.1, which will be the closest IP address of R0. Here it is on one host device:

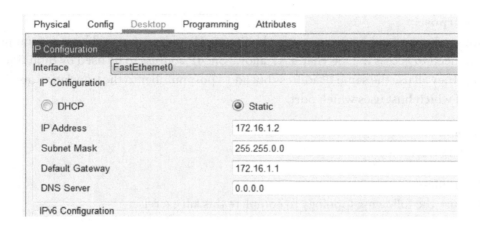

Task 3:

Configure IP addressing on R0 and R1. The routers are connected via G0/1.

```
Router(config)#host R0
R0(config)#int g0/0
R0(config-if)#ip add 172.16.1.1 255.255.0.0
R0(config-if)#no shut
%LINK-5-CHANGED: Interface GigabitEthernet0/0, changed state to up
R0(config-if)#int g0/1
R0(config-if)#ip add 192.168.1.1 255.255.255.0
R0(config-if)#no shut
R0(config-if)#exit

R1(config)#host R1
R1(config)#int g0/1
R1(config-if)#ip add 192.168.1.2 255.255.255.0
R1(config-if)#no shut
R1(config-if)#exit
```

Task 4:

Add a static route on R1 to send all traffic to R0. We do this because the NAT address won't be in any routing tables and will otherwise be dropped by the router.

```
R1(config)#ip route 0.0.0.0 0.0.0.0 192.168.1.1
```

Task 5:

Add your PAT configuration to R0. The network 172.16.0.0 should be NAT-ted to a pool of addresses from the 10.0.0.0/8 network. In this instance, our pool consists of only one address. We would usually use a routable address, but I don't want to take the risk here, so we'll stick to private IP addresses. Note also that you must tell the router which is the inside/outside of your network for the purposes of NAT.

For a NAT pool we must add a bit more configuration. We create a NAT pool, a source list which tells the router which pool to use, and then an access list. This access list is used by NAT to decide which subnets or networks to NAT. We add the 'overload' command to enable PAT. Without this we would be able to translate only one IP address.

Note that we are using the same IP address twice; this would be the case when we have only one IP address allocated by our ISP.

```
R0(config)#ip nat pool 101labs 10.0.0.1 10.0.0.1 netmask 255.0.0.0
R0(config)#ip nat inside source list 1 pool 101labs overload
R0(config)#access-list 1 permit 172.16.0.0 0.0.255.255
R0(config)#int g0/0
R0(config-if)#ip nat inside
R0(config-if)#int g0/1
R0(config-if)#ip nat outside
R0(config-if)#end
```

Task 6:

Test your configuration by pinging 192.168.1.2 from your hosts. R0 should swap (PAT) this address for an address from the pool but tag a port number onto it. Quickly do the same from the second host machine.

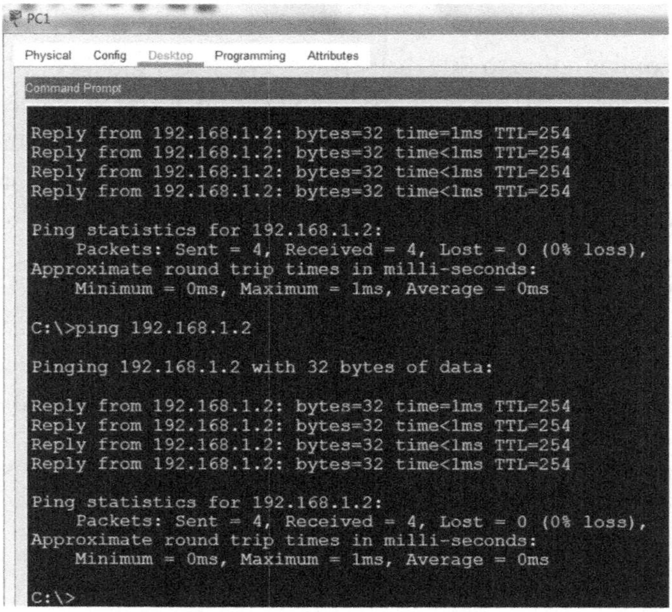

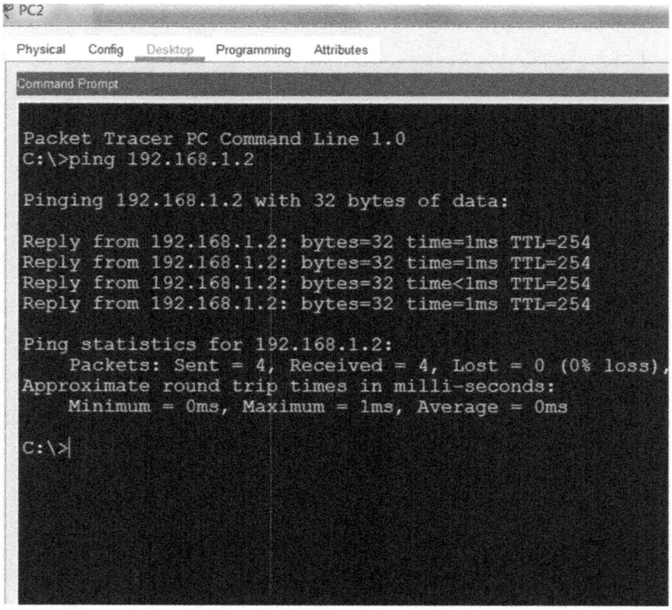

Check the NAT table on R0. The inside global address is the NAT address. The inside local is your host, and the outside local is the destination address. You should see your 172.16.1.2 and .3 hosts using addresses from the NAT pool, but all translations are tagged with a port number. You also get this with a NAT pool, but this is a limitation of Packet Tracer, I'm afraid.

```
R0#show ip nat tran
Pro Inside global Inside local Outside local Outside global
icmp 10.0.0.1:1024 172.16.1.3:1 192.168.1.2:1 192.168.1.2:1024
icmp 10.0.0.1:1025 172.16.1.3:2 192.168.1.2:2 192.168.1.2:1025
icmp 10.0.0.1:1026 172.16.1.3:3 192.168.1.2:3 192.168.1.2:1026
icmp 10.0.0.1:1027 172.16.1.3:4 192.168.1.2:4 192.168.1.2:1027
icmp 10.0.0.1:1 172.16.1.2:1 192.168.1.2:1 192.168.1.2:1
icmp 10.0.0.1:2 172.16.1.2:2 192.168.1.2:2 192.168.1.2:2
icmp 10.0.0.1:3 172.16.1.2:3 192.168.1.2:3 192.168.1.2:3
icmp 10.0.0.1:4 172.16.1.2:4 192.168.1.2:4 192.168.1.2:4

R0#show ip nat statistics
Total translations: 8 (0 static, 8 dynamic, 8 extended)
Outside Interfaces: GigabitEthernet0/1
Inside Interfaces: GigabitEthernet0/0
Hits: 8  Misses: 8
Expired translations: 0
Dynamic mappings:
-- Inside Source
access-list 1 pool 101labs refCount 8
 pool 101labs: netmask 255.0.0.0
        start 10.0.0.1 end 10.0.0.1
        type generic, total addresses 1 , allocated 1 (100%), misses 00
start 10.0.0.0 end 10.0.0.254
type generic, total addresses 255 , allocated 1 (0%), misses 0
```

Note:

PAT is used on every network running IPv4, including your home network.

Port Forwarding

Lab Objective:
Learn how to configure port forwarding.

Lab Purpose:
With NAT, you have no easy way of ensuring outside hosts can connect to internal web servers or email servers on the correct port, such as 80 and 110. Port forwarding solves this problem by ensuring the correct port is attached to the servers.

Lab Tool:
Packet Tracer

Lab Topology:
Please use the following topology to complete this lab exercise:

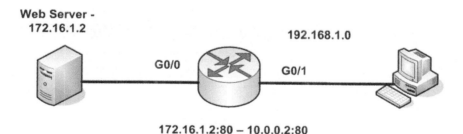

Lab Walkthrough:

Task 1:
Connect a server and a PC to a router using crossover cables. The PC will browse to the web server, and the router will perform port forwarding.

Task 2:

Set the IP configuration for the host and server. The server Ethernet interface should be 172.16.1.2 and the default gateway 172.16.1.1, which will be the closest IP address of R0. The PC will be 192.168.1.2 and gateway of 192.168.1.1. Here it is:

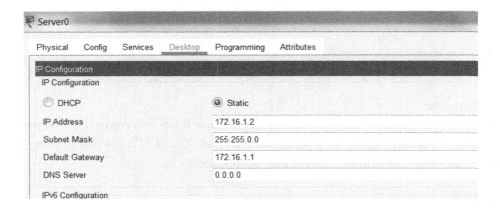

And on the PC:

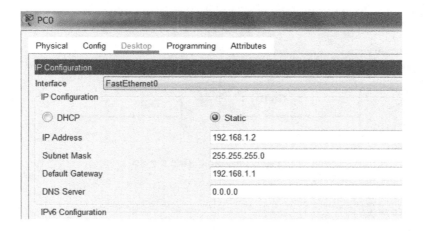

Task 3:

Configure IP addressing on R0.

```
Router(config)#host R0
R0(config)#int g0/0
R0(config-if)#ip add 172.16.1.1 255.255.0.0
R0(config-if)#no shut
%LINK-5-CHANGED: Interface GigabitEthernet0/0, changed state to up
```

```
RO(config-if)#int g0/1
RO(config-if)#ip add 192.168.1.1 255.255.255.0
RO(config-if)#no shut
RO(config-if)#end
```

Task 4:

Ping the server and PC from the router to ensure IP connectivity.

```
RO#ping 172.16.1.2

Type escape sequence to abort.
Sending 5, 100-byte ICMP Echos to 172.16.1.2, timeout is 2 seconds:
!!!!!
Success rate is 100 percent (5/5), round-trip min/avg/max = 0/0/1 ms

RO#ping 192.168.1.2

Type escape sequence to abort.
Sending 5, 100-byte ICMP Echos to 192.168.1.2, timeout is 2 seconds:
!!!!!
Success rate is 100 percent (5/5), round-trip min/avg/max = 0/0/1 ms
```

Task 5:

The HTTP service is turned on by default on Packet Tracer servers, so all we need to do now is add the port forwarding and NAT configurations to the router. We want incoming connections on port 80 for IP 10.0.0.2 to be forwarded to the web server IP of 172.16.1.2.

```
RO(config)#ip nat inside source static tcp 172.16.1.2 80 10.0.0.2 80
RO(config)#int g0/0
RO(config-if)#ip nat inside
RO(config-if)#int g0/1
RO(config-if)#ip nat outside
RO(config-if)#end
```

Task 6:

Test your configuration by connecting to 10.0.0.2 from the web browser on the PC. We won't add any DNS into this lab to keep it simple.

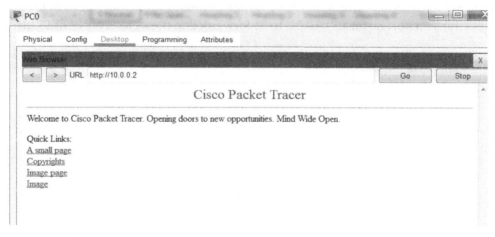

We can connect to the web server from its outside address.

Task 7:

Check the NAT table on the router. Bear in mind that the source port usually won't be 80, but the destination port will be. That's what's important.

```
R0#show ip nat tran
Pro  Inside global   Inside local    Outside local    Outside global
tcp 10.0.0.2:80     172.16.1.2:80   ---              ---
tcp 10.0.0.2:80     172.16.1.2:80   192.168.1.2:1029 192.168.1.2:1029
tcp 10.0.0.2:80     172.16.1.2:80   192.168.1.2:1030 192.168.1.2:1030
```

Note:

You would use port forwarding for web and email servers, live chat, gaming, and many other port-dependent services and protocols.

LAB 27

Standard Access Control Lists (ACLs)

Lab Objective:

Learn how to configure a standard access list.

Lab Purpose:

Access lists are a series of permit or deny statements which determine if traffic is allowed into or blocked from your network. Due to various rules, they can be complicated. Just bear in mind that any traffic which matches a rule will not progress any further down the list; it will first be permitted or denied. At the end of every ACL is an implicit deny statement. It's there even if you can't see it in the configuration.

Lab Tool:

Packet Tracer

Lab Topology:

Please use the following topology to complete this lab exercise:

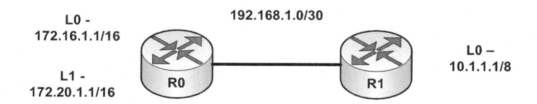

Lab Walkthrough:

Task 1:

Connect two routers with a crossover cable. We will use loopback interfaces to simulate networks/hosts. You already know how to change the router hostnames.

```
R0(config)#int g0/0
R0(config-if)#ip add 192.168.1.1 255.255.255.252
R0(config-if)#no shut
R0(config-if)#int lo0
R0(config-if)#ip add 172.16.1.1 255.255.0.0
```

```
R0(config-if)#int lo1
R0(config-if)#ip add 172.20.1.1 255.255.0.0
R0(config-if)#end

R1(config)#int g0/0
R1(config-if)#ip add 192.168.1.2 255.255.255.252
R1(config-if)#no shut
R1(config-if)#int lo0
R1(config-if)#ip add 10.1.1.1 255.0.0.0
R1(config-if)#end
```

Task 2:

Ping across the link.

```
R0#ping 192.168.1.2

Type escape sequence to abort.
Sending 5, 100-byte ICMP Echos to 192.168.1.2, timeout is 2 seconds:
.!!!!
Success rate is 80 percent (4/5), round-trip min/avg/max = 0/0/0 ms
```

Task 3:

Configure a static route on R0 and R1 so each can reach the network on the other side, and then test with the 'ping' command.

```
R0(config)#ip route 0.0.0.0 0.0.0.0 192.168.1.2
R1(config)#ip route 0.0.0.0 0.0.0.0 192.168.1.1

R0#ping 10.1.1.1

Type escape sequence to abort.
Sending 5, 100-byte ICMP Echos to 10.1.1.1, timeout is 2 seconds:
!!!!!
Success rate is 100 percent (5/5), round-trip min/avg/max = 0/0/1 ms

R1#ping 172.16.1.1

Type escape sequence to abort.
Sending 5, 100-byte ICMP Echos to 172.16.1.1, timeout is 2 seconds:
!!!!!
Success rate is 100 percent (5/5), round-trip min/avg/max = 0/0/1 ms

R1#ping 172.20.1.1

Type escape sequence to abort.
Sending 5, 100-byte ICMP Echos to 172.20.1.1, timeout is 2 seconds:
!!!!!
Success rate is 100 percent (5/5), round-trip min/avg/max = 0/0/1 ms
```

Task 4:

Configure an access list on R0. Traffic from 10.1.1.1 should be blocked, but any other traffic should be permitted. Remember that any traffic is blocked by default at the end of an ACL, so we need to permit everything else. We also need to apply the access list to an interface.

```
R0(config)#access-list 1 deny host 10.1.1.1
R0(config)#access-list 1 permit any
R0(config)#int g0/0
R0(config-if)#ip access-group 1 in
```

Task 5:

Test the access list by pinging from 192.168.1.2 to 172.16.1.1 and then from 10.1.1.1. The U response means the traffic has been blocked.

```
R1#ping 172.16.1.1

Type escape sequence to abort.
Sending 5, 100-byte ICMP Echos to 172.16.1.1, timeout is 2 seconds:
!!!!!
Success rate is 100 percent (5/5), round-trip min/avg/max = 0/0/1 ms

R1#ping
Protocol [ip]:
Target IP address: 172.16.1.1
Repeat count [5]:
Datagram size [100]:
Timeout in seconds [2]:
Extended commands [n]: y
Source address or interface: loopback0
Type of service [0]:
Set DF bit in IP header? [no]:
Validate reply data? [no]:
Data pattern [0xABCD]:
Loose, Strict, Record, Timestamp, Verbose[none]:
Sweep range of sizes [n]:
Type escape sequence to abort.
Sending 5, 100-byte ICMP Echos to 172.16.1.1, timeout is 2 seconds:
Packet sent with a source address of 10.1.1.1
UUUUU
Success rate is 0 percent (0/5)
```

Task 6:

You can check the ACL for hits on the router if you wish.

```
R0#show ip access-lists
Standard IP access list 1
    10 deny host 10.1.1.1 (10 match(es))
    20 permit any (10 match(es))
```

Notes:

ACLs are pretty tricky, and each vendor has its own way of configuring them, so don't sweat the commands too much. Just bear in mind that they are processed from top to bottom, and if there is a match, the traffic stops. At the end of each ACL is an implicit 'deny all' command.

LAB 28

Extended Access Control Lists

Lab Objective:

Learn how to configure an extended access list.

Lab Purpose:

Extended lists offer far more granularity than standard lists. Standard ACLs can block only source hosts or networks, whereas extended ACLs can block sources/destinations as well as many ports and protocols.

The entire basic configuration is the same as that in the previous lab, so if you want a quick fix, then remove the ACL configuration and configure the new ACL.

```
R0(config)#no access-list 1
R0(config)#int g0/0
R0(config-if)#no ip access-group 1 in
```

By now I'm sure you know how to use the end and exit commands to get back to the correct router prompt so I'll leave that part to you.

Lab Tool:

Packet Tracer

Lab Topology:

Please use the following topology to complete this lab exercise:

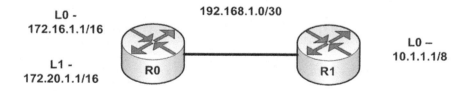

Lab Walkthrough:

Task 1:

Connect two routers with a crossover cable. We will use loopback interfaces to simulate networks/hosts. You already know how to change the router hostnames.

```
R0(config)#int g0/0
R0(config-if)#ip add 192.168.1.1 255.255.255.252
R0(config-if)#no shut
R0(config-if)#int lo0
R0(config-if)#ip add 172.16.1.1 255.255.0.0
R0(config-if)#int lo1
R0(config-if)#ip add 172.20.1.1 255.255.0.0

R1(config)#int g0/0
R1(config-if)#ip add 192.168.1.2 255.255.255.252
R1(config-if)#no shut
R1(config-if)#int lo0
R1(config-if)#ip add 10.1.1.1 255.0.0.0
R1(config-if)#exi
```

Task 2:

Ping across the link.

```
R0#ping 192.168.1.2

Type escape sequence to abort.
Sending 5, 100-byte ICMP Echos to 192.168.1.2, timeout is 2 seconds:
.!!!!
Success rate is 80 percent (4/5), round-trip min/avg/max = 0/0/0 ms
```

Task 3:

Configure a static route on R0 and R1 so each can reach the network on the other side, and then test with the 'ping' command.

```
R0(config)#ip route 0.0.0.0 0.0.0.0 192.168.1.2
R1(config)#ip route 0.0.0.0 0.0.0.0 192.168.1.1

R0#ping 10.1.1.1

Type escape sequence to abort.
Sending 5, 100-byte ICMP Echos to 10.1.1.1, timeout is 2 seconds:
!!!!!
Success rate is 100 percent (5/5), round-trip min/avg/max = 0/0/1 ms

R1#ping 172.16.1.1

Type escape sequence to abort.
```

```
Sending 5, 100-byte ICMP Echos to 172.16.1.1, timeout is 2 seconds:
!!!!!
Success rate is 100 percent (5/5), round-trip min/avg/max = 0/0/1 ms

R1#ping 172.20.1.1

Type escape sequence to abort.
Sending 5, 100-byte ICMP Echos to 172.20.1.1, timeout is 2 seconds:
!!!!!
Success rate is 100 percent (5/5), round-trip min/avg/max = 0/0/1 ms
```

Task 4:

Configure an access list on R0. Traffic from 10.1.1.1 should be blocked if it's trying to access the 172.16.0.0 network. Any other traffic from this or other host should be permitted.

```
R0(config)#access-list 100 deny ip host 10.1.1.1 172.16.0.0 0.0.255.255
R0(config)#access-list 100 permit ip any any
R0(config)#int g0/0
R0(config-if)#ip access-group 100 in
```

Task 5:

Test the access list by pinging to 172.16.1.1 from 192.168.1.2 (which it will automatically do because it's the closest interface) and then from 172.16.1.1 (loopback 0). The U response means the traffic has been blocked.

```
R1#ping 172.16.1.1

Type escape sequence to abort.
Sending 5, 100-byte ICMP Echos to 172.16.1.1, timeout is 2 seconds:
!!!!!
Success rate is 100 percent (5/5), round-trip min/avg/max = 0/0/1 ms

R1#ping
Protocol [ip]:
Target IP address: 172.16.1.1
Repeat count [5]:
Datagram size [100]:
Timeout in seconds [2]:
Extended commands [n]: y
Source address or interface: loopback0
Type of service [0]:
Set DF bit in IP header? [no]:
Validate reply data? [no]:
Data pattern [0xABCD]:
Loose, Strict, Record, Timestamp, Verbose[none]:
Sweep range of sizes [n]:
Type escape sequence to abort.
```

```
Sending 5, 100-byte ICMP Echos to 172.16.1.1, timeout is 2 seconds:
Packet sent with a source address of 10.1.1.1
UUUUU
Success rate is 0 percent (0/5)
```

Task 6:

You can check the ACL for hits on the router if you wish.

```
R0#show ip access-lists
Extended IP access list 100
    10 deny ip host 10.1.1.1 172.16.0.0 0.0.255.255 (5 match(es))
    20 permit ip any any (5 match(es))
```

Notes:

ACLs are pretty tricky, and each vendor has its own way of configuring them, so don't sweat the commands too much. Just bear in mind that they are processed from top to bottom, and if there is a match, the traffic stops. At the end of each ACL is an implicit 'deny all' command.

LAB 29

Named Access Control Lists

Lab Objective:
Learn how to configure named access lists.

Lab Purpose:
Named ACLs can be either standard or extended. You would use named ACLs if you had to apply several of them to your router and needed an easy way to remember what they do.

The entire basic configuration is the same as that in the previous lab, so if you want a quick fix, then remove the ACL configuration and configure the new ACL.

```
R0(config)#no access-list 100
R0(config)#int g0/0
R0(config-if)#no ip access-group 100 in
```

Lab Tool:
Packet Tracer

Lab Topology:
Please use the following topology to complete this lab exercise:

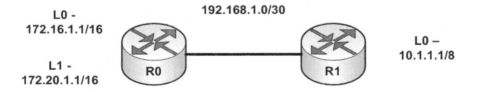

Lab Walkthrough:

Task 1:

Connect two routers with a crossover cable. We will use loopback interfaces to simulate networks/hosts. You already know how to change the router hostnames.

```
R0(config)#int g0/0
R0(config-if)#ip add 192.168.1.1 255.255.255.252
R0(config-if)#no shut
R0(config-if)#int lo0
R0(config-if)#ip add 172.16.1.1 255.255.0.0
R0(config-if)#int lo1
R0(config-if)#ip add 172.20.1.1 255.255.0.0

R1(config)#int g0/0
R1(config-if)#ip add 192.168.1.2 255.255.255.252
R1(config-if)#no shut
R1(config-if)#int lo0
R1(config-if)#ip add 10.1.1.1 255.0.0.0
R1(config-if)#exi
```

Task 2:

Ping across the link.

```
R0#ping 192.168.1.2

Type escape sequence to abort.
Sending 5, 100-byte ICMP Echos to 192.168.1.2, timeout is 2 seconds:
.!!!!
Success rate is 80 percent (4/5), round-trip min/avg/max = 0/0/0 ms
```

Task 3:

Configure a static route on R0 and R1 so each can reach the network on the other side, and then test with the 'ping' command.

```
R0(config)#ip route 0.0.0.0 0.0.0.0 192.168.1.2
R1(config)#ip route 0.0.0.0 0.0.0.0 192.168.1.1

R0#ping 10.1.1.1

Type escape sequence to abort.
Sending 5, 100-byte ICMP Echos to 10.1.1.1, timeout is 2 seconds:
!!!!!
Success rate is 100 percent (5/5), round-trip min/avg/max = 0/0/1 ms

R1#ping 172.16.1.1

Type escape sequence to abort.
```

```
Sending 5, 100-byte ICMP Echos to 172.16.1.1, timeout is 2 seconds:
!!!!!
Success rate is 100 percent (5/5), round-trip min/avg/max = 0/0/1 ms

R1#ping 172.20.1.1

Type escape sequence to abort.
Sending 5, 100-byte ICMP Echos to 172.20.1.1, timeout is 2 seconds:
!!!!!
Success rate is 100 percent (5/5), round-trip min/avg/max = 0/0/1 ms
```

Task 4:

Configure an access list on R0. Traffic from 10.1.1.1 should be blocked if it's trying to ping the 172.16.0.0 network. Any other traffic from this or other host should be permitted. Ping uses the ICMP protocol.

```
R0(config)#ip access-list extended BLOCK_ICMP
R0(config-ext-nacl)#deny icmp host 10.1.1.1 172.16.0.0 0.0.255.255
R0(config-ext-nacl)#permit ip any any
R0(config-ext-nacl)#int g0/0
R0(config-if)#ip access-group BLOCK_ICMP in
```

Task 5:

Test the access list by pinging from 10.1.1.1 to 172.20.1.1 and then from 172.16.1.1. The U response means the traffic has been blocked.

```
R1#ping
Protocol [ip]:
Target IP address: 172.20.1.1
Repeat count [5]:
Datagram size [100]:
Timeout in seconds [2]:
Extended commands [n]: y
Source address or interface: loopback0
Type of service [0]:
Set DF bit in IP header? [no]:
Validate reply data? [no]:
Data pattern [0xABCD]:
Loose, Strict, Record, Timestamp, Verbose[none]:
Sweep range of sizes [n]:
Type escape sequence to abort.
Sending 5, 100-byte ICMP Echos to 172.20.1.1, timeout is 2 seconds:
Packet sent with a source address of 10.1.1.1
!!!!!
Success rate is 100 percent (5/5), round-trip min/avg/max = 0/0/0 ms

R1#ping
Protocol [ip]:
```

```
Target IP address: 172.16.1.1
Repeat count [5]:
Datagram size [100]:
Timeout in seconds [2]:
Extended commands [n]: y
Source address or interface: loopback0
Type of service [0]:
Set DF bit in IP header? [no]:
Validate reply data? [no]:
Data pattern [0xABCD]:
Loose, Strict, Record, Timestamp, Verbose[none]:
Sweep range of sizes [n]:
Type escape sequence to abort.
Sending 5, 100-byte ICMP Echos to 172.16.1.1, timeout is 2 seconds:
Packet sent with a source address of 10.1.1.1
UUUUU
Success rate is 0 percent (0/5)
```

Task 6:

You can check the ACL for hits on the router if you wish.

```
R0#show ip access-lists
Extended IP access list BLOCK_ICMP
    10 deny icmp host 10.1.1.1 172.16.0.0 0.0.255.255 (5 match(es))
    20 permit ip any any (10 match(es))
```

Notes:

Extended ACLs give you far more options but of course are much harder to configure. At the end of each ACL is an implicit 'deny all' command, which is why I had to permit all other IP traffic.

Subnetting 1

Lab Objective:
Learn how to answer subnetting questions.

Lab Purpose:
In the exam, you may be asked to answer a subnetting question. They could ask you to determine which subnet a host address is in, what the subnet/broadcast address is in a particular network, or how many subnets/hosts you would have with a particular subnet mask.

I've added my Subnetting Cheat Sheet at the end of the VLSM lab. Use it to quickly answer subnetting and VLSM questions. You can write it out from memory on scratch paper in any exam you take or use it in technical interviews.

Lab Tool:
Pen and paper

Lab Topology:
NA

Lab Walkthrough:
How many subnets and hosts does 192.168.2.0/26 give you?

First, take an extra 2 bits from the normal 24-bit mask. Tick off two numbers down in the upper portion of the subnetting chart (128 and then 192), giving you a mask of 192, or to be more specific, 255.255.255.192.

You can work out that it is two bits being used for subnetting if you remember that each octet count is eight. 255.0.0.0 is 8 binary bits, 255.255.0.0 is 16, and 255.255.255.0 is 24. If you have a /26 mask, then you need to add two onto the 255.255.255.0 mask, which is 24 bits plus 2 more (or 255.255.255.192).

You've taken two bits for the subnet, so in the Subnets column at the bottom, tick down two numbers (2 and then 4). This gives you four subnets.

Now you know you have six bits left for the hosts (8 − 2 = 6 bits remaining), so tick off six places down in the Hosts Minus 2 column to get the number of hosts. You will always use the bottom part of the chart first when trying to work out how many subnets and hosts per subnet there are. If you're trying to work out which subnet a host address is in, use the top part of the chart.

Six down in the Hosts Minus 2 column gives you 64; take 2 away for the subnet and broadcast and that gives you 62 hosts per subnet. You can see I also ticked two across the top bits row so you can see that our subnets go up in increments of 64.

The subnet mask given provides you then, with four subnets each with 62 hosts. Easy, isn't it?

Subnetting Cheat Chart

	Bits	128	64	32	16	8	4	2	1
Subnets		✓	✓						
128	✓								
192	✓								
224									
240									
248									
252									
254									
255									
Powers of Two	Subnets	Hosts Minus 2							
2	✓	✓							
4	✓	✓							
8		✓							
16		✓							
32		✓							
64		✓							
128									
256									
512									
1024									
2048									
4096									
8192									
16,384									

Notes:

Hopefully, this has helped you understand subnetting a bit more. Please use the Subnetting Cheat Chart in the VLSM lab and learn how to write it out by heart.

Subnetting 2

Lab Objective:
Learn how to answer subnetting questions.

Lab Purpose:
Here is another subnetting question. If you learn subnetting, you will easily get good marks in the exam. You will also be asked this type of question in technical interviews, so you must learn it.

Lab Tool:
Pen and paper

Lab Topology:
NA

Lab Walkthrough:
Which subnet is host 172.16.100.118/29 in?

This is a Class B address, but for subnetting you don't need to concern yourself with that. You just need to look at which octet the subnetting is happening in. The Subnetting Cheat Chart will work with all address classes.

Because the third octet is already filled in with binary 1s, we will disregard it (to save time) and look only at the last octet.

/29 is five places into the last octet, so start by ticking five places across the upper portion of the chart and then five down. You can now see that you have a subnet mask of 255.255.255.248 and the subnets are going up in increments of 8.

Subnetting Cheat Chart

	Bits	128	64	32	16	8	4	2	1
Subnets		✓	✓	✓	✓	✓			
128	✓								
192	✓								
224	✓								
240	✓								
248	✓								
252									
254									
255									
Powers of Two	Subnets	Hosts Minus 2							
2									
4									
8									
16									
32									
64									
128									
256									
512									

Unfortunately, you are counting up in increments of 8, meaning that if you were creating a chart for allocating subnets, you would start with 172.16.0.0, then use 172.16.0.8, and so on (until you've worked out all 8,192 subnets), but you need to answer the exam question quickly. With this in mind, let's focus only on the last octet since this is where you'll find the host address:

172.16.100.0
172.16.100.8

This will still take too long, so jump from values of 8 to 80.

172.16.100.80
172.16.100.88

172.16.100.96
172.16.100.104
172.16.100.112 ⇦ **Host 172.16.100.118 is in this subnet**
172.16.100.120

Notes:

Subnetting is hard to begin with, but with a few hours of practice you will master it. I have a subnetting course at howtonetwork.com if you need to learn it, or check out my 'IP Subnetting—Zero to Guru' and '101 Labs—IP Subnetting' books on Amazon.

VLSM

Lab Objective:
Learn how to design a network using VLSM.

Lab Purpose:
You will often be given a network or network segment to design and manage. Whoever is responsible for IP addressing in your company may allocate you an address range you can use. It will be down to you to create an efficient addressing scheme which avoids discontinuous addressing (bad for routing protocols) and allows you to send a summary address to upstream routers to reduce traffic.

I've added my Subnetting Cheat Sheet at the end. Use it to quickly answer subnetting and VLSM questions. You can write it out from memory on scratch paper in any exam you take or use it in technical interviews.

Lab Tool:
Pen and paper

Lab Topology:
Please use the below diagram. Bear in mind that there are several ways to address this network, so use my example as a suggestion and then come up with your own. Your Network+ study guide should cover VLSM.

Here is a network you have been asked to design an addressing scheme for:

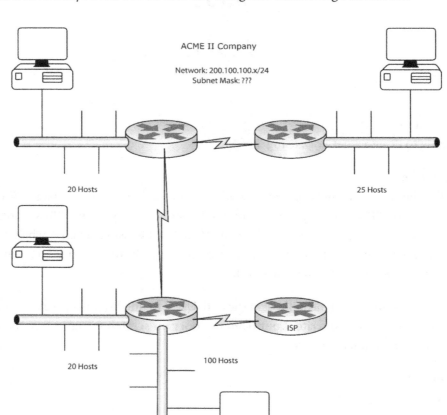

In the figure above, ACME II Company has been allocated the 200.100.100.x network, with a default mask of 255.255.255.0. If you keep the standard mask, you will be left with one network with 254 usable hosts. Using the bottom half of the Subnetting Cheat Chart introduced earlier, tick down eight places in the Hosts Minus 2 column, which will give you one subnet with 256 − 2 hosts, or 254 hosts.

The challenge is this: You have three serial connections, and each requires only two usable host addresses. You also have four LANs that need between 20 and 100 hosts. If you design a mask to give you 20 to 100 hosts, you will be wasting a lot of addresses. To get 100 hosts, tick down seven places in the Hosts Minus 2 column, which will give you a mask of 255.255.255.128 (because you have only one bit left to tick down in the

Subnets column). This gives you 126 hosts (128 − 2). You will then have two networks: one starting at 200.100.100.0 and one starting at 200.100.100.128. Not great, to be honest, because you need seven subnets (three WANs and four LANs) and some require only 20 hosts—so why waste 108 addresses?

Referencing the bottom half of the Subnetting Cheat Chart below, tick down in the Hosts Minus 2 column until you find a number close enough to give you 100 hosts. The only number you can use is 128, which is seven ticks down, so you are stealing seven bits from the host portion, leaving you one bit for subnetting.

Powers of Two	Subnets	Hosts Minus 2
2	✓	✓
4		✓
8		✓
16		✓
32		✓
64		✓
128		✓
256		
512		

Using the upper portion of the Subnetting Cheat Chart, tick down one place to reveal a subnet mask of 128.

Subnets	
128	✓
192	
224	
248	
252	
254	
255	

When you use the 128 subnet with ACME II Company's IP address, you get subnet 200.100.100.0 and subnet 200.100.100.128, both with a mask of /25, or 255.255.255.128. For a network needing 100 hosts, you can use the 200.100.100.128 subnet. For the first host, you will use 200.100.100.129, and so on up to 200.100.100.229. So now you have

200.100.100.128/25 – LAN (hosts 129–254)
200.100.100.0/25 – available for use or for VLSM

You need to allocate hosts to the three remaining LANs and the three WANs. The other three LANs all need between 20 and 30 hosts. If you tick down five places in the Hosts Minus 2 column, you will get 32 – 2, or 30 hosts. If you steal five bits from the host portion, you are left with three bits for the subnet (because there are eight bits in every octet).

Powers of Two	Subnets	Hosts Minus 2
2	✓	✓
4	✓	✓
8	✓	✓
16		✓
32		✓
64		
128		
256		
512		

Tick down three places in the upper portion of the Subnetting Cheat Chart to reveal a subnet mask of 224. This mask will give you eight subnets (you need only three for the LANs), and each subnet will have up to 30 available host addresses. Can you see how this will fit ACME II Company's requirements?

Subnets	
128	✓
192	✓
224	✓
240	
248	
252	
254	
255	

If you tick across three places in the upper portion of the Subnetting Cheat Chart, you will see that the subnets go up in increments of 32, so the subnets will be 0, 32, 64, and 96; you cannot use 128 because this was used for the large LAN.

Bits	128	64	32	16	8	4	2	1
	✓	✓	✓					

So now you have

200.100.100.0/27—Reserve this for the WAN links
200.100.100.32/27—LAN 1 (hosts 33–62)
200.100.100.64/27—LAN 2 (hosts 65–94)
200.100.100.96/27—LAN 3 (hosts 97–126)

Next, you need IP addresses for the three WAN connections. WAN IP addressing is fairly easy because you need only two IP addresses if it is a point-to-point link. In the Hosts Minus 2 column, tick down two places to get 4 – 2, or 2 hosts. This leaves six bits for the subnet.

Powers of Two	Subnets	Hosts Minus 2
2	✓	✓
4	✓	✓
8	✓	
16	✓	
32	✓	
64	✓	
128		
256		
512		

Tick down six places in the upper portion of the Subnetting Cheat Chart to get 252 as the subnet mask.

Subnet	
128	✓
192	✓
224	✓
240	✓
248	✓
252	✓
254	
255	

Network Addresses

As a network administrator, you will need to keep a record of the IP addresses and subnets used. So far, you have allocated the following addresses:

WAN links
> 200.100.100.0/30—WAN link 1 (hosts 1–2)
> 200.100.100.4/30 – WAN link 2 (hosts 5–6)
> 200.100.100.8/30—WAN link 3 (hosts 9–10)

LAN hosts
> 200.100.100.32/27—LAN 1 (hosts 33–62)
> 200.100.100.64/27—LAN 2 (hosts 65–94)
> 200.100.100.96/27—LAN 3 (hosts 97–126)

Large LAN hosts
> 200.100.100.128/25—LAN (hosts 129–254)

Chopping Down

VLSM principles will let you take a network and slice it down into smaller chunks. Those chunks can then be sliced into smaller chunks and so on. You will reach the limit only when you get to the mask 255.255.255.252, or /30, because this gives you two usable hosts, which is the minimum you would need for any network.

Consider network 200.100.100.0/24. If you change the mask from /24 to /25, this is what happens:

Original mask (last octet)	00000000	1 subnet	254 hosts
New mask (Subnet 1)	00000000	200.100.100.0 – Subnet 1	126 hosts
New mask (Subnet 2)	10000000	200.100.100.128 – Subnet 2	126 hosts

Now you have two subnets. If you take the new Subnet 2 of 200.100.100.128 and break it down further by changing the mask from /25 to /26, you get this:

Original mask (last octet)	10000000	1 subnet	126 hosts
New mask (Subnet 1)	10000000	200.100.100.128 – Subnet 1	62 hosts
New mask (Subnet 2)	11000000	200.100.100.192 – Subnet 2	62 hosts

If you take the second subnet and break it down further by changing the mask from /26 to /28 (for example), you get this:

Original mask (last octet)	11000000	1 subnet	62 hosts
New mask (Subnet 1)	11**00**0000	200.100.100.192 – Subnet 1	14 hosts
New mask (Subnet 2)	11**01**0000	200.100.100.208 – Subnet 2	14 hosts
New mask (Subnet 3)	11**10**0000	200.100.100.224 – Subnet 3	14 hosts
New mask (Subnet 4)	11**11**0000	200.100.100.240 – Subnet 4	14 hosts

Notes:

Hopefully, this has helped you understand VLSM a bit more. It's no mystery really. Please take the time to go over the examples above again and then have a go at a few of your own challenges. I doubt you will be asked to design a network in the exam, but they do mention VLSM in the exam syllabus.

Subnetting Cheat Chart

	Bits	128	64	32	16	8	4	2	1
Subnets									
128									
192									
224									
240									
248									
252									
254									
255									
Powers of Two	**Subnets**	**Hosts Minus 2**							
2									
4									
8									
16									
32									
64									
128									
256									
512									
1024									
2048									
4096									
8192									
16,384									

IoT Configuration

Lab Objective:
Learn how to configure an IoT server and devices for home.

Lab Purpose:
The Internet of Things is the network of sensors, devices, servers, and software which enables things to exchange data. You can use it to turn on the aircon at home as you are leaving work, or your car can signal your garage that a part is wearing out and needs replacing.

All major software and hardware vendors have embraced this technology as the future, so you need to understand it if you are to work in the IT industry in the coming years.

Lab Tool:
Packet Tracer

Lab Topology:
Please use the following topology to complete this lab exercise:

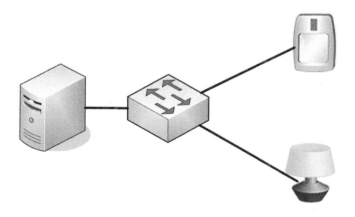

Lab Walkthrough:

Task 1:
Drag a server and switch onto the canvas. Under 'End Devices/Home/Smart City' drag up a light and a sensor. Link them all with Ethernet cables to the switch (any interface will do fine).

Task 2:
Add IP address 192.168.1.1 to the server configuration.

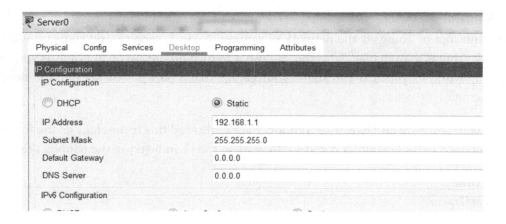

Task 3:
On the server, enable the IoT service.

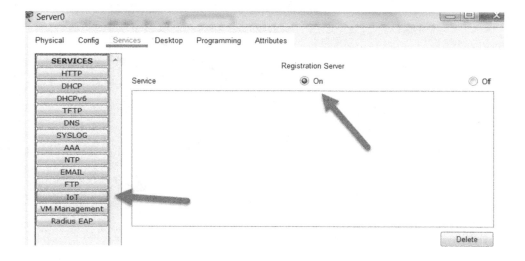

Task 4:

Open a web browser window on the server. Configure username '101labs' and password 'hello'. You will need to press the 'Sign up now' link in order to create this account.

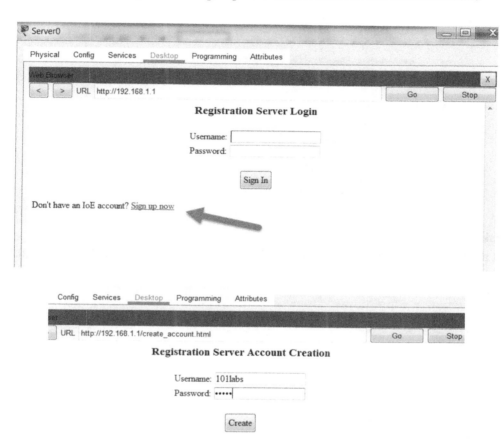

Task 5:

On the Motion Detector panel click on 'Settings' and change the name to 'Motion'. On the Light panel change the name to 'Light'.

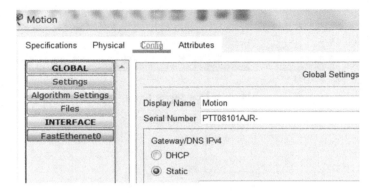

Task 6:

Set the IP address of the motion sensor to 192.168.1.2 and that of the light to 192.168.1.3.

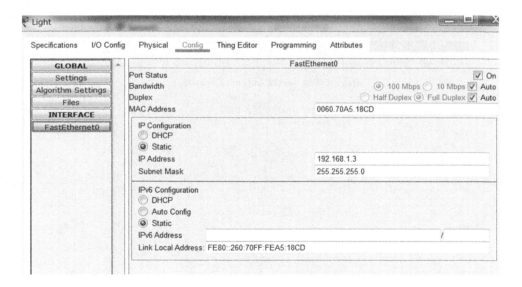

Task 6:

Under 'Settings' for both devices, set the IoT registration server to the server address. Add the username '101labs' and the password 'hello'.

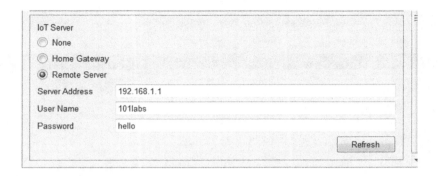

Task 7:

Go back to the server; both devices should be registered.

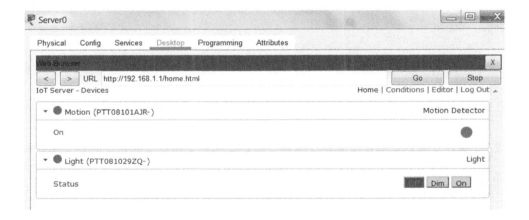

Task 8:

Press 'Conditions' and name the new condition 'light on'. Set it as below. If Motion On is true, then set light to on. Then press 'OK' at the bottom.

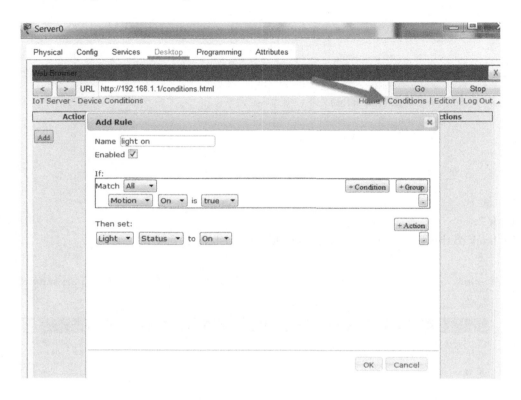

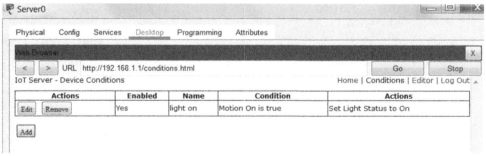

Task 9:

If we tested now, the light would come on and stay on, so add another condition. If Motion On is false, then set the light status to off.

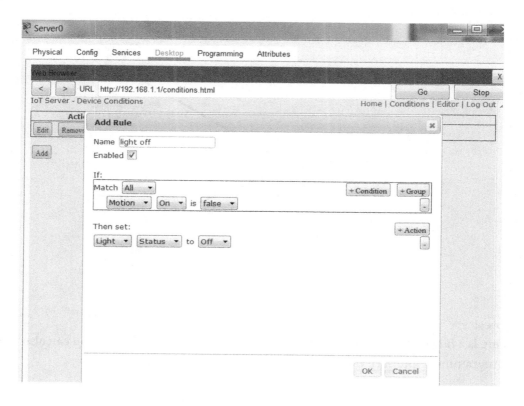

Task 10:

Hold down your Alt key and move your mouse in front of the movement sensor. This should activate the light. The red LED should show on the motion detector when it detects movement.

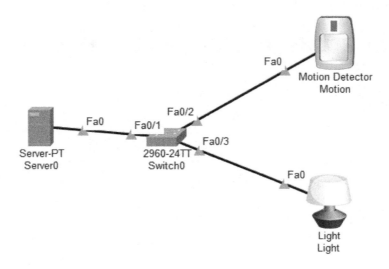

Notes:

There is a huge range of options and devices with IoT in Packet Tracer. You can also use a programming interface called Blockly to program events.

2.0 Infrastructure

LAB 34

Configuring a Firewall

Lab Objective:
Learn how to install a firewall.

Lab Purpose:
The CompTIA Net+ exam asks you to install/configure a firewall but also adds the fact that the exam is vendor-neutral. They do list several tools you should spend time learning to use at the end of the syllabus, and one of these is a firewall.

Lab Tool:
Virtual Ubuntu machine

Lab Topology:
You can install pfsense on hardware, on your home PC, or as I have, into a virtual network. Please refer to the resources page at **https://www.101labs.net/resources** for how I set this environment up.

Lab Walkthrough:

Task 1:

If you have set up pfsense correctly, it will indicate the interfaces it has recognized. Mine are shown below (LAN interface marked).

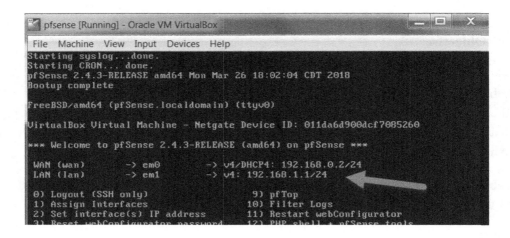

Task 2:

Open a web browser and navigate to your LAN interface IP address; you may need to add a security exception if there is a warning pop up. The default credentials for pfsense are:

> Username—admin
> Password—pfsense

Task 3:

Navigate to Status/Dashboard to find the dashboard. Here you can see all the general settings, including the machine the firewall is running on and available interfaces. You would usually have LAN, WAN, and a DMZ, but we haven't set the latter up for this lab.

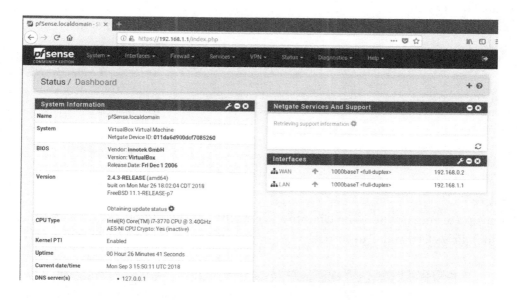

Task 4:

Go to Firewall/Rules and then WAN. You will see all networks are blocked by default.

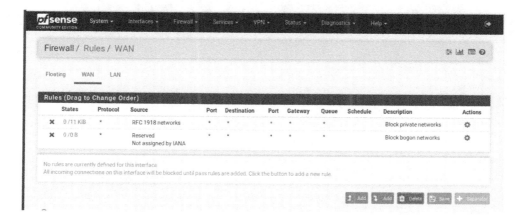

Task 5:

Check the LAN rules for the firewall. Note that by default, all traffic is allowed out of the LAN. An asterisk (*) indicates 'any' in pfsense. The very first rule for 'LAN Address' allows us to connect to the firewall via a browser on port 80 or port 443 if we want a secure connection.

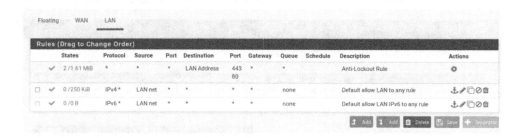

Task 6:

Open up a terminal window on Ubuntu and ping the firewall address (which is 192.168.1.1 for me). Press Ctrl and C to stop it.

```
paul@paul-VirtualBox:~$ ping 192.168.1.1
PING 192.168.1.1 (192.168.1.1) 56(84) bytes of data.
64 bytes from 192.168.1.1: icmp_seq=23 ttl=64 time=0.417 ms
64 bytes from 192.168.1.1: icmp_seq=24 ttl=64 time=0.245 ms
64 bytes from 192.168.1.1: icmp_seq=25 ttl=64 time=0.432 ms
64 bytes from 192.168.1.1: icmp_seq=26 ttl=64 time=0.788 ms
64 bytes from 192.168.1.1: icmp_seq=27 ttl=64 time=0.449 ms
64 bytes from 192.168.1.1: icmp_seq=28 ttl=64 time=0.304 ms
64 bytes from 192.168.1.1: icmp_seq=29 ttl=64 time=0.783 ms
^C
--- 192.168.1.1 ping statistics ---
```

Task 7:

Add a firewall rule blocking all ICMP traffic out of the LAN.

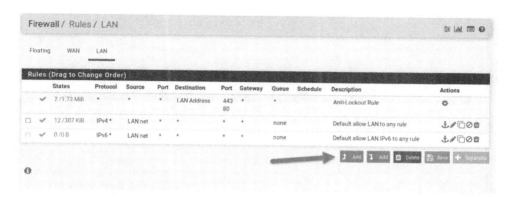

Block ICMP from the LAN from anywhere to anywhere. Click 'Save' and note the red cross shows the rule is a blocking rule.

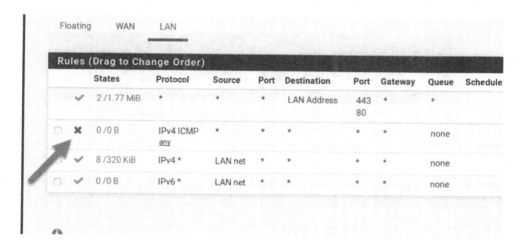

Apply by pressing the 'Apply Changes' button.

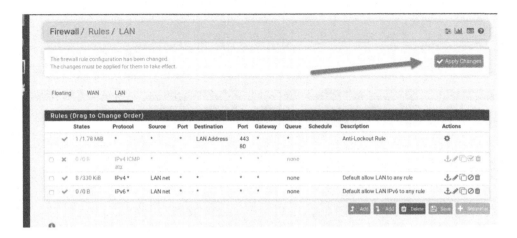

Task 8:

Ping the firewall again. It should be blocked.

```
paul@paul-VirtualBox:~$ ping 192.168.1.1
PING 192.168.1.1 (192.168.1.1) 56(84) bytes of data.
^C
--- 192.168.1.1 ping statistics ---
21 packets transmitted, 0 received, 100% packet loss, time 20462ms
```

Notes:

This is a very quick dip into the world of firewalls. Usually, SMEs have a dedicated firewall engineer to plan, install, configure, and troubleshoot firewalls. In the Network+ exam you should not be asked to configure a firewall, but you may be asked about placement and rules.

LAB 35

Installing and Configuring a Router

Lab Objective:
Learn how to install a branch office and HQ router.

Lab Purpose:
Routers can take several hours to install and configure. This lab will cover just a few of the basic steps you need to follow to connect your router in a branch office (R1) and your HQ (R0). I've scaled everything down for simplicity.

Lab Tool:
Packet Tracer

Lab Topology:
Please use the following topology to complete this lab exercise:

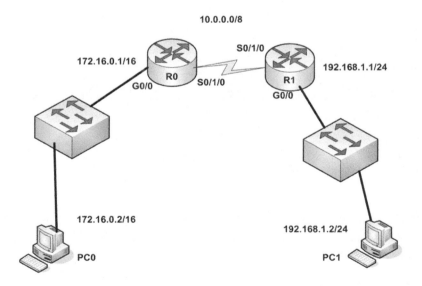

Lab Walkthrough:

Task 1:

Build the network shown in the topology above (I used 1941 models for this lab). Power down the routers and add (drag) a WAN card to each router, connect the routers with a serial cable, and then power up the routers.

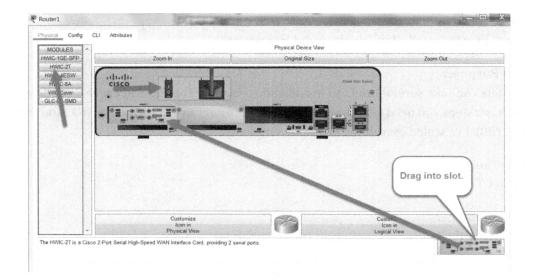

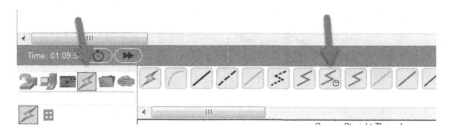

Task 2:

Change the hostname on the router and then check the interfaces for the correct name/number/slot so you configure the correct one. You will use a serial cable to connect the two routers.

```
Router#conf t
Router(config)#hostname R0
Router(config)#exit
R0#show ip int brief
Interface IP-Address OK? Method Status Protocol
```

```
GigabitEthernet0/0 unassigned YES unset administratively down down
GigabitEthernet0/1 unassigned YES unset administratively down down
Serial0/1/0 unassigned YES unset administratively down down
Serial0/1/1 unassigned YES unset administratively down down
Vlan1 unassigned YES unset administratively down down
R0#
```

Task 2:

One of the routers will have a DCE cable end. This provides the clocking for the connection, so you need to add a speed command. The 'show controllers interface X' command will tell you which cable type you have. Packet Tracer appears to automatically add a clock rate, so we need not worry about that step, but bear it in mind for live routers or remote racks.

```
R0#show controllers s0/1/0
Interface Serial0/1/0
Hardware is PowerQUICC MPC860
DCE V.35, clock rate 2000000
```

Task 3:

Configure the IP address on either router and then ping across the link.

```
R0#config t
R0(config)#int s0/1/0
R0(config-if)#ip add 10.0.0.1 255.0.0.0
R0(config-if)#no shut
```

For Router1:

```
Router#config t
Router(config)#hostname R1
R1(config)#
R1(config)#int s0/1/0
R1(config-if)#ip add 10.0.0.2 255.0.0.0
R1(config-if)#no shut
R1(config-if)#end
R1#ping 10.0.0.1
Type escape sequence to abort.
Sending 5, 100-byte ICMP Echos to 10.0.0.1, timeout is 2 seconds:
%LINEPROTO-5-UPDOWN: Line protocol on Interface Serial0/1/0, changed
state to up
.!!!!
Success rate is 80 percent (4/5), round-trip min/avg/max = 1/1/1 ms
```

Task 4:

Configure the Ethernet interfaces on the routers and add the IP addresses and default gateways on the hosts. Here is the config for R0. On R1 remember that it's using the 192.168.1.0 network on the LAN side.

```
R0(config-if)#int g0/1
R0(config-if)#ip add 172.16.0.1 255.255.0.0
R0(config-if)#no shut
```

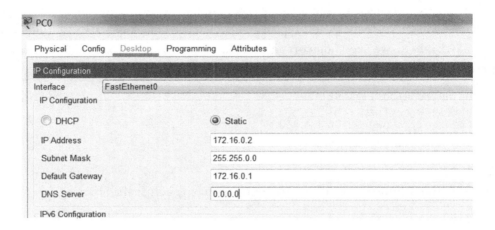

```
R0#ping 172.16.0.2

Type escape sequence to abort.
Sending 5, 100-byte ICMP Echos to 172.16.0.2, timeout is 2 seconds:
.!!!!
Success rate is 80 percent (4/5), round-trip min/avg/max = 0/0/2 ms
```

Task 5:

Configure RIP version 2 on the network so that each router has a map of the entire topology.

```
R0(config)#router rip
R0(config-router)#version 2
R0(config-router)#network 10.0.0.0
R0(config-router)#network 172.16.0.0

R1(config)#router rip
R1(config-router)#ver 2
R1(config-router)#network 10.0.0.0
R1(config-router)#net 192.168.1.0
R1(config-router)#end
```

Task 6:

Check your routing tables.

```
R0#show ip route
Codes: L - local, C - connected, S - static, R - RIP, M - mobile, B
- BGP
        D - EIGRP, EX - EIGRP external, O - OSPF, IA - OSPF inter area
        N1 - OSPF NSSA external type 1, N2 - OSPF NSSA external type 2
        E1 - OSPF external type 1, E2 - OSPF external type 2, E - EGP
        i - IS-IS, L1 - IS-IS level-1, L2 - IS-IS level-2, ia - IS-IS
inter area
        * - candidate default, U - per-user static route, o - ODR
        P - periodic downloaded static route

Gateway of last resort is not set

      10.0.0.0/8 is variably subnetted, 2 subnets, 2 masks
C        10.0.0.0/8 is directly connected, Serial0/1/0
L        10.0.0.1/32 is directly connected, Serial0/1/0
      172.16.0.0/16 is variably subnetted, 2 subnets, 2 masks
C        172.16.0.0/16 is directly connected, GigabitEthernet0/1
L        172.16.0.1/32 is directly connected, GigabitEthernet0/1
R     192.168.1.0/24 [120/1] via 10.0.0.2, 00:00:15, Serial0/1/0

R1#show ip route
Codes: L - local, C - connected, S - static, R - RIP, M - mobile, B
- BGP
        D - EIGRP, EX - EIGRP external, O - OSPF, IA - OSPF inter area
        N1 - OSPF NSSA external type 1, N2 - OSPF NSSA external type 2
        E1 - OSPF external type 1, E2 - OSPF external type 2, E - EGP
        i - IS-IS, L1 - IS-IS level-1, L2 - IS-IS level-2, ia - IS-IS
inter area
        * - candidate default, U - per-user static route, o - ODR
        P - periodic downloaded static route

Gateway of last resort is not set

      10.0.0.0/8 is variably subnetted, 2 subnets, 2 masks
C        10.0.0.0/8 is directly connected, Serial0/1/0
L        10.0.0.2/32 is directly connected, Serial0/1/0
R     172.16.0.0/16 [120/1] via 10.0.0.1, 00:00:28, Serial0/1/0
      192.168.1.0/24 is variably subnetted, 2 subnets, 2 masks
C        192.168.1.0/24 is directly connected, GigabitEthernet0/0
L        192.168.1.1/32 is directly connected, GigabitEthernet0/0
```

Task 7:

Ping the remote PC from one end to the other: PC0's to PC1's IP address.

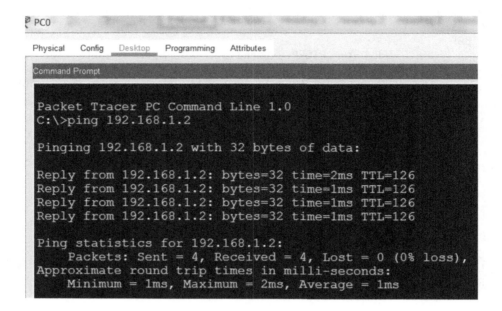

Task 8:

Configure R0 to allow remote access via Telnet. Add a username and password so the administrator can telnet to the router. Add an enable password so that the admin can get into enable mode to do any configurations. The command 'login local' tells the router to check the user against the local database of usernames and passwords. Then test your connection from the PC.

```
R0#conf t
Enter configuration commands, one per line. End with CNTL/Z.
R0(config)#enable secret hello
R0(config)#username 101labs password cisco
R0(config)#line vty 0 15
R0(config-line)#transport input telnet
R0(config-line)#login local
```

```
C:\>telnet 172.16.0.1
Trying 172.16.0.1 ...Open


User Access Verification

Username: 101labs
Password:
R0>enable
Password:
R0#
```

Notes:

This is a very basic setup. There is far more detail if you plan to take Cisco CCNA and other advanced exams. Feel free to redo this lab, but skip the 'enable secret' password. Now you can still telnet but can't configure the router.

LAB 36

Configuring a Layer 2 Switch

Lab Objective:

Learn how to configure layer 2 switches.

Lab Purpose:

Installing, configuring, and troubleshooting layer 2 switches will be part of your day-to-day routine as a network engineer. In this lab we cover basic VLAN and trunk configuration. Our two VLANs will use the trunk to connect. To keep things simple, each switch has only one host per VLAN.

Lab Tool:

Packet Tracer

Lab Topology:

Please use the following topology to complete this lab exercise:

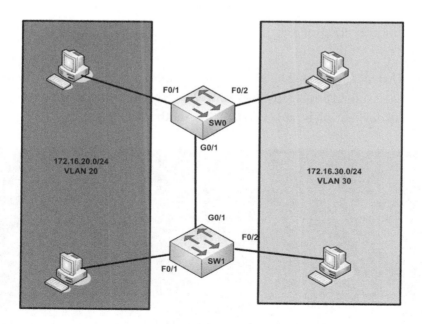

Lab Walkthrough:

Task 1:

Drag two Cisco switches (2960) onto the canvas and attach four PCs as per the diagram.

Task 2:

Add IP addresses of 172.16.20.2 and .3 to the devices going into VLAN 20. For the devices in VLAN 30 the IP addresses will be 172.16.30.2 and .3. We are using VLSM here, so make sure you use a subnet mask of 255.255.255.0.

Here is the configuration for one of the devices:

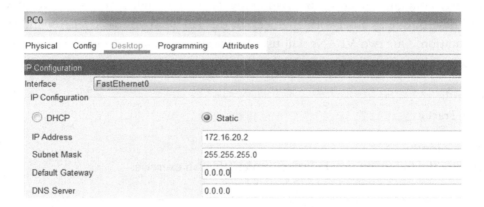

Task 3:

Remember that all devices will be placed into VLAN1 (the native VLAN) by default, so host 172.16.20.2 should be able to ping 172.16.20.3. This means that whenever you install any switch, all devices will be able to reach one another by default.

```
C:\>ping 172.16.20.3

Pinging 172.16.20.3 with 32 bytes of data:

Reply from 172.16.20.3: bytes=32 time=1ms TTL=128
Reply from 172.16.20.3: bytes=32 time<1ms TTL=128
Reply from 172.16.20.3: bytes=32 time<1ms TTL=128
Reply from 172.16.20.3: bytes=32 time<1ms TTL=128

Ping statistics for 172.16.20.3:
    Packets: Sent = 4, Received = 4, Lost = 0 (0% loss),
Approximate round trip times in milli-seconds:
    Minimum = 0ms, Maximum = 1ms, Average = 0ms
```

When all devices are configured, you will be able to ping devices in the same network but not across networks, even though they may be connected to the same VLAN. Here is a ping source from host 172.16.30.3.

```
Command Prompt

Packet Tracer PC Command Line 1.0
C:\>ping 172.16.30.2

Pinging 172.16.30.2 with 32 bytes of data:

Reply from 172.16.30.2: bytes=32 time=1ms TTL=128
Reply from 172.16.30.2: bytes=32 time<1ms TTL=128
Reply from 172.16.30.2: bytes=32 time<1ms TTL=128
Reply from 172.16.30.2: bytes=32 time<1ms TTL=128

Ping statistics for 172.16.30.2:
    Packets: Sent = 4, Received = 4, Lost = 0 (0% loss),
Approximate round trip times in milli-seconds:
    Minimum = 0ms, Maximum = 1ms, Average = 0ms

C:\>ping 172.16.20.2

Pinging 172.16.20.2 with 32 bytes of data:

Request timed out.
Request timed out.
```

This lab isn't concerned with inter-VLAN routing though, so we will just focus on connecting hosts in the same VLAN across switches using trunk links. The 'show vlan brief' command demonstrates the fact that all ports are in the same VLAN.

```
Switch#show vlan brief

VLAN Name                             Status    Ports
---- -------------------------------- --------- -------------------------------
1    default                          active    Fa0/1, Fa0/2, Fa0/3, Fa0/4
                                                Fa0/5, Fa0/6, Fa0/7, Fa0/8
                                                Fa0/9, Fa0/10, Fa0/11, Fa0/12
                                                Fa0/13, Fa0/14, Fa0/15, Fa0/16
                                                Fa0/17, Fa0/18, Fa0/19, Fa0/20
                                                Fa0/21, Fa0/22, Fa0/23, Fa0/24
                                                Gig0/1, Gig0/2
1002 fddi-default                     active
1003 token-ring-default               active
1004 fddinet-default                  active
1005 trnet-default                    active
```

Task 4:

Create VLAN 20 and 30 on the switches. Assign F0/1 on both switches to VLAN 20 and F0/2 to VLAN 30. Set the interfaces to access. Here is the configuration for Switch0; do the same for Switch1.

```
Switch#conf t
Enter configuration commands, one per line. End with CNTL/Z.
Switch(config)#host Switch0
Switch0(config)#vlan 20
Switch0(config-vlan)#vlan 30
Switch0(config-vlan)#int f0/1
Switch0(config-if)#switchport mode access
Switch0(config-if)#switchport access vlan 20
Switch0(config-if)#int f0/2
Switch0(config-if)#switchport mode access
Switch0(config-if)#switchport access vlan 30
Switch0(config-if)#
```

Task 5:

When you are done with this part, check the layer 2 settings for the interfaces with the 'show interfaces X switchport' command. We are most interested in the parts highlighted in bold.

```
Switch1#show int f0/1 switchport
Name: Fa0/1
Switchport: Enabled
Administrative Mode: static access
Operational Mode: static access
Administrative Trunking Encapsulation: dot1q
Operational Trunking Encapsulation: native
Negotiation of Trunking: Off
Access Mode VLAN: 20 (VLAN0020)
Trunking Native Mode VLAN: 1 (default)
Voice VLAN: none
Administrative private-vlan host-association: none
Administrative private-vlan mapping: none
Administrative private-vlan trunk native VLAN: none
Administrative private-vlan trunk encapsulation: dot1q
Administrative private-vlan trunk normal VLANs: none
Administrative private-vlan trunk private VLANs: none
Operational private-vlan: none
Trunking VLANs Enabled: All
Pruning VLANs Enabled: 2-1001
Capture Mode Disabled
Capture VLANs Allowed: ALL
Protected: false
Unknown unicast blocked: disabled
Unknown multicast blocked: disabled
Appliance trust: none
```

Task 6:

From 172.16.20.2 ping .3. It should fail because there is no trunk link between Switch0 and Switch1. The link connecting the two will be at the default setting of VLAN1 and an access port.

```
C:\>ping 172.16.20.3

Pinging 172.16.20.3 with 32 bytes of data:

Request timed out.
Request timed out.
Request timed out.
Request timed out.

Ping statistics for 172.16.20.3:
    Packets: Sent = 4, Received = 0, Lost = 4 (100% loss),
```

```
Switch0#show interfaces g0/1 switchport
Name: Gig0/1
Switchport: Enabled
Administrative Mode: dynamic auto
Operational Mode: static access
Administrative Trunking Encapsulation: dot1q
Operational Trunking Encapsulation: native
Negotiation of Trunking: On
Access Mode VLAN: 1 (default)
Trunking Native Mode VLAN: 1 (default)
Voice VLAN: none
```

Task 7:

Configure Switch0 interface G0/1 as a trunk. Because the setting for these models of switches is 'dynamic auto' as you can see above, the other end will respond by becoming a trunk link. 'Auto' means it will passively wait to become a trunk interface.

```
Switch0(config)#int g0/1
Switch0(config-if)#switchport mode trunk
%LINEPROTO-5-UPDOWN: Line protocol on Interface GigabitEthernet0/1,
changed state to up

Switch0#show interfaces g0/1 switchport
Name: Gig0/1
Switchport: Enabled
Administrative Mode: trunk
Operational Mode: trunk
Administrative Trunking Encapsulation: dot1q
Operational Trunking Encapsulation: dot1q
```

```
Negotiation of Trunking: On
Access Mode VLAN: 1 (default)
Trunking Native Mode VLAN: 1 (default)

Switch0#show interfaces trunk
Port Mode Encapsulation Status Native vlan
Gig0/1 on 802.1q trunking 1

Port Vlans allowed on trunk
Gig0/1 1-1005

Port Vlans allowed and active in management domain
Gig0/1 1,20,30

Port Vlans in spanning tree forwarding state and not pruned
Gig0/1 1,20,30
```

Task 8:

Finally, ping from 172.16.20.2 to .3. It should be successful.

```
C:\>ping 172.16.20.3

Pinging 172.16.20.3 with 32 bytes of data:

Reply from 172.16.20.3: bytes=32 time=1ms TTL=128
Reply from 172.16.20.3: bytes=32 time<1ms TTL=128
Reply from 172.16.20.3: bytes=32 time<1ms TTL=128
Reply from 172.16.20.3: bytes=32 time<1ms TTL=128

Ping statistics for 172.16.20.3:
    Packets: Sent = 4, Received = 4, Lost = 0 (0% loss),
Approximate round trip times in milli-seconds:
    Minimum = 0ms, Maximum = 1ms, Average = 0ms
```

Note:

There are many features we could go into, but we will be covering more switching features later in the relevant sections.

LAB 37

Installing a Bridge

Lab Objective:

Learn how to install a bridge.

Lab Purpose:

A bridge is a network switch for all intents and purposes; it does, however, feature fewer ports (usually two). In this lab we will see the bridge learn and store the device MAC address, preventing the packet from crossing to the next hub. The hubs have no capacity to store a MAC address, so they will continue to forward packets out of all ports.

Lab Tool:

Packet Tracer

Lab Topology:

Please use the following topology to complete this lab exercise:

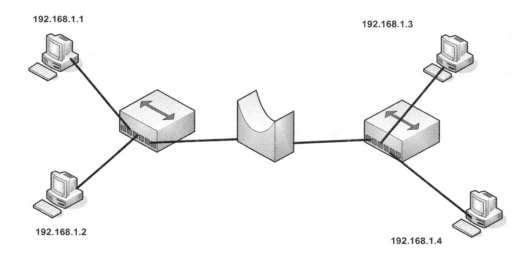

Lab Walkthrough:

Task 1:

Drag two hubs onto the canvas and attach two PCs to each using straight cables. Connect the hubs to a bridge using crossover cables.

Task 2:

Add IP addresses to the devices, starting at 192.168.1.1 and ending with .4 as per the diagram. Here is the configuration for one of the devices:

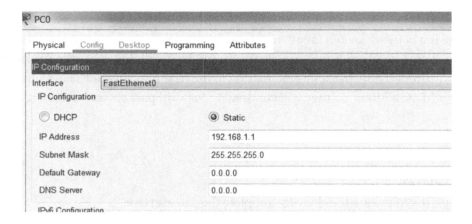

Task 3:

Click on the 'Simulation' tab in Packet Tracer. This gives you a window showing packets moving across the network.

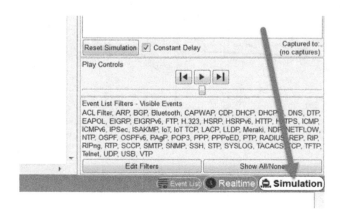

Task 4:

Resize your canvas so you can see the icons, command prompt, and packet outputs.

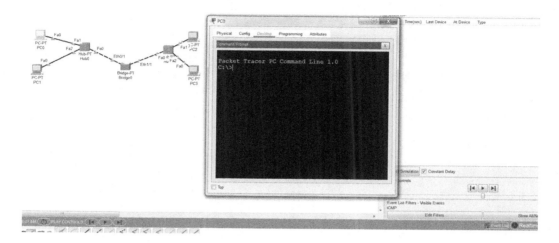

Note an envelope icon has appeared on the PC you are going to ping 192.168.1.2 from (which is .1).

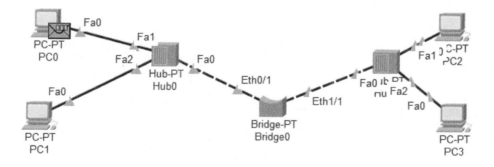

Task 5:

In order to reduce the amount of information you see click on 'Show All/None' and then 'Edit Filters' and select IPv4 ICMP, which is used by ping.

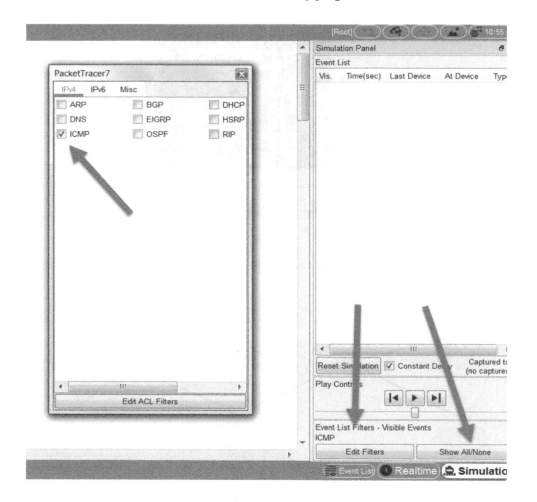

Task 6:

From host 192.168.1.1 issue a ping to host 192.168.1.2. In simulation mode it won't send the packet until you press the play button. You should see the ping envelope go to the hub, which will forward it to the bridge and host .2.

With the first ping you may see the bridge forward the packet, but after this you will see it blocked, as indicated by a red cross on the envelope. It will continue to do this because it has stored a mapping of the correct port host .2 is connected to.

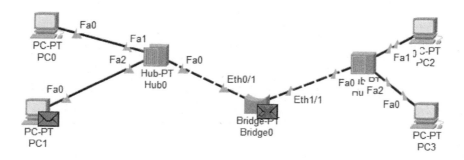

Feel free to ping other hosts and note the activity of the hubs and bridge.

Note:

Bridges store MAC addresses, as do switches. Hubs do not.

LAB 38

Installing a Hub

Lab Objective:
Learn how to install a simple hub.

Lab Purpose:
You have already learned in your study guide no doubt that hubs have no facility to store a table of which devices are connected to which interface, meaning every packet or frame is repeated out of each port. In this lab we will see this happening.

Lab Tool:
Packet Tracer

Lab Topology:
Please use the following topology to complete this lab exercise:

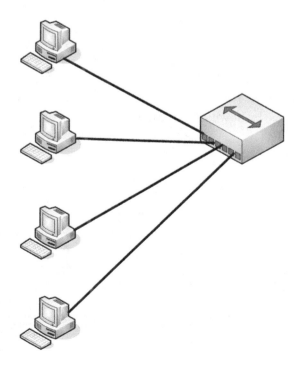

Lab Walkthrough:

Task 1:

Drag a hub onto the canvas and connect four PCs to any port on it. There is no facility to name or configure the ports on a hub.

Task 2:

Add IP addresses to the devices, starting at 192.168.1.1 and ending with .4. Here is the configuration for one of the devices:

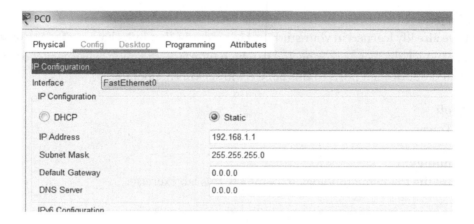

Task 3:

Click on the 'Simulation' tab in Packet Tracer. This gives you a window showing packets moving across the network. You can select (deselect) those you want (don't want) to see, but for now I'll just leave it showing everything until the next step.

Task 4:

Resize your canvas so you can see the icons, command prompt, and packet outputs. Note a green envelope icon has appeared on the PC you are going to ping 192.168.1.4 from (which is .1).

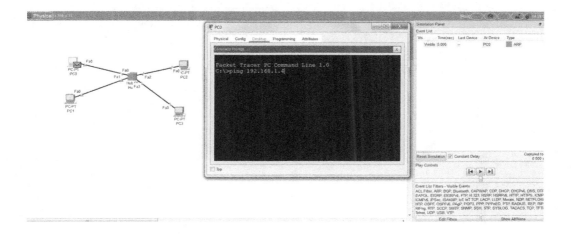

Task 5:

In order to reduce the amount of information you see click on 'Show All/None' and 'Edit Filters' and then select IPv4 ICMP, which is used by ping.

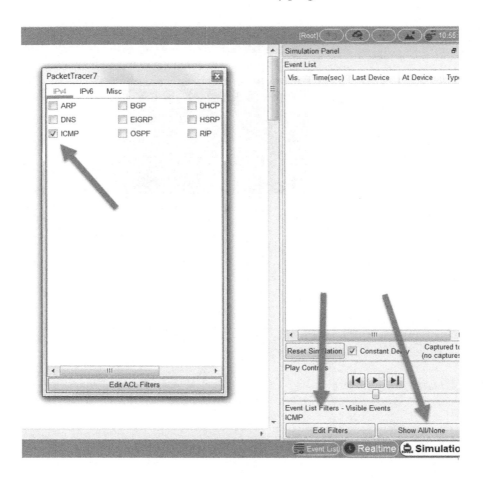

Task 6:

From host 192.168.1.1 issue a ping to host 192.168.1.4. In simulation mode it won't send the packet until you press the play button. You should see the ping envelope go to the hub and then being sent to all connected hosts. Hosts .2 and .3 will have to receive the packet, process it, and drop it (as signified by red crosses on the envelopes).

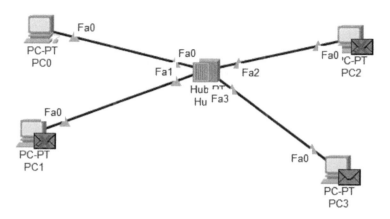

Only host .4 will respond. The response is sent to the hub, which again sends it out of all ports despite the fact only .1 need receive it.

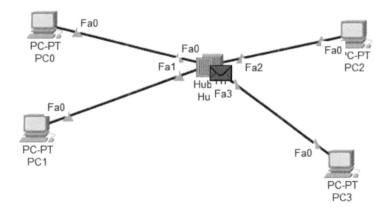

Task 7:

Issue another ping command and watch the same thing happen. The hub has no way of storing host information and so will continue to forward traffic destined for host .4 out of all ports (apart from the one it received the packet on).

Note:

There are many features we could go into, but we will be covering more switching features later in the relevant sections.

LAB 39

Installing a Wireless Access Point

Lab Objective:
Learn how to install a WAP.

Lab Purpose:
WAPs are ubiquitous and you are more than likely to be required to install them as part of your job as a network engineer. This lab will cover the basics; we will look into wireless security later in this guide.

Lab Tool:
Packet Tracer

Lab Topology:
Please use the following topology to complete this lab exercise:

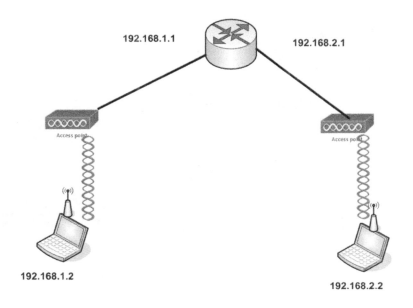

Lab Walkthrough:

Task 1:

Drag WAPs onto the canvas. I used 'Access-Point PT'. Connect them to the Ethernet ports of a router. Use the lightning strike cable icon to connect cables from the WAPs to the router. I used an 1841 router in my lab, but you can use any model with Ethernet ports.

Drag two laptops to the canvas and under the 'Physical' tab drag a wireless module to the empty slot on the side of both. You will need to press the power button first and remember to power back on. In order to do this, you first need to remove the wired Ethernet port by dragging it away.

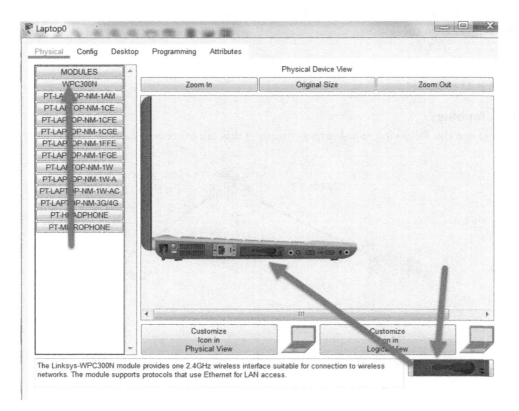

Task 2:

Add IP addresses to the relevant router ports: 192.168.1.1 to the left port and 192.168.2.1 to the right. We usually use the command line, but this time I used the GUI to find the Ethernet port. You need to tick the 'On' box to enable the interface.

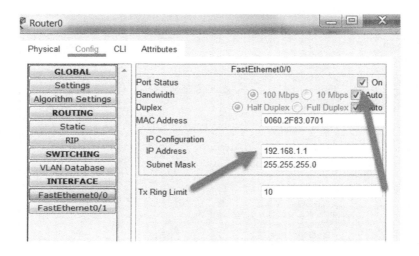

The interface for the right WAP will be 192.168.2.1.

Task 3:

Configure the SSID for the WAPs. Use 'leftwap' and 'rightwap' for the respective devices. Here it is on the left WAP. Make sure you enter the correct SSID per device.

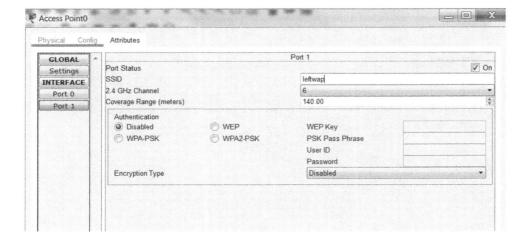

Task 4:

Configure the correct SSID for the left and right laptops and add the 192.168.1.2 IP address to the left and 192.168.2.2 to the right (which connects to 'rightwap' AP).

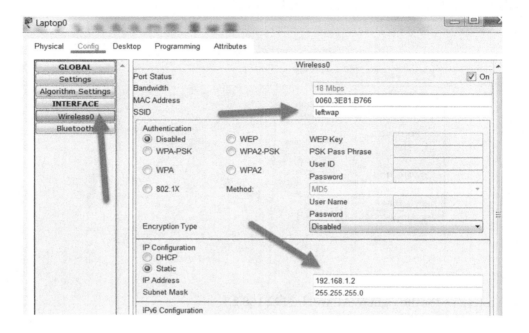

You also need to set the default gateway of the local router Ethernet interface. Here it is for the left laptop:

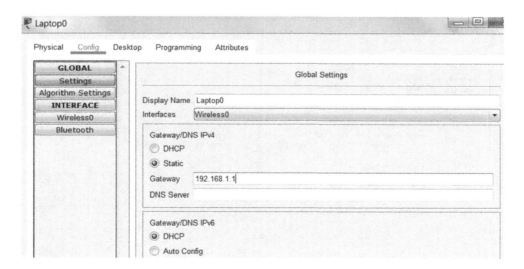

Task 5:

From the left laptop, ping the default gateway, the remote router interface address, and then the remote laptop.

```
C:\> ping 192.168.1.1

Pinging 192.168.1.1 with 32 bytes of data:

Reply from 192.168.1.1: bytes=32 time=38ms TTL=255
Reply from 192.168.1.1: bytes=32 time=25ms TTL=255
Reply from 192.168.1.1: bytes=32 time=21ms TTL=255
Reply from 192.168.1.1: bytes=32 time=15ms TTL=255

Ping statistics for 192.168.1.1:
    Packets: Sent = 4, Received = 4, Lost = 0 (0% loss),
Approximate round trip times in milli-seconds:
    Minimum = 15ms, Maximum = 38ms, Average = 24ms

C:\> ping 192.168.2.1

Pinging 192.168.2.1 with 32 bytes of data:

Reply from 192.168.2.1: bytes=32 time=37ms TTL=255
Reply from 192.168.2.1: bytes=32 time=20ms TTL=255
Reply from 192.168.2.1: bytes=32 time=20ms TTL=255
Reply from 192.168.2.1: bytes=32 time=21ms TTL=255

Ping statistics for 192.168.2.1:
    Packets: Sent = 4, Received = 4, Lost = 0 (0% loss),
Approximate round trip times in milli-seconds:
    Minimum = 20ms, Maximum = 37ms, Average = 24ms

C:\> ping 192.168.2.2

Pinging 192.168.2.2 with 32 bytes of data:

Request timed out.
Reply from 192.168.2.2: bytes=32 time=16ms TTL=127
Reply from 192.168.2.2: bytes=32 time=28ms TTL=127
Reply from 192.168.2.2: bytes=32 time=18ms TTL=127

Ping statistics for 192.168.2.2:
```

Notes:

This is a very basic install. Security comes later on.

LAB 40

Installing a VoIP Endpoint

Lab Objective:

Learn how to install and configure voice over IP endpoints.

Lab Purpose:

Installing VoIP devices is a somewhat specialized task; however, you may be required to do it even in small companies.

Lab Tool:

Packet Tracer

Lab Topology:

Please use the following topology to complete this lab exercise:

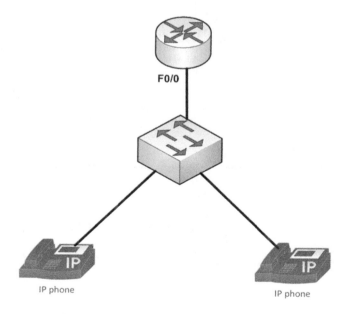

Lab Walkthrough:

Task 1:

Drag a voice-capable router to the canvas; I used a 2811. Also drag one switch and two IP phones. You must manually drag the power cord to the power port on the IP phone in order for it to boot.

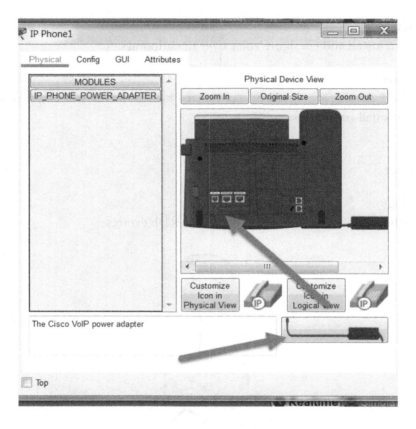

Task 2:

Add IP addresses on the Ethernet interface of the router. I'll leave you to input 'exit' or 'end' wherever you need to.

```
Router>enable
Router#configure terminal
Router(config)#interface FastEthernet0/0
Router(config-if)#ip address 192.168.10.1 255.255.255.0
Router(config-if)#no shutdown
```

Task 3:

Configure the router to allocate addresses via DHCP. Also, add an option for the phones to download their configuration files from the router (option 150). Ensure the router doesn't allocate its own IP address from the DHCP pool.

```
Router(config)#ip dhcp excluded-address 192.168.10.1
Router(config)#ip dhcp pool VOICE
Router(dhcp-config)#network 192.168.10.0 255.255.255.0
Router(dhcp-config)#default-router 192.168.10.1
Router(dhcp-config)#option 150 ip 192.168.10.1
Router(dhcp-config)#exit
```

Task 4:

Configure the switch. Configure the ports as access ports and define the VLAN the voice traffic will use. For simplicity we'll stick to VLAN1.

```
Switch(config)#interface range fa0/1 - 5
Switch(config-if-range)#switchport mode access
Switch(config-if-range)#switchport voice vlan 1
```

Task 5:

Add the voice configuration on the router. The commands are specific to Cisco, so you will not be expected to recall them in the exam. We have 10 directory numbers, 10 phones, the source IP address, and a method to auto-assign extension numbers to buttons.

```
Router(config)#telephony-service
Router(config-telephony)#max-dn 10
Router(config-telephony)#max-ephones 10
Router(config-telephony)#ip source-address 192.168.10.1 port 2000
Router(config-telephony)#auto assign 4 to 6
Router(config-telephony)#auto assign 1 to 5
Router(config-telephony)#exit
```

Task 6:

Assign the first directory entry and then the number associated with that entry. Then do the next number.

```
Router(config)#ephone-dn 1
Router(config-ephone-dn)#number 54001
Router(config-ephone-dn)#exit
Router(config)#ephone-dn 2
Router(config-ephone-dn)#number 54002
```

Task 7:

Hover your mouse over the phone and check the configuration has been applied. It may take a short while.

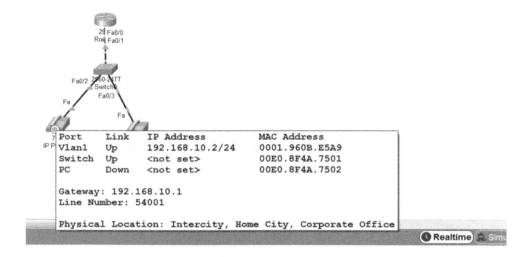

Task 8:

Finally, click on the handset and call the other phone by pressing its extension number. The other phone should ring, and you should see the light flash.

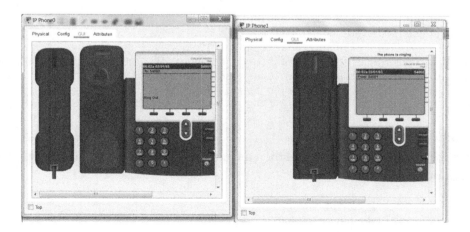

Notes:

The idea of doing these labs is to get a bit of confidence and have some fun. You may well end up configuring VoIP at your work using Cisco or some other provider.

LAB 41

Installing a Wireless LAN Controller

Lab Objective:
Learn how to install a WLC.

Lab Purpose:
Wireless LAN controllers (depending on the model) can control several access points, allocate DHCP information, and provide internet access for your network. We will configure a simple WLC in this lab.

Lab Tool:
Packet Tracer

Lab Topology:
Please use the following topology to complete this lab exercise:

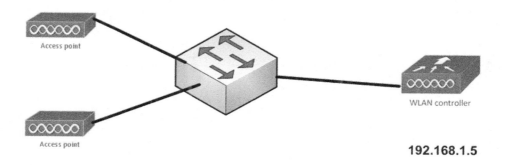

Lab Walkthrough:

Task 1:
Drag two lightweight access points onto the dashboard and one wireless LAN controller. Connect them to a switch. The port numbers don't matter. You need to drag the power leads for the LWAPs.

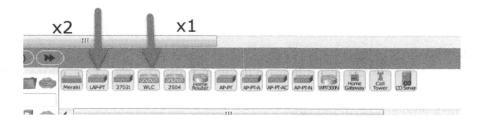

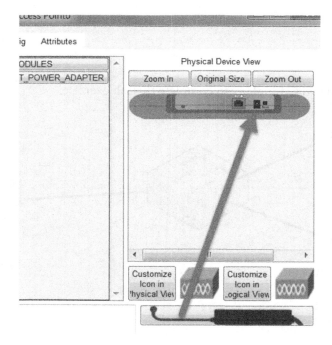

Task 2:

Change the display name of the top AP to 'AP 1' and that of the bottom AP to 'AP 2'.

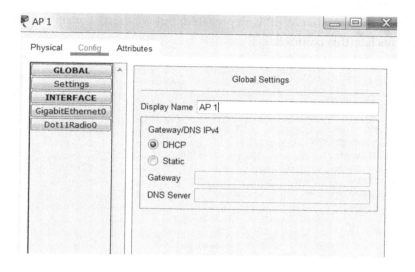

Task 3:

For the management interface add the IP address of the WLC, which is 192.168.1.5. The gateway and DNS server will be .1. Leave the default subnet mask (255.255.255.0).

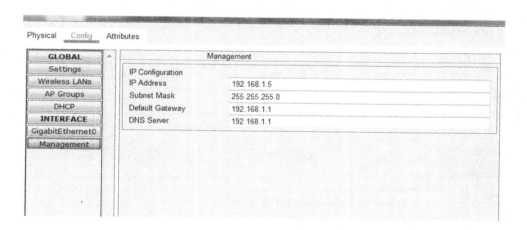

Task 4:

Under 'Wireless LANs' create AP 1 with WEP and an SSID of AP1 and then AP 2 with WEP and a passphrase of 0123456789 for AP1 and 1234567890 for AP2 (please note the difference). I know that WEP is deprecated, but we aren't concerned with wireless security in this lab (this comes later).

Task 5:

Check under 'AP Groups' that both are present.

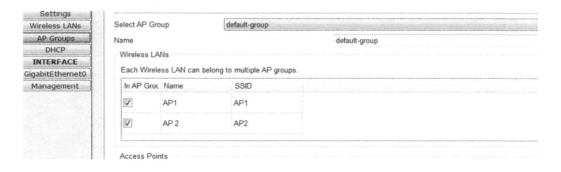

Task 6:

Configure DHCP on the WLC. Make sure you turn DHCP on and click on 'Add' and then 'Save'.

Pool Name—101labs
Gateway—192.168.1.1
DNS Server—192.168.1.1
Start IP—192.168.1.10
Users—100
WLC Address—192.168.1.5

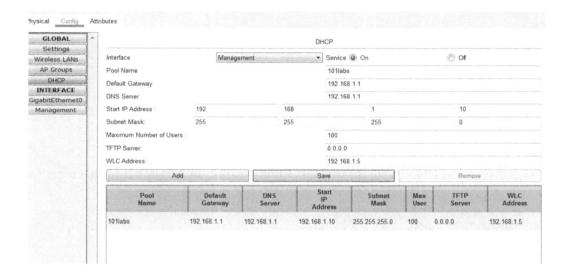

Task 7:

In order to instigate traffic on the network (because it's virtual) go to simulation mode and press the play button. It could take some time for DHCP to allocate addresses. Simulation mode runs very slowly. I suggest you filter to DHCP traffic only to prevent Packet Tracer from crashing.

Task 8:

Under 'AP Groups' create AP1 and AP2. Put AP1 under its own group and AP2 under its own group.

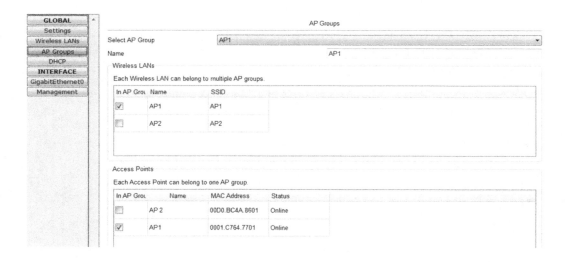

Task 9:

Drag two wireless tablets onto the desktop. Configure one for AP1 and the other for AP2.

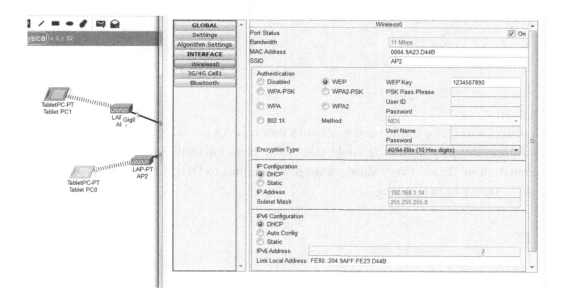

Task 10:

Hover your mouse over the smart tablets. Check that their IP addresses have been allocated from the DHCP pool.

```
TabletP
Tablet  Port            Link    IP Address              IPv6 Address
        Wireless0       Up      192.168.1.17/24         <not set>
        3G/4G Cell1     Up      169.254.183.176/16 <not set>
        Bluetooth       Down    <not set>               <not set>

        Gateway: 192.168.1.1
        DNS Server: 192.168.1.1
        Line Number:  <not set>

        Wireless Best Data Rate: 300 Mbps
        Wireless Signal Strength: 73%

        Physical Location: Intercity, Home City, Corporate Office
```

Note:

This is a very basic install. Security comes later on.

Installing a Multilayer Switch

Lab Objective:

Learn how to install and configure a multilayer switch.

Lab Purpose:

Many vendors supply basic (layer 2) switches but also higher-specification switches which can perform routing (layer 3) or content switching (layers 4–7). The main difference between the way switches route traffic and the way routers do it is that switches use application-specific integrated circuits (ASICs) and routers use software/CPU.

Lab Tool:

Packet Tracer

Lab Topology:

Please use the following topology to complete this lab exercise:

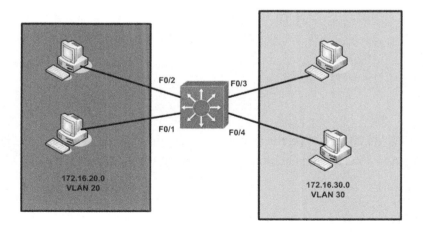

Lab Walkthrough:

Task 1:
Drag a Cisco 3560 model multilayer switch onto the canvas and attach four PCs as per the diagram.

Task 2:
Add IP addresses of 172.16.20.2 and .3 to the devices going into VLAN 20. The default gateway will be 172.16.20.1 (the switch VLAN interface). For the devices in VLAN 30 the IP addresses will be 172.16.30.2 and .3, and the default gateway will be 172.16.30.1.

We are using VLSM here, so make sure you use a subnet mask of 255.255.255.0.

Here is the configuration for one of the devices:

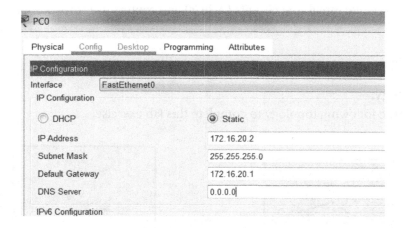

Task 3:
Configure VLAN 20 and 30 on the switch. Also, create a switched virtual interface (SVI) for each VLAN. SVIs are logical interfaces which allow routing to take place.

```
Switch>en
Switch#conf t
Enter configuration commands, one per line.  End with CNTL/Z.
Switch(config)#vlan 20
Switch(config-vlan)#vlan 30
Switch(config-vlan)#interface vlan 20
%LINK-5-CHANGED: Interface Vlan20, changed state to up

Switch(config-if)#ip add 172.16.20.1 255.255.255.0
Switch(config-if)#no shut
```

```
Switch(config-if)#interface vlan 30
Switch(config-if)#
%LINK-5-CHANGED: Interface Vlan30, changed state to up

Switch(config-if)#ip add 172.16.30.1 255.255.255.0
Switch(config-if)#no shut
Switch(config-if)#
```

Task 4:

Assign F0/1 and F0/2 to VLAN 20 and F0/3 and F0/4 to VLAN 30. Set the interfaces to access.

```
Switch(config-if)#int f0/1
Switch(config-if)#switchport mode access
Switch(config-if)#switchport access vlan 20
%LINEPROTO-5-UPDOWN: Line protocol on Interface Vlan20, changed state
to up
Switch(config-if)#int f0/2
Switch(config-if)#switchport mode access
Switch(config-if)#switchport access vlan 20
Switch(config-if)#int f0/3
Switch(config-if)#switchport mode access
Switch(config-if)#switchport access vlan 30
Switch(config-if)# int f0/4
%LINEPROTO-5-UPDOWN: Line protocol on Interface Vlan30, changed state
to up
Switch(config-if)#switchport mode access
Switch(config-if)#switchport access vlan 30
```

Task 5:

Configure the switch to route traffic. If you miss this command, your VLANs won't be able to communicate.

```
Switch(config)#ip routing
```

Task 6:

From 172.16.20.2 ping .3. Then, ping a device in VLAN 30, such as 172.16.30.2.

```
C:\>ping 172.16.20.3

Pinging 172.16.20.3 with 32 bytes of data:

Reply from 172.16.20.3: bytes=32 time=1ms TTL=128
Reply from 172.16.20.3: bytes=32 time<1ms TTL=128
Reply from 172.16.20.3: bytes=32 time<1ms TTL=128
Reply from 172.16.20.3: bytes=32 time<1ms TTL=128

Ping statistics for 172.16.20.3:
    Packets: Sent = 4, Received = 4, Lost = 0 (0% loss),
Approximate round trip times in milli-seconds:
    Minimum = 0ms, Maximum = 1ms, Average = 0ms

C:\>ping 172.16.30.2

Pinging 172.16.30.2 with 32 bytes of data:

Reply from 172.16.30.2: bytes=32 time=1ms TTL=127
Reply from 172.16.30.2: bytes=32 time<1ms TTL=127
Reply from 172.16.30.2: bytes=32 time<1ms TTL=127
Reply from 172.16.30.2: bytes=32 time<1ms TTL=127

Ping statistics for 172.16.30.2:
    Packets: Sent = 4, Received = 4, Lost = 0 (0% loss),
Approximate round trip times in milli-seconds:
    Minimum = 0ms, Maximum = 1ms, Average = 0ms
```

Note:

There are many features we could go into for the multilayer switch, but this would take another book.

LAB 43

Configuring a Layer 7 Firewall

Lab Objective:
Learn how to configure a layer 7 firewall.

Lab Purpose:
As you can imagine, getting your hands on next-generation firewalls (NGFWs) can be a challenge. At the moment, Meraki (which was recently acquired by Cisco) lets you log in to a web-based installation of its software.

Lab Tool:
Meraki online demo - **https://meraki.cisco.com/form/demo**

Lab Topology:
Please use the following topology to complete this lab exercise:

CASE STU

Meraki Dashboard Demo

Try our network management interface for free.

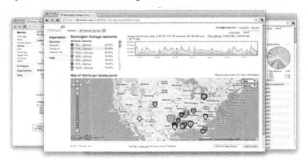

Lab Walkthrough:

Task 1:
Go to the Meraki demo website, register your email address, and then verify your email address by clicking on the verification link. This will unlock all the features.

https://meraki.cisco.com/form/demo

Task 2:
Navigate to 'Security appliance / Firewall'.

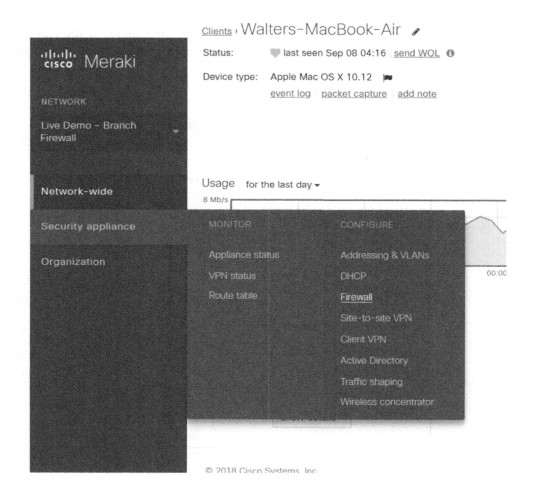

Task 3:

Feel free to peruse all the available features. We will be applying some layer 7 blocking rules for this lab. Click on 'Add a layer 7 firewall rule'.

Layer 7

Firewall rules   There are no rules defined for this network.
                        Add a layer 7 firewall rule

Forwarding rules

Port forwarding ℹ️   There are no port forwarding rules on this network.
                        Add a port forwarding rule

1:1 NAT ℹ️   There are no 1:1 NAT mappings.

Task 4:

The first rule will block 'Video & music / YouTube'.

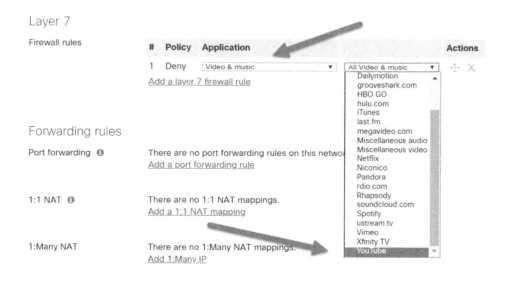

Layer 7

Firewall rules

#	Policy	Application		Actions
1	Deny	Video & music ▼	All Video & music ▼	✛ ✕

Add a layer 7 firewall rule

Dailymotion
grooveshark.com
HBO GO
hulu.com
iTunes
last.fm
megavideo.com
Miscellaneous audio
Miscellaneous video
Netflix
Niconico
Pandora
rdio.com
Rhapsody
soundcloud.com
Spotify
ustream.tv
Vimeo
Xfinity TV
YouTube

Forwarding rules

Port forwarding ℹ️   There are no port forwarding rules on this netwo
                        Add a port forwarding rule

1:1 NAT ℹ️   There are no 1:1 NAT mappings.
                        Add a 1:1 NAT mapping

1:Many NAT   There are no 1:Many NAT mappings.
                        Add 1:Many IP

Task 5:

Add two more rules. Block online backups to Backblaze and deny a host—101labs.net. You can use the crosshairs to move the rules up or down. Rules are processed top-down.

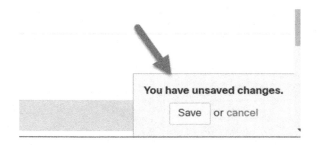

Task 6:

Click 'Save' at the bottom of the page.

Task 7:

Go to 'Network-wide / Clients' and then click on the top client.

Task 8:

Scroll down and check the policy brief. Then click on 'show details' to check the layer 7 rules are active.

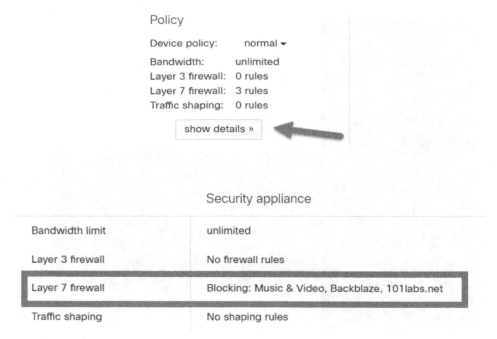

Bandwidth limit	unlimited
Layer 3 firewall	No firewall rules
Layer 7 firewall	Blocking: Music & Video, Backblaze, 101labs.net
Traffic shaping	No shaping rules

Note:

There are many other features available in the online demo.

LAB 44

UTM Appliance Tour

Lab Objective:
Download and explore the features of a UTM.

Lab Purpose:
Unified threat management is an approach to security whereby a single hardware or software device provides multiple functions, such as firewall, VPN, wireless, intrusion detection/prevention, antivirus, web proxy, and more.

It helps users reduce costs and avoid having to train on multiple platforms. It can of course represent a single point of failure (SPF).

Lab Tool:
Korugan Lite

Lab Topology:
Please download Korugan Lite from https://www.korugan.com/koruganlite.php.

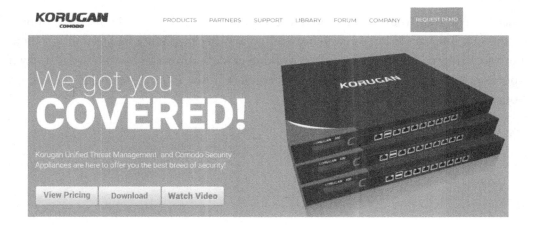

Lab Walkthrough:

Task 1:
Download the software. If you are using VirtualBox (as I did), then click 'File / Import Appliance' and find the installation file.

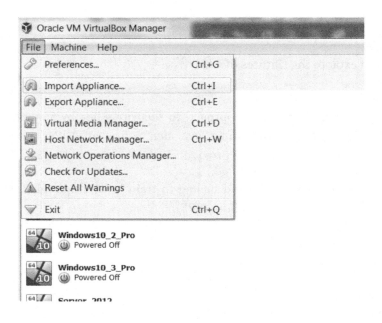

Task 2:
I had to set the software installation to use an internal network. But in order to connect to the web interface using the web browser on another machine I had to then set them both to 'Bridged Adapter'. Internal networking in VirtualBox can be somewhat tricky if you want to connect virtual machines or connect to the internet or to files hosted on your real machines.

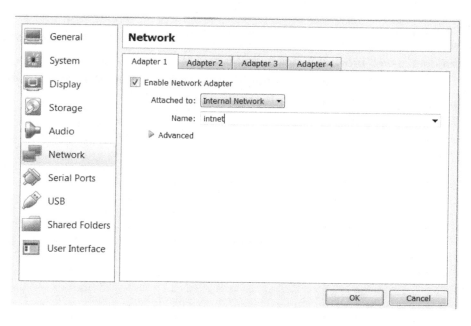

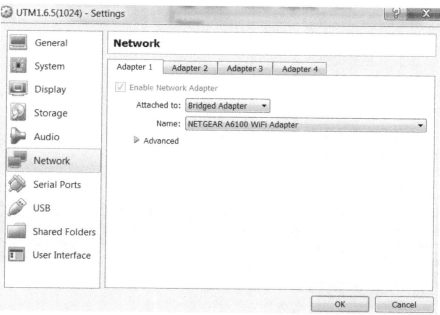

Task 3:

Make sure you have your internal machines (your UTM and Virtual PC) set to 'Bridged' and then open a web browser Navigate to **https://192.168.0.15:10443**. You may have to add a security exception, and the connection may be slow. **Note that your IP address may differ, so please check on your local machine first.**

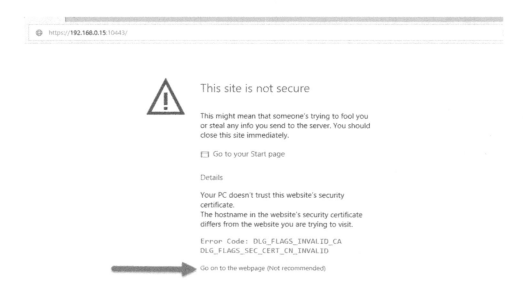

Task 4:

Add any exceptions (see above) and then log in at the login screen with username 'admin' and password 'comodo'.

Task 5:

You will then be taken to the main page, the dashboard.

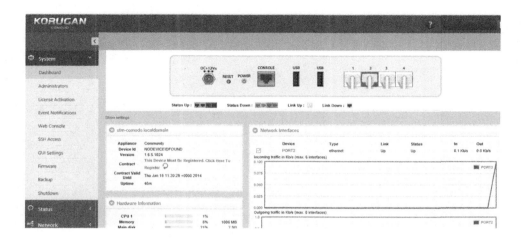

Task 6:

Go through each of the settings. If you set this up on your home computer, you will be able to set up and test rules for the firewall. It's not so easy on the virtual network, but peruse all the options and features.

Notes:

This is just a brief tour of the features available with one downloadable UTM.

Some users have found that their Chrome settings block the web page, but got Firefox to work. I used the default IE browser on my VM for this lab.

LAB 45

Jumbo Frames

Lab Objective:
Learn how jumbo frames work, and configure an interface to send them.

Lab Purpose:
Ethernet traffic is encapsulated inside frames. The maximum size (MTU) of this frame is 1500 bytes. Any packet larger than this is referred to as a jumbo frame. An interface receiving a jumbo frame can either fragment it or drop it unless it's configured to receive them.

Please configure your interfaces for jumbo frames only after speaking to your equipment vendor because it may actually slow your network down.

Lab Tool:
Packet Tracer

Lab Topology:
Please use the following topology to complete this lab exercise:

192.168.1.0/30

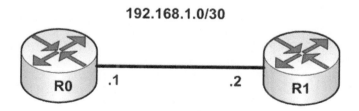

Lab Walkthrough:

Task 1:
Connect the above network devices. Use a crossover cable to connect the routers.

Task 2:

Change the hostnames as indicated and add the IP addresses. Here is the config for R0.

```
Router>en
Router#conf t
Enter configuration commands, one per line. End with CNTL/Z.
Router(config)#host R0
R0(config)#int f0/0
R0(config-if)#ip add 192.168.1.1 255.255.255.252
R0(config-if)#no shut
R0(config-if)#end
```

Task 3:

Check the maximum transmission unit for the Ethernet interface. It should be 1500 bytes.

```
R0#show int f0/0
FastEthernet0/0 is up, line protocol is down (disabled)
Hardware is Lance, address is 0060.3e01.9601 (bia 0060.3e01.9601)
Internet address is 192.168.1.1/30
MTU 1500 bytes, BW 100000 Kbit, DLY 100 usec,
reliability 255/255, txload 1/255, rxload 1/255
Encapsulation ARPA, loopback not set
Full-duplex, 100Mb/s, media type is RJ45
[Output Truncated]
```

Task 4:

Change the MTU. Different models and interface types may give different options. Here are your options for this model. Match the configuration on R1.

```
R0(config)#int f0/0
R0(config-if)#mtu ?
<64-1600> MTU size in bytes
R0(config-if)#mtu 1600
```

Task 5:

Unfortunately, Packet Tracer's sniffer is somewhat limited, but below are two Wireshark packet captures for an Ethernet frame. The top is normal, and the bottom is a jumbo frame showing the amount of data it contains. The bottom capture is from two Ethernet frames, which normally would never be able to move this volume of data.

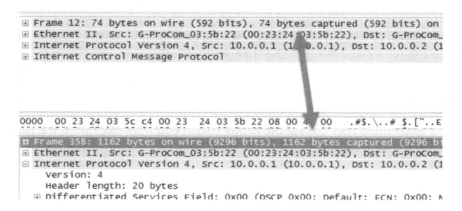

```
⊞ Frame 12: 74 bytes on wire (592 bits), 74 bytes captured (592 bits) on
⊞ Ethernet II, Src: G-ProCom_03:5b:22 (00:23:24:03:5b:22), Dst: G-ProCom_
⊞ Internet Protocol Version 4, Src: 10.0.0.1 (10.0.0.1), Dst: 10.0.0.2 (1
⊞ Internet Control Message Protocol

0000   00 23 24 03 5c c4 00 23   24 03 5b 22 08 00 4  00     .#$.\..# $.["..E
⊟ Frame 358: 1162 bytes on wire (9296 bits), 1162 bytes captured (9296 b
⊞ Ethernet II, Src: G-ProCom_03:5b:22 (00:23:24:03:5b:22), Dst: G-ProCom_
⊟ Internet Protocol Version 4, Src: 10.0.0.1 (10.0.0.1), Dst: 10.0.0.2 (1
      Version: 4
      Header length: 20 bytes
   ⊞ Differentiated Services Field: 0x00 (DSCP 0x00: Default; ECN: 0x00: N
```

Image copyright: samsclass.info

Task 6:

You can set jumbo frames on your network card if it supports them.

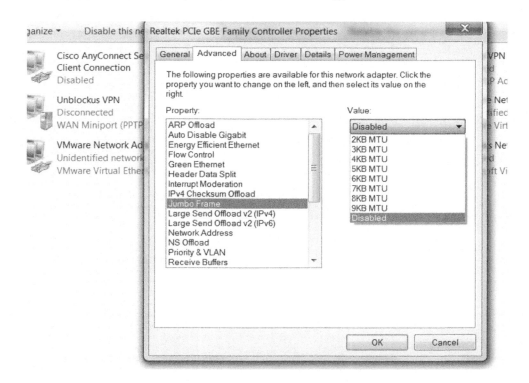

Notes:

On a live router you could run a ping test telling the router to not fragment the ping packet or change its size. Below is the 'do not fragment' option.

```
Type of service [0]:
Set DF bit in IP header? [no]: Yes
```

There is a nice jumbo frame lab at the below URL if you want to capture the packets for real on your home or virtual network.

https://samsclass.info/106/proj13/p1x_jumbo-frames.htm

LAB 46

Configuring Frame Relay

Lab Objective:

Learn how to install and configure Frame Relay.

Lab Purpose:

Frame Relay was once a hugely popular WAN protocol. It offers an inexpensive and easy-to-configure solution for small to medium-sized businesses. It has lost popularity due to DSL and other technologies.

Lab Tool:

Packet Tracer

Lab Topology:

Please use the following topology to complete this lab exercise:

Lab Walkthrough:

Task 1:

Add two routers to the canvas and add WAN cards. As before, you need to power down the router first and then drag the modules into the chassis. Connect the routers to the Packet Tracer cloud using a DCE cable with the DCE end on the cloud side.

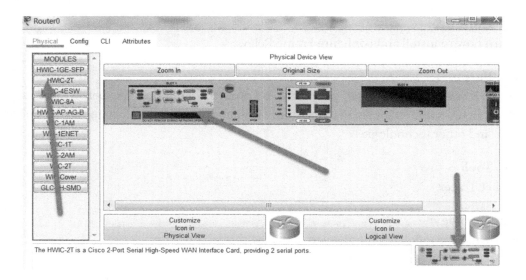

The HWIC-2T is a Cisco 2-Port Serial High-Speed WAN Interface Card, providing 2 serial ports.

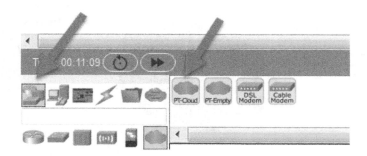

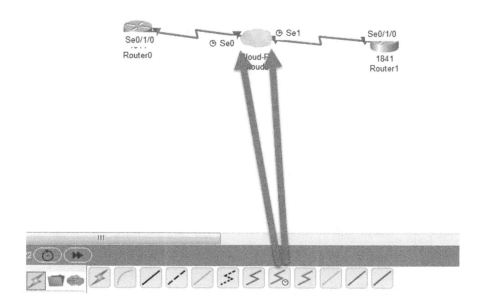

Task 2:

The Frame Relay cloud would normally be the concern of your provider, but we are doing it here because we are doing this lab on Packet Tracer. You need to assign a connection number to each interface and then map them. The number is known as a data link connection identifier or DLCI.

For Serial0 on the PT cloud allocate DLCI 100 and for Serial1 allocate DLCI 200.

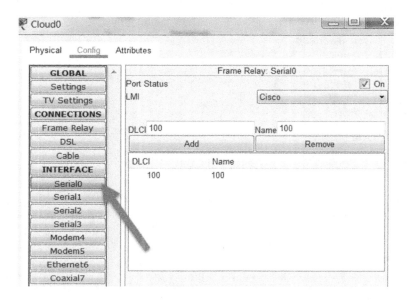

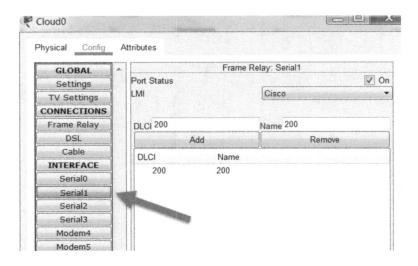

Under 'Frame Relay' create a map so DLCI 100 goes into S0 and out of S1 as DLCI 200. Press 'Add' when done.

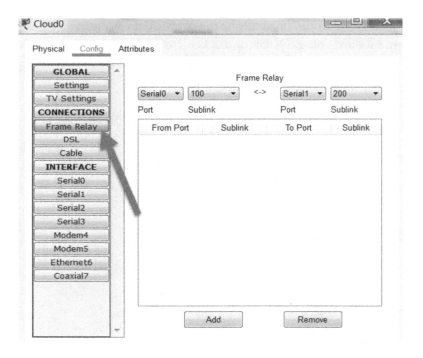

Task 3:

Configure your IP address on R0 and set your encapsulation and DLCI, which you would have allocated by your Frame Relay service provider. Here is the config for R0; for R1 use DLCI 200 and of course IP address .2.

```
Router#conf t
Router(config)#host R0
R0(config)#int s0/1/0
R0(config-if)#encapsulation frame-relay
R0(config-if)#ip address 192.168.1.1 255.255.255.252
R0(config-if)#frame-relay interface-dlci 100
R0(config-if)#no shut
```

Task 4:

We can use some show commands in order to establish if the connection is active.

```
R1#show frame-relay map
Serial0/1/0 (up): ip 192.168.1.1 dlci 200, dynamic,
broadcast,
CISCO, status defined, active
```

LMI stands for local management interface. It's a keepalive between your router and the service provider. LMIs sent should be almost as many as those received.

```
R1#show frame-relay lmi
LMI Statistics for interface Serial0/1/0 (Frame Relay DTE) LMI TYPE =
CISCO
Invalid Unnumbered info 0 Invalid Prot Disc 0
Invalid dummy Call Ref 0 Invalid Msg Type 0
Invalid Status Message 0 Invalid Lock Shift 0
Invalid Information ID 0 Invalid Report IE Len 0
Invalid Report Request 0 Invalid Keep IE Len 0
Num Status Enq. Sent 25 Num Status msgs Rcvd 24
Num Update Status Rcvd 0 Num Status Timeouts 16
```

The Frame Relay PVC is a permanent virtual circuit. It's the end-to-end connection between your routers. It should of course be active.

```
R1#show frame-relay pvc

PVC Statistics for interface Serial0/1/0 (Frame Relay DTE)
DLCI = 200, DLCI USAGE = LOCAL, PVC STATUS = ACTIVE, INTERFACE =
Serial0/1/0

input pkts 14055 output pkts 32795 in bytes 1096228
out bytes 6216155 dropped pkts 0 in FECN pkts 0
in BECN pkts 0 out FECN pkts 0 out BECN pkts 0
```

```
in DE pkts 0 out DE pkts 0
out bcast pkts 32795 out bcast bytes 6216155
```

Task 5:

I'll leave you to ping across the link, but I'm sure you already know that it's working.

Note:

Frame Relay is rarely used nowadays, but it's in the exam syllabus, so you need to be familiar with how it works and the various terms associated with it.

Configuring PPP

Lab Objective:

Learn how to install a PPP.

Lab Purpose:

PPP is a hugely popular WAN protocol. It works on both synchronous and asynchronous links, offers security (authentication and encryption), and can be configured on routers for many vendors due to the fact it is an open standard.

Lab Tool:

Packet Tracer

Lab Topology:

Please use the following topology to complete this lab exercise:

192.168.1.0/30

Lab Walkthrough:

Task 1:

Drag two routers onto the canvas. You will need to power down and then add a WAN module. My hardware setup is shown below:

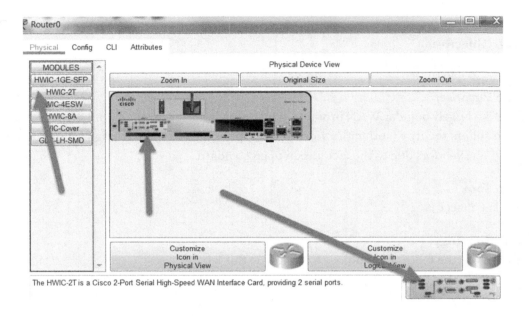

The HWIC-2T is a Cisco 2-Port Serial High-Speed WAN Interface Card, providing 2 serial ports.

You can issue a 'show ip int brief' command to see which interfaces you have available.

```
R0#show ip int brief
Interface IP-Address OK? Method Status Protocol
GigabitEthernet0/0 unassigned YES unset administratively down down
GigabitEthernet0/1 unassigned YES unset administratively down down
Serial0/1/0 unassigned YES unset administratively down down
Serial0/1/1 unassigned YES unset administratively down down
Vlan1 unassigned YES unset administratively down down
R0#
```

Task 2:

Drag a serial cable across the WAN link and then add IP address .1 on R0 and .2 on R1. Here is the configuration for R0:

```
R0(config)#interface s0/1/0
R0(config-if)#ip add 192.168.1.1 255.255.255.252
R0(config-if)#no shut
```

Task 3:

Most routers have a default WAN encapsulation, so the link will come up if you connect them. Ping across the link.

```
R1#ping 192.168.1.1

Type escape sequence to abort.
Sending 5, 100-byte ICMP Echos to 192.168.1.1, timeout is 2 seconds:
!!!!!
Success rate is 100 percent (5/5), round-trip min/avg/max = 1/11/55 ms
```

Task 4:

Issue a 'show interface X' command to see the interface settings. 'X' is whatever your interface name is for your device. Cisco defaults to HDLC.

```
R1#show interface s0/1/0
Serial0/1/0 is up, line protocol is up (connected)
Hardware is HD64570
Internet address is 192.168.1.2/30
MTU 1500 bytes, BW 1544 Kbit, DLY 20000 usec,
reliability 255/255, txload 1/255, rxload 1/255
Encapsulation HDLC, loopback not set, keepalive set (10 sec)
```

Task 5:

Change the encapsulation type to PPP. Add security so the router checks the calling router username and password. Turn on PPP debugs so you see the link come up. Also, after you configure R0, check that the link to R1 is down. It will be physically up, but the line protocol is down due to the fact that R1 is using HDLC and R0 is using PPP.

```
R0(config-if)#encapsulation ppp
R0(config-if)#ppp authentication chap
R0(config-if)#exit
R0(config)#username R1 password cisco
R0(config)#end

R1#debug ppp authentication
PPP authentication debugging is on
R1#debug ppp negotiation
PPP protocol negotiation debugging is on

R1#show int s0/1/0
Serial0/1/0 is up, line protocol is down (disabled)
Hardware is HD64570
Internet address is 192.168.1.2/30
MTU 1500 bytes, BW 1544 Kbit, DLY 20000 usec,
reliability 255/255, txload 1/255, rxload 1/255
```

```
R1(config)#interface s0/1/0
R1(config-if)#encapsulation ppp
R1(config-if)#ppp authentication chap
R1(config-if)#exit
R1(config)#username R0 password cisco
R1(config)#end

Serial0/1/0 PPP: Phase is AUTHENTICATING
Serial0/1/0 LCP: State is Open
Serial0/1/0 PPP: Phase is AUTHENTICATING
```

Task 6:

Turn all debugging off.

```
R1#un all
All possible debugging has been turned off
```

Task 7:

Check the interface on R1 is up and the encapsulation is PPP.

```
R1#show int s0/1/0
Serial0/1/0 is up, line protocol is up (connected)
Hardware is HD64570
Internet address is 192.168.1.2/30
MTU 1500 bytes, BW 1544 Kbit, DLY 20000 usec,
reliability 255/255, txload 1/255, rxload 1/255
Encapsulation PPP, loopback not set, keepalive set (10 sec)
LCP Open
Open: IPCP, CDPCP
```

Ping across the link if you wish.

Note:

PPP is regularly used on WAN links, and if you are ever asked to connect routers from different vendors, you will almost certainly use it.

LAB 48

Configuring PPPoE

Lab Objective:

Learn how to install and configure a PPPoE connection.

Lab Purpose:

PPP over Ethernet encapsulates PPP frames over an Ethernet connection. It is most frequently used with DSL, where individual users connect.

Lab Tool:

Packet Tracer

Lab Topology:

Please use the following topology to complete this lab exercise:

Lab Walkthrough:

Task 1:

Connect a PC to a DSL modem in Packet Tracer. Connect the modem (port) to a PT cloud (phone interface). Finally, connect the cloud (Ethernet) to the router Ethernet interface (I used an 1841 model). On the PT cloud, connect the modem port to the Ethernet. Here is the DSL modem:

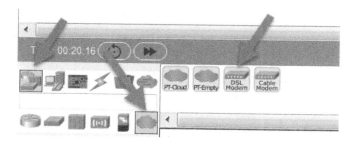

And the cloud:

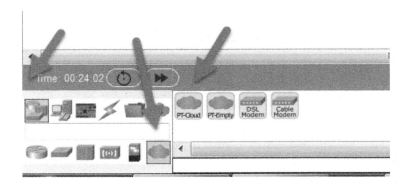

And the connection you need to make on the cloud:

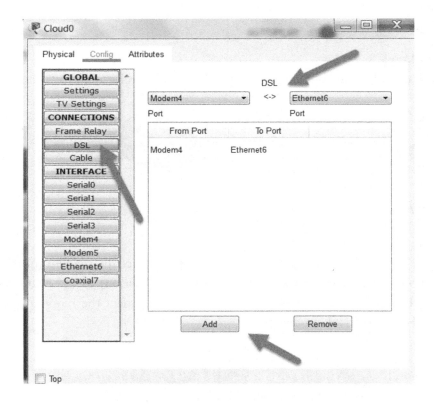

Task 2:

Add IP address 192.168.1.1 to the Ethernet interface on the router.

```
Router(config)#int f0/0
Router(config-if)#ip address 192.168.1.1 255.255.255.0
Router(config-if)#no shut
Router(config-if)#exit
```

Task 3:

Configure the virtual interface and PPPoE profile (with the 'bba-group' command). Have it use the IP address associated with F0/0. Link the interface with the pool of addresses called 'POOL', which we will create shortly, and finally, enable PPP authentication CHAP. Ignore any error warning message you might see.

```
Router(config)#bba-group pppoe 101labs
%LINK-5-CHANGED: Interface Virtual-Access1, changed state to up
Router(config-bba)#virtual-template 1
Router(config-bba)#exit
Router(config)#interface virtual-Template 1
Router(config-if)#ip unnumbered f0/0
Router(config-if)#peer default ip address pool POOL
Router(config-if)#ppp authentication chap
```

Task 4:

Configure a username and password the host will use to authenticate with. Then create a local pool which will be used to allocate to hosts dialing in.

```
Router(config-if)#exit
Router(config)#username cisco password labs
Router(config)#ip local pool POOL 192.168.1.2 192.168.1.10
```

Task 5:

Under interface F0/0, add the PPPoE group.

```
Router(config)#int f0/0
Router(config-if)#pppoe enable group 101labs
```

Task 6:

On the PC open a PPPoE dialer and enter the username and password you configured.

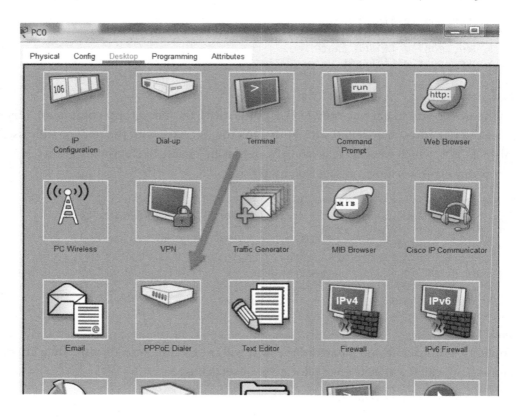

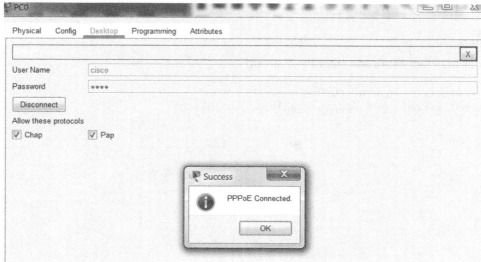

Task 7:

Check that an IP address has been allocated to the PC from the local pool.

```
Physical    Config    Desktop    Programming    Attributes

Command Prompt

Packet Tracer PC Command Line 1.0
C:\>ipconfig

FastEthernet0 Connection:(default port)

   Link-local IPv6 Address.........: FE80::2E0:F9FF:FE07:8489
   IP Address......................: 0.0.0.0
   Subnet Mask.....................: 0.0.0.0
   Default Gateway.................: 0.0.0.0

Bluetooth Connection:

   Link-local IPv6 Address.........: ::
   IP Address......................: 0.0.0.0
   Subnet Mask.....................: 0.0.0.0
   Default Gateway.................: 0.0.0.0

Dialer1 Connection:

   Link-local IPv6 Address.........: FE80::2E0:F9FF:FE07:8489
   IP Address......................: 192.168.1.2
   Subnet Mask.....................: 255.255.255.255
   Default Gateway.................: 0.0.0.0
```

Notes:

PPPoE configuration can be a bit tricky, especially on an emulator. Issue show command on the router if you wish: 'show pppoe session'.

3.0 Network Operations

LAB 49

High Availability with HSRP

Lab Objective:
Learn how to configure HA using the Hot Standby Router Protocol (HSRP).

Lab Purpose:
You have covered HA in your study guide, I'm sure. In this example, we'll aim to keep the PC on the LAN able to reach the internet if one of the routers or router interfaces goes down. Of course you would have more switches and IP addresses on the internet side, but I wanted to keep this lab simple.

HSRP allows routers to take over as gateways should one fail for any reason. They share a virtual IP address, and hosts use this address as the gateway. One router is active, and another is on standby.

Lab Tool:
Packet Tracer

Lab Topology:
Please use the following topology to complete this lab exercise:

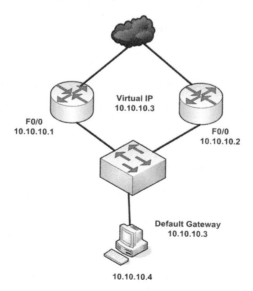

Virtual IP
10.10.10.3

F0/0
10.10.10.1

F0/0
10.10.10.2

Default Gateway
10.10.10.3

10.10.10.4

Lab Walkthrough:

Task 1:
Connect two routers, one switch, and one PC as per the diagram. I put the cloud image up just to illustrate the connection going out to the internet, but you can ignore it. Just connect the routers, switch, and PC.

Task 2:
Configure the Ethernet interfaces on the routers. Here is the config for R0 (on the left).

```
R0(config)#int f0/0
R0(config-if)#ip add 10.10.10.1 255.255.255.0
R0(config-if)#no shut
```

Task 3:
Configure the IP address and default gateway on the PC. The default gateway will be a virtual IP address shared by the routers using HSRP.

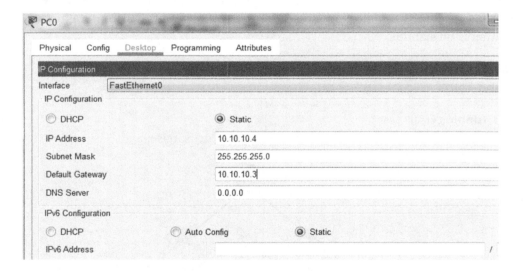

Task 4:

Set up HSRP on the routers. They will share the virtual IP address 10.10.10.3. R0 will be the active router, and R1 will become active should R0 or its interface fail. For R1 it's the same, but skip the 'standby 1 priority 120' command because it will be on standby.

```
R0(config)#int f0/0
R0(config-if)#standby 1 ip 10.10.10.3
R0(config-if)#standby 1 priority 120
%HSRP-6-STATECHANGE: FastEthernet0/0 Grp 1 state Speak -> Standby

%HSRP-6-STATECHANGE: FastEthernet0/0 Grp 1 state Standby -> Active
```

Task 5:

Check the HSRP status of R0 with the 'show standby' command. You can see that this is the active router with the virtual IP address 10.10.10.3. There is also a virtual MAC address, but don't worry about this. Then check that R1 is the standby router. The priority of 120 on R0 makes this router active because the default is 100.

```
R0#show standby
FastEthernet0/0 - Group 1
State is Active
5 state changes, last state change 00:39:19
Virtual IP address is 10.10.10.3
Active virtual MAC address is 0000.0C07.AC01
Local virtual MAC address is 0000.0C07.AC01 (v1 default)
Hello time 3 sec, hold time 10 sec
Next hello sent in 2.639 secs
Preemption disabled
Active router is local
Standby router is 10.10.10.2
Priority 120 (configured 120)
Group name is hsrp-Fa0/0-1 (default)

R1#show standby
FastEthernet0/0 - Group 1
State is Standby
3 state changes, last state change 00:39:50
Virtual IP address is 10.10.10.3
Active virtual MAC address is 0000.0C07.AC01
Local virtual MAC address is 0000.0C07.AC01 (v1 default)
Hello time 3 sec, hold time 10 sec
Next hello sent in 2.255 secs
Preemption disabled
Active router is 10.10.10.1
Standby router is local
Priority 100 (default 100)
Group name is hsrp-Fa0/0-1 (default)
```

Task 6:

Ping the default gateway from the PC.

```
Packet Tracer PC Command Line 1.0
C:\>ping 10.10.10.3

Pinging 10.10.10.3 with 32 bytes of data:

Reply from 10.10.10.3: bytes=32 time<1ms TTL=255
Reply from 10.10.10.3: bytes=32 time<1ms TTL=255
Reply from 10.10.10.3: bytes=32 time=1ms TTL=255
Reply from 10.10.10.3: bytes=32 time<1ms TTL=255

Ping statistics for 10.10.10.3:
    Packets: Sent = 4, Received = 4, Lost = 0 (0% loss),
Approximate round trip times in milli-seconds:
    Minimum = 0ms, Maximum = 1ms, Average = 0ms

C:\>
```

Task 7:

Shut F0/0 on R0. It should trigger R1 to become active almost immediately.

```
R0(config)#int f0/0
R0(config-if)#shut
%HSRP-6-STATECHANGE: FastEthernet0/0 Grp 1 state Active -> Init

%LINK-5-CHANGED: Interface FastEthernet0/0, changed state to
administratively down

%LINEPROTO-5-UPDOWN: Line protocol on Interface FastEthernet0/0,
changed state to down


R1#show standby
FastEthernet0/0 - Group 1
State is Active
4 state changes, last state change 00:46:04
Virtual IP address is 10.10.10.3
Active virtual MAC address is 0000.0C07.AC01
Local virtual MAC address is 0000.0C07.AC01 (v1 default)
Hello time 3 sec, hold time 10 sec
Next hello sent in 1.245 secs
Preemption disabled
Active router is local
Standby router is unknown
Priority 100 (default 100)
Group name is hsrp-Fa0/0-1 (default)
```

Task 8:

Ping the default gateway again from the PC. It will still be reachable.

```
C:\>ping 10.10.10.3

Pinging 10.10.10.3 with 32 bytes of data:

Request timed out.
Reply from 10.10.10.3: bytes=32 time<1ms TTL=255
Reply from 10.10.10.3: bytes=32 time=2ms TTL=255
Reply from 10.10.10.3: bytes=32 time=3ms TTL=255

Ping statistics for 10.10.10.3:
    Packets: Sent = 4, Received = 3, Lost = 1 (25% loss),
Approximate round trip times in milli-seconds:
    Minimum = 0ms, Maximum = 3ms, Average = 1ms
```

Note:

This is a Cisco CCNA level lab, so well done on completing it.

NIC Teaming

Lab Objective:

Learn how to configure NIC teaming on a Windows Server.

Lab Purpose:

NIC teaming is also known as interface bonding, balancing, or aggregation. It allows you (depending on your platform and software) to group 1–32 network cards into one or more virtual network adapters. This provides load balancing and fault tolerance (if there is more than one physical NIC used).

Lab Tool:

VirtualBox running Windows Server 2012

Lab Topology:

Please use the following topology to complete this lab exercise:

Lab Walkthrough:

Task 1:
Configure the settings for the Windows 2012 server (in Virtualbox) so it has four network cards and runs on an internal network. Here is how to do it for the first NIC (the machine must be powered down for this to work). You complete these steps on your virtual machine, NOT on the server.

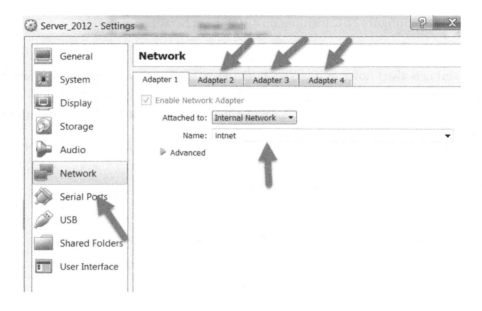

Task 2:
Power up the server. To log in you have to press Ctrl + Alt + Delete, and the easiest way is to send this via the menu.

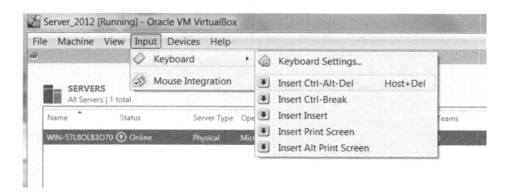

Task 3:

Go to 'Server Manager'. You can reach this via the toolbar or the Windows icon. It usually loads automatically, so you might not have to do this step.

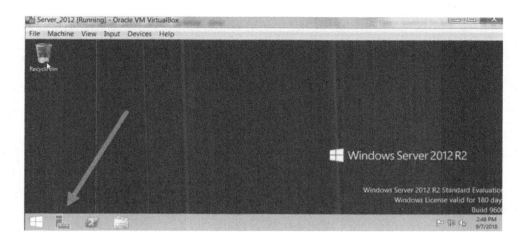

Task 4:

On the local server you can see 'NIC Teaming' is disabled. There are several ways to do this, but I'll click on 'Disabled' and it will allow me to configure it.

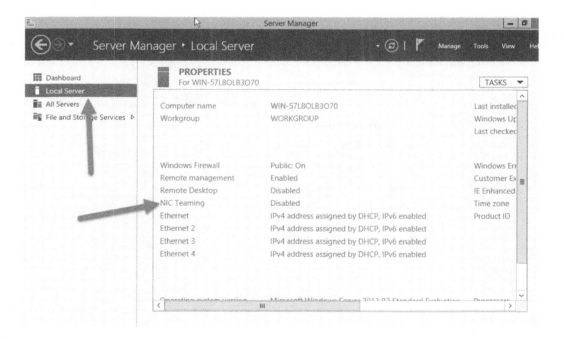

Task 5:

Before you configure NIC teaming, check the network settings under the Control Panel. You should see four NICs. This step is optional; however, it's good to know where to find this information.

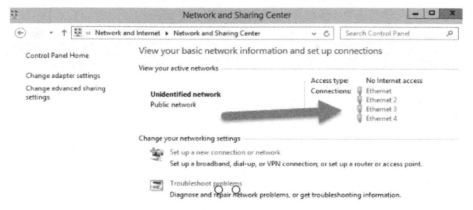

Task 6:

Your list of Ethernet interfaces will be displayed. You can hold the Ctrl key and click on all four.

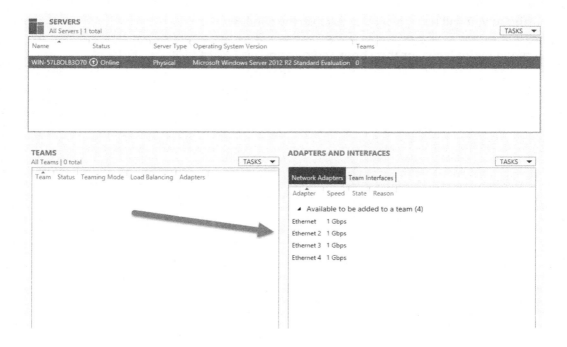

Task 7:

Under 'TASKS' choose 'Add to New Team' and give the team a name.

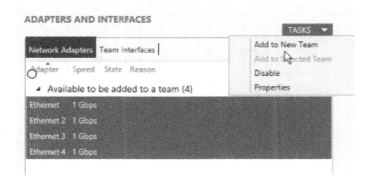

Task 8:

You can save this team and see that a team has been created. You might see various error messages because we are not connected to a switch. If you do get errors, then Windows doesn't automatically close the team window. If you click 'OK', it tries to create the team again, so you will have to click 'x' to close the window.

It might take a while for this command to come into effect.

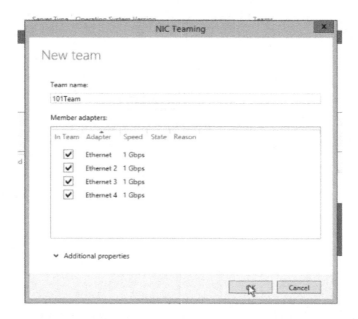

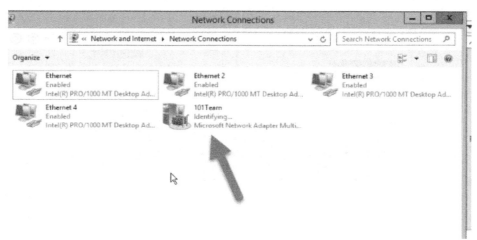

Task 9:

Under 'Network and Internet / Network and Sharing Center' you will see the four adapters have gone and been replaced by the NIC team.

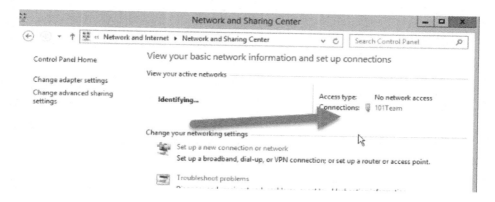

Notes:

Steps may differ if you have a different release of the software. There are several options you can use to create a NIC team, including PowerShell.

Port Aggregation

Lab Objective:

Learn how to configure port aggregation using Port Aggregation Protocol (PAgP).

Lab Purpose:

Collecting interfaces or ports into one big virtual interface is known as link aggregation, link teaming, NIC teaming, or port channeling. The interfaces in the bundle should usually share the same capacity, so you can't bundle a 100 Mbps interface with a 1 Gbps interface to make it 1.1 Gbps, for example.

We will bundle some Cisco switch interfaces into a group using PAgP. This interface will create a port channel interface with a theoretical speed of 400 Mbps. If any of the interfaces in the bundle goes down, the traffic will be load-balanced over the remaining ports.

Lab Tool:

Packet Tracer

Lab Topology:

Please use the following topology to complete this lab exercise:

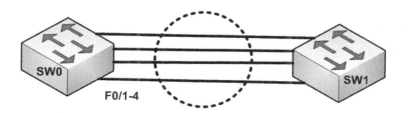

Lab Walkthrough:

Task 1:

Connect two switches together as per the diagram.

Task 2:

Configure the Ethernet interfaces on the switches. The 'interface range' command will save some time. Make them all access interfaces and put them all into VLAN 100. Here is how to do it on Switch0. Do the same on Switch1.

```
Switch(config)#hostname SW0
SW0(config)#interface range f0/1-4
SW0(config-if-range)#switchport mode access
SW0(config-if-range)#switchport access vlan 100
% Access VLAN does not exist. Creating vlan 100
SW0(config-if-range)#
```

Task 3:

Create virtual interface and number it six using the command 'channel-group 6 mode desirable'. At least one side of the link must be active in order for the group to come up. You can use 'auto' on Switch1.

```
SW0(config-if-range)#channel-group 6 mode ?
active Enable LACP unconditionally
auto Enable PAgP only if a PAgP device is detected
desirable Enable PAgP unconditionally
on Enable Etherchannel only
passive Enable LACP only if a LACP device is detected

SW0(config-if-range)#channel-group 6 mode desirable
Creating a port-channel interface Port-channel 6

Sw1(config-if-range)#channel-group 6 mode auto
```

Task 4:

Check the interfaces on Switch0 to see if the port channel interface has been created.

```
SW0#show ip interface brief
Interface IP-Address OK? Method Status Protocol
Port-channel6 unassigned YES manual up up
FastEthernet0/1 unassigned YES manual up up
FastEthernet0/2 unassigned YES manual up
[output truncated]
```

Task 5:

There are several commands you can issue to check the status of the port channel, including

```
SW0#show etherchannel ?
load-balance Load-balance/frame-distribution scheme among ports in
port-channel
```

```
port-channel Port-channel information
summary One-line summary per channel-group
<cr>
```

Notes:

The ports will load-balance traffic based on factors such as destination/source IP/MAC, etc. You can alter this behavior, but it's beyond the scope of the exam.

Dual Power Supplies

Lab Objective:
Learn how to configure a dual power supply on a Cisco switch.

Lab Purpose:
Business continuity is a hot topic for any corporate network. One aspect of this is dual power supplies, whereby your device can continue to operate when one of the supplies fails. Many are hot-swappable, meaning you can remove and insert them while the device is live.

Lab Tool:
Packet Tracer

Lab Topology:
Please use a Cisco 3650 switch for this lab:

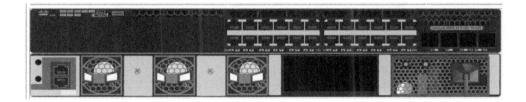

Lab Walkthrough:

Task 1:

Drag a Cisco 3650 model switch onto the canvas. By default, it will have no power supplies connected. Drag two into the blank power bays. The switch should power up.

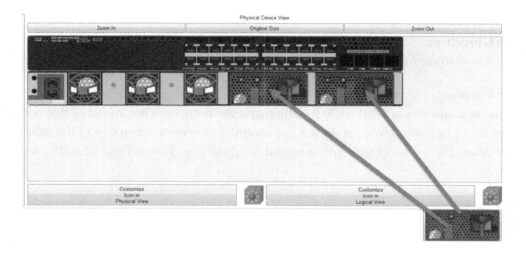

Task 2:

At the command line, run the 'show power inline' command. Note the available wattage.

```
Switch#show power inline
Available:780.0(w) Used:0.0(w) Remaining:780.0(w)

Interface Admin Oper Power Device Class Max
(Watts)
--------- ------ ---------- ------- -------------------- ----- ----
Gig1/0/1 auto off 0.0 n/a n/a 30.0
Gig1/0/2 auto off 0.0 n/a n/a 30.0
Gig1/0/3 auto off 0.0 n/a n/a 30.0
Gig1/0/4 auto off 0.0 n/a n/a 30.0
[output truncated]
```

Task 3:

Execute the 'show environment power' command. Note the slot naming convention of 1A and 1B, the model number (you would use 'PWR-C2-640WAC' to order the replacement), and the serial number (you would quote 'QIBQWVUF8UX' for a warranty or support contract). Drops or surges in available power will usually trigger an alert if you have configured monitoring for your devices.

```
Switch#show environment power
SW PID Serial# Status Sys Pwr PoE Pwr Watts
-- ------------------ ---------- ---------------- ------- ------- ---
1A PWR-C2-640WAC QIBQWVUF8UX OK Good Good 640
1B PWR-C2-640WAC DSBEPETTTHB OK Good Good 640
```

Task 4:

Drag one of the power supplies off the chassis (back to where it came from) and then run the two commands again. Note any changes.

```
Switch#
Mar 1 00:26:01.678 : %PLATFORM_FEP - 6 - FRU_PS_OIR : Switch 1 : FRU
power supply A removed

Switch#show environment power
SW PID Serial# Status Sys Pwr PoE Pwr Watts
-- ------------------ ---------- ---------------- ------- ------- ---
1A Not Present
1B PWR-C2-640WAC DSBEPETTTHB OK Good Good 640

Switch#show power inline
Available:390.0(w) Used:0.0(w) Remaining:390.0(w)

Interface Admin Oper Power Device Class Max
(Watts)
--------- ------ ---------- ------- -------------------- ----- ----
Gig1/0/1 auto off 0.0 n/a n/a 30.0
Gig1/0/2 auto off 0.0 n/a n/a 30.0
Gig1/0/3 auto off 0.0 n/a n/a 30.0
Gig1/0/4 auto off 0.0 n/a n/a 30.0
[output truncated]
```

Notes:

Your device may ship with only one power supply (such as the above switch), and you would have to pay for others. There are command line instructions you can input to disable/enable the PSU; however, these are not available on Packet Tracer.

Backups–Incremental Backups

Lab Objective:

Learn how to configure incremental backups on a Windows Server.

Lab Purpose:

There are a few options for configuring backups. We will cover incremental backups in this lab. The method of course will differ between platforms and operating systems. Incremental backups only back up changes made since the last backup. Please check your study guide for details on full, differential, and incremental backups.

Lab Tool:

VirtualBox running Windows Server 2012. Please prep your server by adding a virtual disk where you can set your backups to be sent to. When you boot to Windows Server, please format this volume using Disk Manager (found by right-clicking the Windows icon on the home screen).

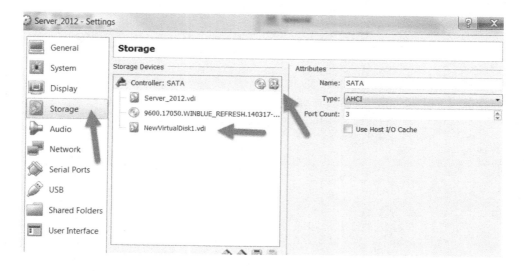

Lab Topology:

Please use the following topology to complete this lab exercise:

Lab Walkthrough:

Task 1:

If this is a new install, you will need to enable the Windows Backup feature. Do so under 'Server Manager / Dashboard'.

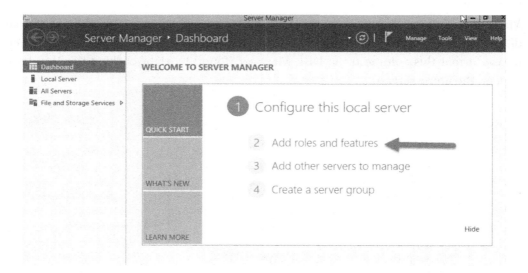

Task 2:

Go to 'Features' and choose 'Windows Server Backup'.

You need to click on 'Next' and 'Install'; it will take a few seconds to install this feature.

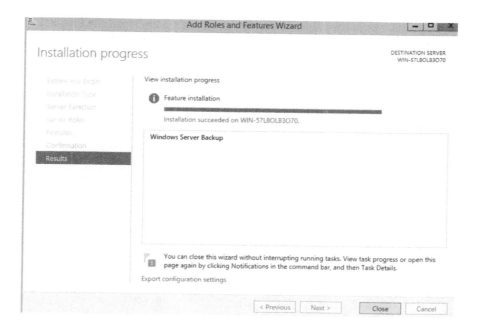

Task 3:

You can access the backup management area by typing 'wbadmin.msc' into a command prompt or through 'Administrative Tools'.

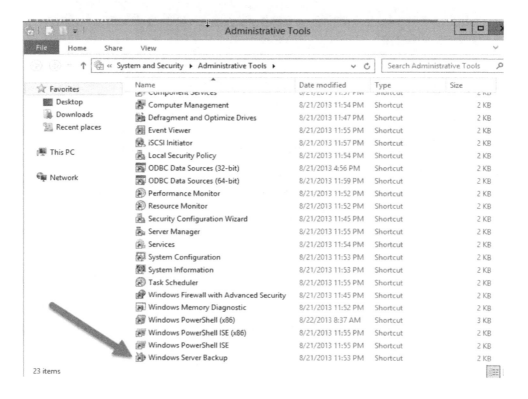

Task 4:

Click on 'Local Backup' and then 'Backup Schedule'. You will see a wizard appear.

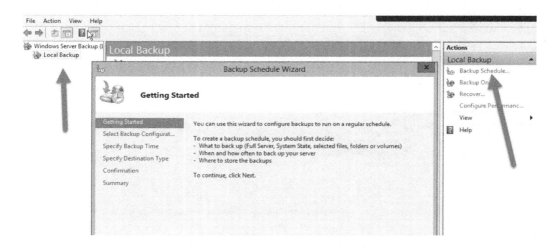

Task 5:

You will be taken through the wizard. Choose 'Custom,' preferably choose a small folder you want to back up, and choose any time you wish.

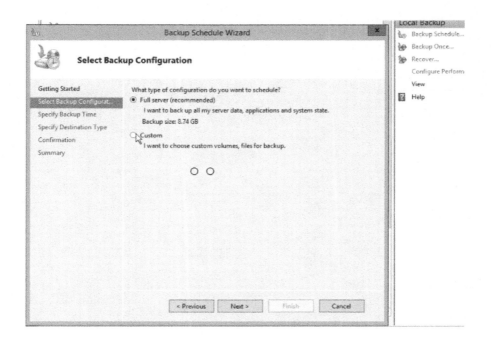

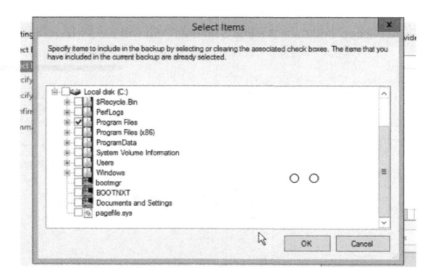

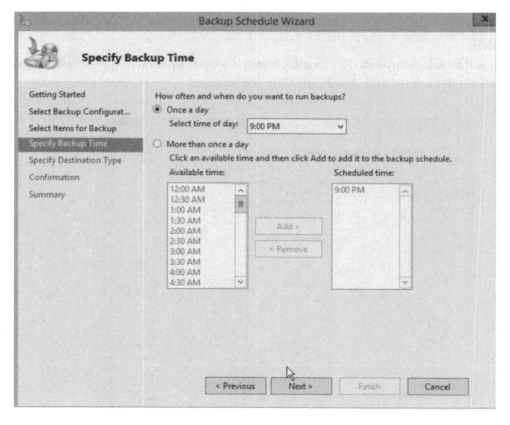

Task 6:

Back up to the volume you created earlier.

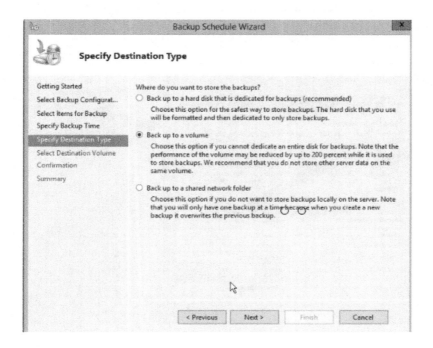

And choose the volume you added before you started the backup configuration.

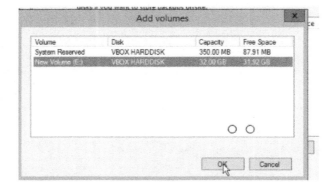

Task 7:

When you have finished, the wizard will run. Then you can click on 'Configure Performance Settings', click on 'Custom', and set the backups to 'Incremental'.

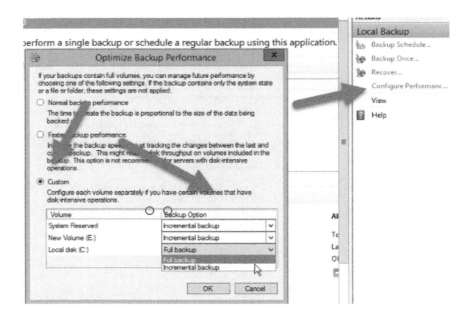

Note:

Please take some time to explore the various backup options available.

LAB 54

Snapshots

Lab Objective:
Learn how to create a snapshot of a virtual machine.

Lab Purpose:
Snapshots capture the state of a system at a certain point in time. They allow a system to be restored to where it was. They are useful if you want to test something. They can be done while the system is running or offline.

Lab Tool:
VirtualBox running Windows 10, but any OS will work fine.

Lab Topology:
Please use the following topology to complete this lab exercise:

Lab Walkthrough:

Task 1:

Open VirtualBox and click on your Windows 10 install. Then from the top right choose 'Machine Tools / Snapshots'. Bear in mind that this button may move as they release new versions of VB.

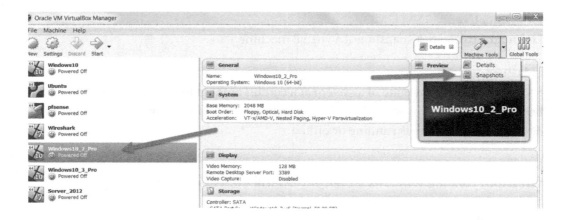

Task 2:

Click on 'Take [Snapshot]' and give the snapshot a name.

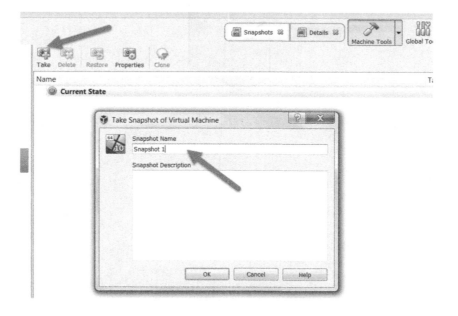

Task 3:

Click 'OK' and you will see the snapshot captured.

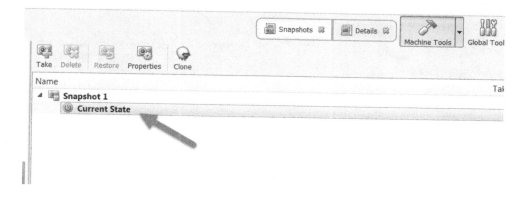

Task 4:

Start the VM, open Notepad, and save a file onto the desktop. Then power off the machine.

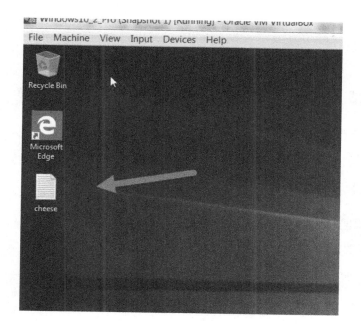

Task 5:

Restore the snapshot. You can right-click it and press 'Restore' or click once and hit the 'Restore' button.

You can save a new snapshot if you wish.

Task 6:

Start the machine with Snapshot1.

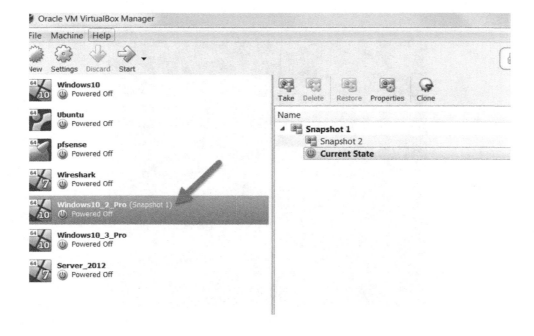

Task 7:

When it boots, you will see the file isn't there.

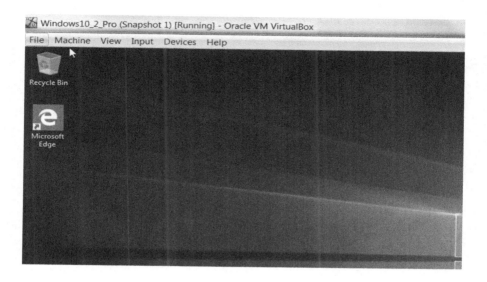

Note:

Most VM software has snapshot capability built in.

Port Scanning

Lab Objective:

Learn how to connect using a port scanner to find possible vulnerabilities.

WARNING—Please use this only on your own home network for study purposes. It may well be illegal in your country to scan a network you do not own, so please check first.

Lab Purpose:

Run a port scan on your network to find open ports. If you have time, check on YouTube for 'Neighbours loud party going down'. The uploader used a port scanner (the same one we use here) and MAC address killer to bring down a neighbor's noisy party.

Lab Tool:

PC with Advanced Port Scanner installed—http://www.advanced-port-scanner.com/

Lab Topology:

Please use the following topology to complete this lab exercise:

ADVANCED PORT SCANNER

Lab Walkthrough:

Task 1:

Install the software on your home PC or virtual PC if you are using VirtualBox or VMware. Ideally, have other devices connected to it.

Task 2:

Launch the port scanner and let it run by pressing the play button. You can enter a network range if you wish.

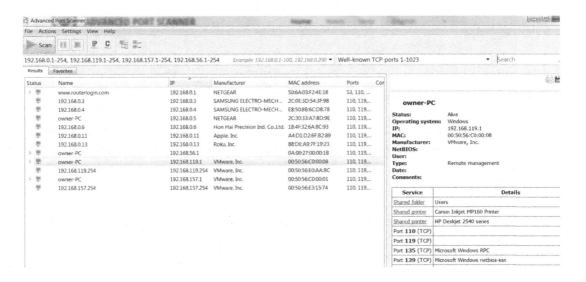

Task 3:

Choose a device you know is on your LAN and click on it to see open ports displayed on the right.

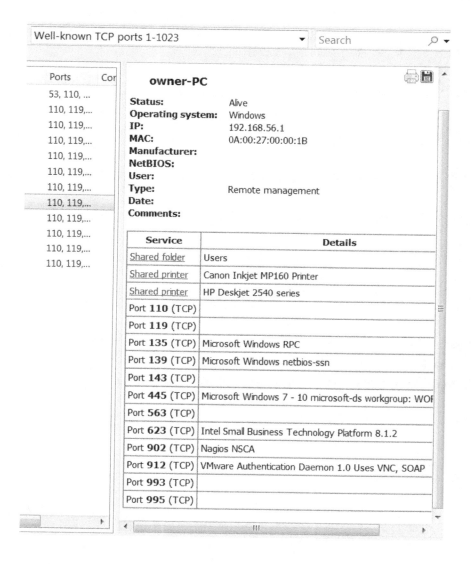

Task 4:

Right-click the device IP address and explore the options. Some are only available if you purchase remote-control software.

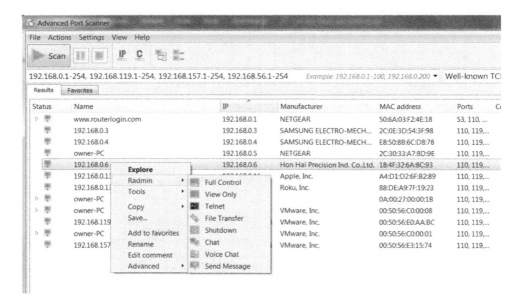

Notes:

Ethical hacking is an entire branch of networking you can explore and become certified in. CompTIA has also launched a penetration testing certification.

LAB 56

Logging Events with Syslog Server

Lab Objective:

Learn how to configure a syslog server.

Lab Purpose:

Syslog is a standard for message logging. It can be used for system management, security, and auditing as well as for general troubleshooting. Syslog can be installed on printers, routers, and many other device types. It offers a number of severity levels from debug up to emergency level.

Lab Tool:

Packet Tracer

Lab Topology:

Please use the following topology to complete this lab exercise:

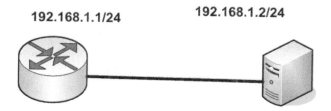

192.168.1.1/24   192.168.1.2/24

Lab Walkthrough:

Task 1:

Use one router and one server; connect them using a crossover cable.

Task 2:

Configure the IP address on the router and server.

```
Router(config)#host R0
R0(config)#int f0/0
R0(config-if)#ip add 192.168.1.1 255.255.255.0
R0(config-if)#no shut
```

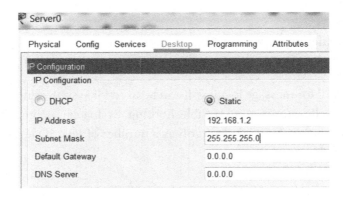

Task 3:

Ensure the 'SYSLOG' feature on the server is turned on (it should be by default).

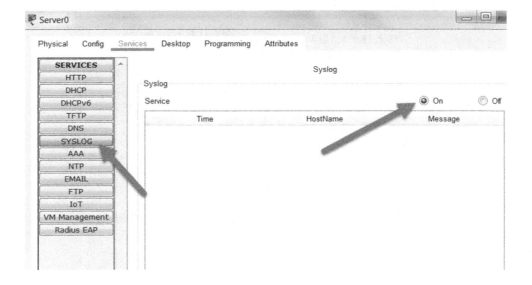

Task 4:

Add the IP address of the syslog server to the router. Then set the logging level. The options are somewhat limited on Packet Tracer.

```
RO(config)#logging host 192.168.1.2
RO(config)#logging ?
A.B.C.D IP address of the logging host
buffered Set buffered logging parameters
console Set console logging parameters
host Set syslog server IP address and parameters
on Enable logging to all enabled destinations
trap Set syslog server logging level
userinfo Enable logging of user info on privileged mode enabling
RO(config)#logging trap ?
debugging Debugging messages (severity=7)
<cr>
RO(config)#logging trap debugging
```

Task 5:

We are not logging debug messages on the router. We just need to turn on debugs for ping traffic, which uses ICMP.

```
RO#debug ip icmp
ICMP packet debugging is on
```

Task 6:

Ping the syslog server and then check to see if the log has been updated.

```
RO#ping 192.168.1.2

Type escape sequence to abort.
Sending 5, 100-byte ICMP Echos to 192.168.1.2, timeout is 2 seconds:
!
ICMP: echo reply rcvd, src 192.168.1.2, dst 192.168.1.1
!
ICMP: echo reply rcvd, src 192.168.1.2, dst 192.168.1.1
!
ICMP: echo reply rcvd, src 192.168.1.2, dst 192.168.1.1
!
ICMP: echo reply rcvd, src 192.168.1.2, dst 192.168.1.1
!
Success rate is 100 percent (5/5), round-trip min/avg/max = 0/0/1 ms
```

Note:

Of course there are many levels and services we can log; this is just an introduction.

LAB 57

SNMP

Lab Objective:

Learn how to configure SNMP on a Cisco router.

Lab Purpose:

SNMP is a very powerful protocol used to monitor and manage network devices. Ideally, you would run it on a dedicated server and use it to monitor traffic, outages, and impending port or device failures. In this lab we will use a Cisco router with a PC and use SNMP to change a router setting.

Lab Tool:

Packet Tracer

Lab Topology:

Please use a Cisco router and generic PC:

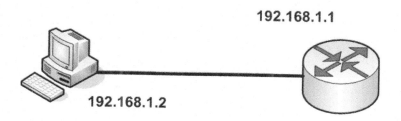

192.168.1.1

192.168.1.2

Lab Walkthrough:

Task 1:

Configure an IP address on the router and bring the interface up.

```
Router(config)#int f0/0
Router(config-if)#ip add 192.168.1.1 255.255.255.0
Router(config-if)#no shut
```

Task 2:

Configure the IP address on the PC and the default gateway as the router interface.

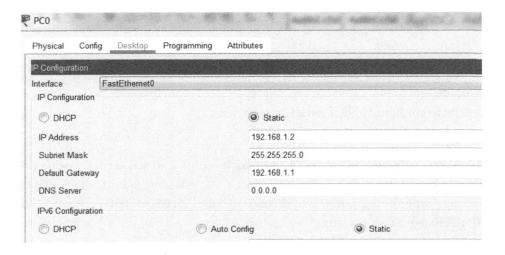

Task 3:

Set up a SNMP read/write access and the string as '101labs'. The string acts like a password and permits access to SNMP.

```
Router(config)#snmp-server community 101labs rw
%SNMP-5-WARMSTART: SNMP agent on host Router is undergoing a warm start
```

Task 4:

On the PC, open the MIB browser. You should have learned about MIBs in your study guide. Enter the router IP address and then under 'Advanced' enter the password '101labs' in both sections.

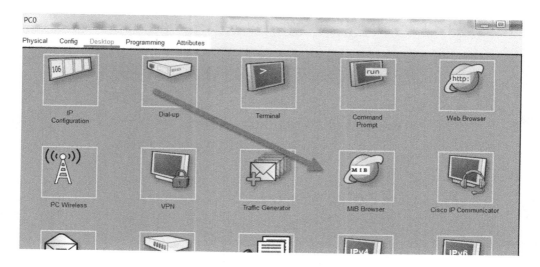

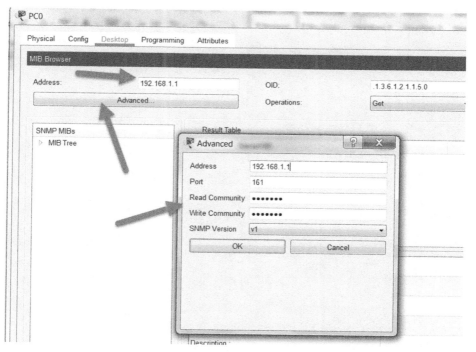

Task 5:

Drill down to the '.sysName' MIB by clicking on the triangles (as indicated below). This populates the name of the remote device. Then press 'GO.' You will see the value populate with the name of the router, which is set to the default of 'Router.'

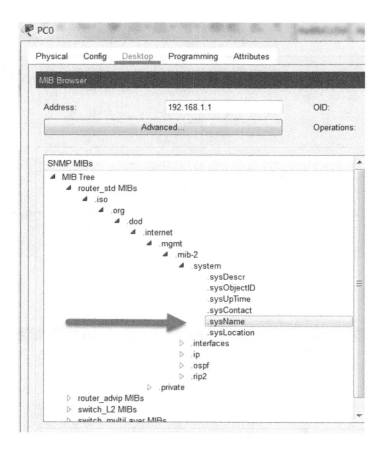

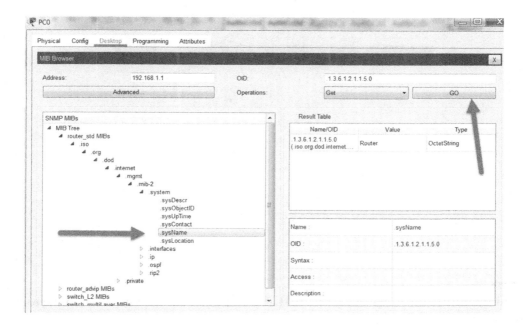

Task 6:

Use SNMP to change the router name to '101Labs'. Back in the MIB browser change the operation to 'Set' and the data type to 'OctetString', set the value to '101Labs', and press the 'OK' button. Finally, press the 'GO' button.

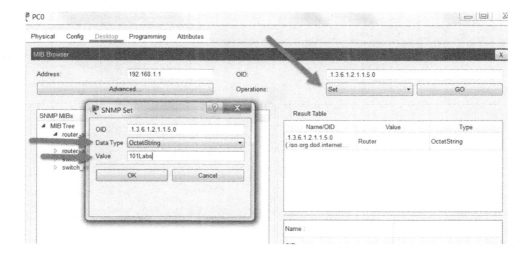

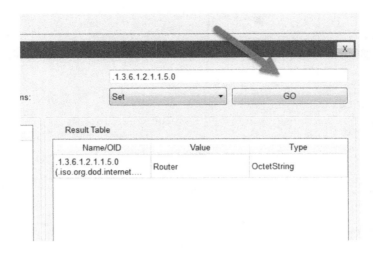

Task 7:

You should see the value change to '101Labs'. You can press the Enter key on the router to check the command worked.

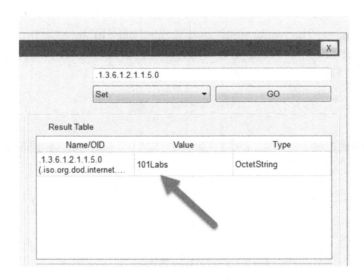

```
101Labs>
```

Notes:

SNMP (as you can see) can not only monitor your network but also make configuration changes. Most SNMP software is sold with a GUI, so you can click on an image of your device and configure ports and interfaces and much more.

LAB 58

Site-to-Site VPN

Lab Objective:
Learn how to configure a site-to-site VPN.

Lab Purpose:
VPNs feature in the syllabus in more than one place and more than one type. You certainly won't be asked to configure one in the exam, but doing so will certainly help you put your theory into practice.

Lab Tool:
Packet Tracer

Lab Topology:
Please use the following topology to complete this lab exercise:

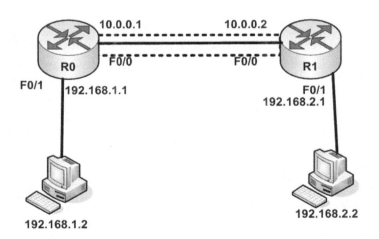

Lab Walkthrough:

Task 1:
Connect two routers together with a crossover cable. Attach one PC to either end with a crossover cable. The dotted lines represent the VPN we will create.

Task 2:

Configure the host with the IP address and default gateway of the local router interface. The image below shows PC0; do the same on PC1, but the IP and the default gateway should match the diagram above.

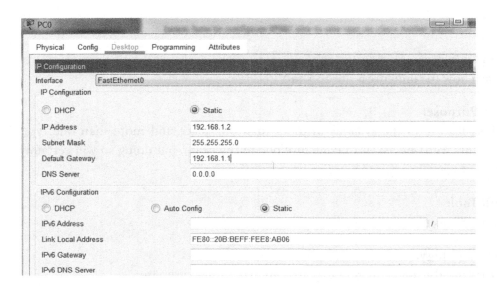

Task 3:

Configure the IP addresses on the routers. Here is how to do it on R0. When you have configured R1, ping across the 10.0.0.0 link. Make sure you configure R1!

```
Router>en
Router#conf t
Enter configuration commands, one per line.  End with CNTL/Z.
Router(config)#host R0
R0(config)#int f0/1
R0(config-if)#ip add 192.168.1.1 255.255.255.0
R0(config-if)#no shut
R0(config-if)#int f0/0
R0(config-if)#ip add 10.0.0.1 255.0.0.0
R0(config-if)#no shut
```

Task 4:

Configure RIP on both routers. Remember to put in the correct network numbers. Here is the config for R0. Remember to configure R1 with the attached networks!

```
R0(config)#router rip
R0(config-router)#network 10.0.0.0
R0(config-router)#network 192.168.1.0
```

Task 5:

After configuring R1 and R0, check the routing table to ensure all routes are visible.

```
R0#show ip route
Codes: C - connected, S - static, I - IGRP, R - RIP, M - mobile, B
- BGP
D - EIGRP, EX - EIGRP external, O - OSPF, IA - OSPF inter area
N1 - OSPF NSSA external type 1, N2 - OSPF NSSA external type 2
E1 - OSPF external type 1, E2 - OSPF external type 2, E - EGP
i - IS-IS, L1 - IS-IS level-1, L2 - IS-IS level-2, ia - IS-IS inter area
* - candidate default, U - per-user static route, o - ODR
P - periodic downloaded static route

Gateway of last resort is not set

C 10.0.0.0/8 is directly connected, FastEthernet0/0
C 192.168.1.0/24 is directly connected, FastEthernet0/1
R 192.168.2.0/24 [120/1] via 10.0.0.2, 00:00:15, FastEthernet0/0
```

Task 6:

Now configure phase 1 of the IKE (Internet Key Exchange) tunnel. This defines how IKE authenticates IPSec peers and negotiates IKE SAs during this phase, setting up a secure channel for negotiating IPSec SAs in phase 2. Here is R0; repeat this on R1.

```
R0#conf t
Enter configuration commands, one per line. End with CNTL/Z.
R0(config)#crypto isakmp policy 10
R0(config-isakmp)#authentication pre-share
R0(config-isakmp)#encryption aes 256
R0(config-isakmp)#group 2
R0(config-isakmp)#lifetime 86400
```

Task 7:

Now we configure phase 2. The purpose of IKE phase 2 is to negotiate IPSec SAs (security associations) to set up the IPSec tunnel. Do this on R1 also, but of course the address is 10.0.0.1.

```
R0(config)#crypto isakmp key 101labs address 10.0.0.2
R0(config)#crypto ipsec transform-set TEST esp-aes esp-sha-hmac
```

Task 8:

Define what traffic will bring up the VPN. We want all the LAN-to-LAN traffic to be encrypted.

```
R0(config)#access-list 100 permit ip 192.168.1.0 0.0.0.255 192.168.2.0
0.0.0.255
```

On R1 the ACL will be

```
R1(config)#access-list 100 permit ip 192.168.2.0 0.0.0.255 192.168.1.0
0.0.0.255
```

Task 9:

A crypto map is a software configuration which selects data flows that need security processing, and defines the policy for these flows and the crypto peer to which that traffic needs to go. Please repeat on R1 (but change the peer address of course).

```
R0(config)#crypto map LABS 10 ipsec-isakmp
% NOTE: This new crypto map will remain disabled until a peer
        and a valid access list have been configured.
R0(config-crypto-map)#set peer 10.0.0.2
R0(config-crypto-map)#match address 100
R0(config-crypto-map)#set transform-set TEST
R0(config-crypto-map)#exit
```

Task 10:

Apply the crypto map to the F0/0 interface. Here is R0; do it on R1 also.

```
R0(config)#int f0/0
R0(config-if)#crypto map LABS
*Jan 3 07:16:26.785: %CRYPTO-6-ISAKMP_ON_OFF: ISAKMP is ON
```

Task 11:

Turn on debugs on R0 so you can see the VPN tunnel come up and authenticate. Don't worry about understanding all the output.

```
R0#debug crypto ipsec
Crypto IPSEC debugging is on
R0#debug crypto isakmp
Crypto ISAKMP debugging is on
```

Task 12:

Ping from PC0 to PC1 and check the debugs on R0.

```
C:\>ping 192.168.2.2

Pinging 192.168.2.2 with 32 bytes of data:

Reply from 192.168.2.2: bytes=32 time=1ms TTL=126
Reply from 192.168.2.2: bytes=32 time<1ms TTL=126
Reply from 192.168.2.2: bytes=32 time<1ms TTL=126
Reply from 192.168.2.2: bytes=32 time<1ms TTL=126

Ping statistics for 192.168.2.2:
    Packets: Sent = 4, Received = 4, Lost = 0 (0% loss),
Approximate round trip times in milli-seconds:
    Minimum = 0ms, Maximum = 1ms, Average = 0ms
```

ISAKMP:(1026):Total payload length: 12

ISAKMP:(1026): sending packet to 10.0.0.2 my_port 500 peer_port 500 (I)
MM_KEY_EXCH

ISAKMP:(1026):Sending an IKE IPv4 Packet.

ISAKMP:(1026):Input = IKE_MESG_INTERNAL, IKE_PROCESS_COMPLETE

ISAKMP:(1026):Old State = IKE_I_MM4 New State = IKE_I_MM5

ISAKMP (0:1026): received packet from 10.0.0.2 dport 500 sport 500
Global (I) MM_KEY_EXCH

ISAKMP:(1026): processing ID payload. message ID = 0

ISAKMP (0:1026): ID payload
next-payload : 8
type   : 1
address   : 10.0.0.2
protocol   : 17
port   : 500
length   : 12

ISAKMP:(1026):SA authentication status:

authenticated

ISAKMP:(1026):SA has been authenticated with 10.0.0.2

ISAKMP: Trying to insert a peer 10.0.0.1/10.0.0.2/500/, and inserted
successfully 47CA9F80.

ISAKMP:(1026):Input = IKE_MESG_FROM_PEER, IKE_MM_EXCH

Task 13:

Issue a show command.

```
RO#show crypto ipsec sa

interface: FastEthernet0/0
Crypto map tag: LABS, local addr 10.0.0.1

protected vrf: (none)
local ident (addr/mask/prot/port): (192.168.1.0/255.255.255.0/0/0)
remote ident (addr/mask/prot/port): (192.168.2.0/255.255.255.0/0/0)
current_peer 10.0.0.2 port 500
PERMIT, flags={origin_is_acl,}
#pkts encaps: 11, #pkts encrypt: 11, #pkts digest: 0
#pkts decaps: 7, #pkts decrypt: 7, #pkts verify: 0
#pkts compressed: 0, #pkts decompressed: 0
#pkts not compressed: 0, #pkts compr. failed: 0
#pkts not decompressed: 0, #pkts decompress failed: 0
#send errors 1, #recv errors 0

local crypto endpt.: 10.0.0.1, remote crypto endpt.:10.0.0.2
path mtu 1500, ip mtu 1500, ip mtu idb FastEthernet0/0
current outbound spi: 0x6A51344B(1783706699)
```

Task 14:

There are several show commands you can try.

```
RO#show crypto ?
ipsec Show IPSEC policy
isakmp Show ISAKMP
key Show long term public keys
map Crypto maps
RO#show crypto map
Crypto Map LABS 10 ipsec-isakmp
Peer = 10.0.0.2
Extended IP access list 100
access-list 100 permit ip 192.168.1.0 0.0.0.255 192.168.2.0 0.0.0.255
Current peer: 10.0.0.2
Security association lifetime: 4608000 kilobytes/3600 seconds
PFS (Y/N): N
Transform sets={
TEST,
}
Interfaces using crypto map LABS:
FastEthernet0/0
```

Notes:

Don't feel overwhelmed by this lab; you won't need to do anything like this in the exam. Come back to it later if you get stuck. If the commands aren't accepted, check that your router model and IOS support them. I used the standard 1841 model with the default IOS of flash:c1841-advipservicesk9-mz.124-15.T1.bin.

Creating an RDC

Lab Objective:

Learn how to set up a Remote Desktop Connection to a Windows device.

Lab Purpose:

Remote Desktop Connection (RDC) is a Microsoft Windows tool installed on most operating systems and servers. It can be installed by default or enabled in the settings. WARNING—Getting this to work with different OSs, from virtual machines to LAN devices, and through firewalls can be tricky! If you can, please use two home computers to save any headaches.

Lab Tool:

Home PCs, VirtualBox, etc.

Lab Topology:

For this lab I used a VirtualBox Windows 10 Pro PC. I connected to it from my home PC running Windows 7. It took some time to get it all working, so you might find it easier to connect two home computers on your LAN.

PC to be
Controlled

Remote
Access PC

Lab Walkthrough:

Task 1:
Enable RDC in your virtual Windows machine settings and set the network to 'Bridged Adapter' so it's on the same network as your home PC.

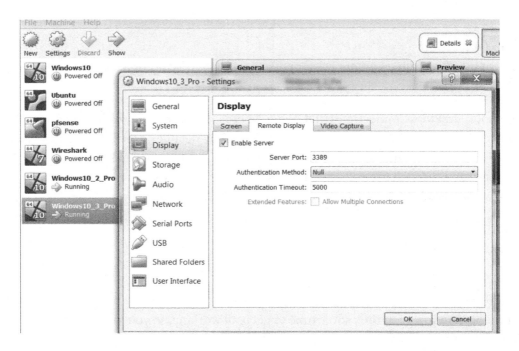

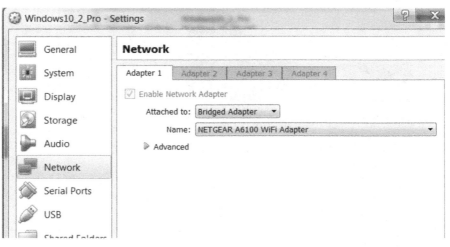

Task 2:

Depending on your Windows version you may have to enable RDC. Here is the setting on my Windows 10 PC.

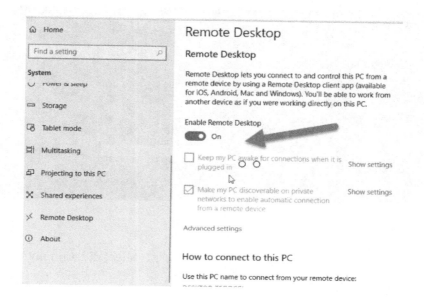

Task 3:

You also need to ensure there is an administrator account on the PC to be connected to as well as a password. For Windows 10 I connected using my Microsoft credentials (see later step).

Task 4:

Check the IP address of your PC (to be controlled).

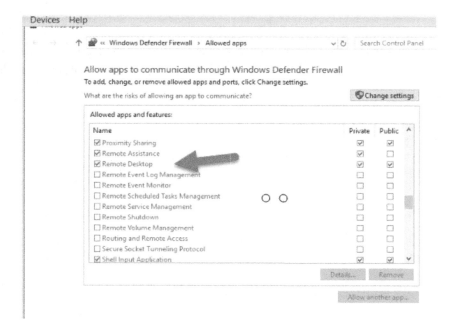

```
Microsoft Windows [Version 10.0.17134.112]
(c) 2018 Microsoft Corporation. All rights reserved.

C:\Users\paulw>ipconfig

Windows IP Configuration


Ethernet adapter Ethernet:

   Connection-specific DNS Suffix  . :
   Link-local IPv6 Address . . . . . : fe80::b91f:4a69:170f:31c6%12
   IPv4 Address. . . . . . . . . . . : 192.168.0.10
   Subnet Mask . . . . . . . . . . . : 255.255.255.0
   Default Gateway . . . . . . . . . : 192.168.0.1

C:\Users\paulw>
```

Task 5:

Ensure RDCs are allowed through your firewall. Here is how I did it on my Windows 10 firewall.

Task 6:

Open an RDC window on your home PC and enter the IP address and port 3389.

Task 7:

You should be challenged to log in. On Windows 10 I used my Microsoft login. On earlier versions of Windows you may need to enter an admin username and password.

Task 8:

I was then taken to the home screen of the remote PC.

Notes:

Getting all of this working through VMs and different versions of Windows took quite some time. You might want to use two home PCs or skip this lab for now if it proves too time-consuming.

Creating a VNC Connection

Lab Objective:

Learn how to set up a VNC connection to a remote device.

Lab Purpose:

Virtual Network Computing is one of a number of remote-access tools. Others include pcAnywhere from Symantec and RDP from Microsoft. These offer a way to remotely access a PC or server and control the desktop with your keyboard and mouse as if you were physically present there. They all offer free versions for home use, free trials, and personal/enterprise options.

Lab Tool:

Home PCs, VirtualBox, etc.

Lab Topology:

In order to complete this lab you need two host devices. One will be the controlled device and the other will be your client. I used a Windows 7 PC on VirtualBox and then my home PC to connect to it as if it were a remote device.

PC to be
Controlled

Remote
Access PC

Lab Walkthrough:

Task 1:
Navigate to the VNC website and download the VNC Connect software onto the device you want to be controlled and the VNC Viewer software onto the PC you want to use for control. In case the download URLs change, you can navigate from the main website or google the above terms.

https://www.realvnc.com

Task 2:

Set up your free account and install the relevant software on the devices.

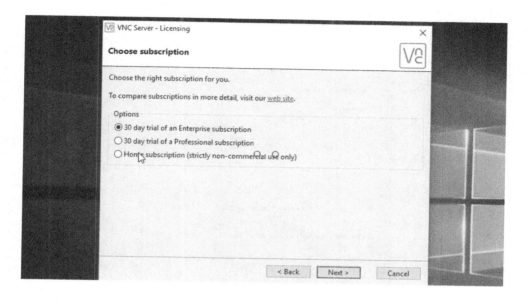

Task 3:

When VNC Connect is finally installed, your device will have a unique ID, which will display on your VNC Viewer device. This is in case you have multiple devices you wish to control.

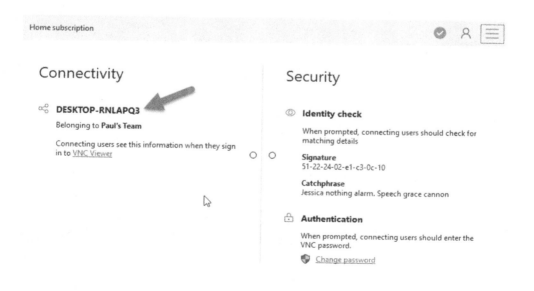

Task 4:

From your VNC Viewer device, log in with your VNC credentials. These will differ from the ones you need to access the remote device (to be controlled).

Task 5:

After you have logged in, you should see the name of the remote device appear as a clickable icon. Click on it and log in.

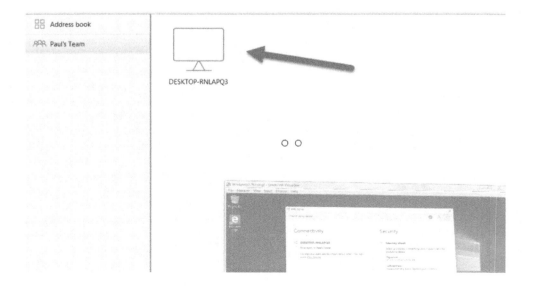

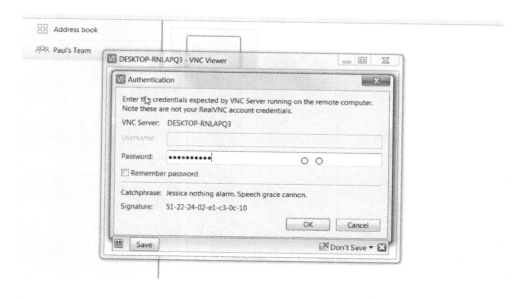

Task 6:

You are now connected to the remote device. Open up Notepad and write a line of text. Now go to the VNC Connect device and you will see it first-hand.

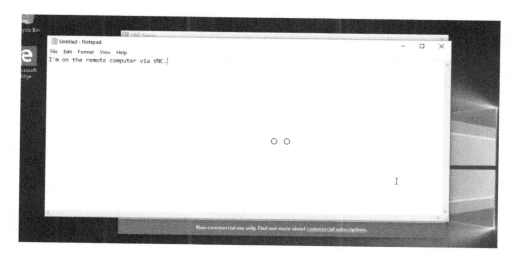

Notes:

Remote-control software is very useful for working while away from home. Bear in mind that you may have to permit it through your firewall and some corporate networks block it so you won't be able to gain access from home.

Remote File Access—FTP

Lab Objective:

Learn how to save configurations using FTP.

Lab Purpose:

Any data which is not backed up you risk losing. On corporate networks you should have a detailed backup and recovery plan. You may well use SFTP or some other secure method. In this lab we will back up your router configuration using the File Transfer Protocol.

Lab Tool:

Packet Tracer

Lab Topology:

Please use the following topology to complete this lab exercise:

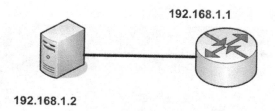

192.168.1.1

192.168.1.2

Lab Walkthrough:

Task 1:

Connect a router to a server using a crossover cable.

Task 2:

Configure an IP address on the Ethernet interface on your router.

```
Router>en
Router#conf t
Enter configuration commands, one per line. End with CNTL/Z.
Router(config)#interface f0/0
```

```
Router(config-if)#ip address 192.168.1.1 255.255.255.0
Router(config-if)#no shut
```

Task 3:

Configure an IP address on your server Ethernet interface. Set the default gateway to the router.

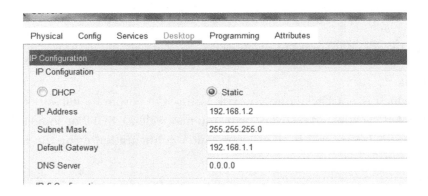

Task 4:

Ping the router from the server.

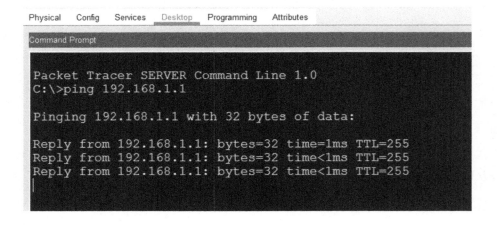

Task 5:

Router configurations are stored in NVRAM, but you need to save the live configuration there in order to populate it. Use the 'copy run start' command. Any value inside square brackets [] is the default, so just press the Enter key.

```
Router#copy run start
Destination filename [startup-config]?
```

```
Building configuration...
[OK]
Router#
```

Task 6:

Configure FTP credentials on the server. Use the username '101labs' and the password 'hello.' Tick all the permission boxes (write, read etc.) and then click 'Add.'

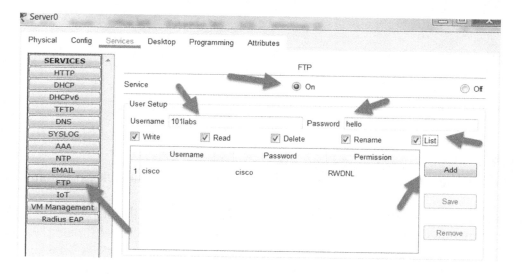

Task 7:

Add the FTP username and password to the router:

```
Router(config)#ip ftp username 101labs
Router(config)#ip ftp password hello
```

Task 8:

Copy the router configuration to the FTP server. Rename the saved file to today's date. If you had to copy it back, you would need to rename it to 'Router-confg,' but don't worry about that for now.

```
Router#copy startup-config ftp:
Address or name of remote host []? 192.168.1.2
Destination filename [Router-confg]? 7sept18

Writing startup-config...
[OK - 566 bytes]
```

Task 9:

Check that the file is on the FTP server. You will have to click on another service and back onto FTP because there is no refresh key.

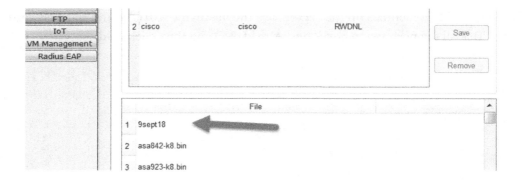

Notes:

Most backups can be identified by the name-date, so you can pull back the relevant file.

The router startup configuration file contains all of your passwords and IP addresses and could amount to hundreds of lines of code. You wouldn't want to lose it!

SFTP File Access

Lab Objective:

Learn how to download a file from a server using SFTP.

Lab Purpose:

SFTP (SSH File Transfer Protocol) was designed as an extension to the SSH protocol. It provides file transfer capabilities and uses SSH for data and control packets. Don't confuse this with FTPS, which is FTP with SSL security. FTPS uses a control channel and opens a new connection for data transfer. It requires an SSL certificate.

Lab Tool:

An online SFTP server and an SFTP client

Lab Topology:

There are a number of SFTP clients you can download for free. You can access files using the command line on terminal clients, such as Putty, but we will stick to a GUI. I found free-to-use SFTP servers at **https://www.sftp.net/public-online-sftp-servers**, and they also provide links to SFTP client software. I used FileZilla.

Lab Walkthrough:

Task 1:
Find a list of free-to-use SFTP servers.

I used https://www.sftp.net/public-online-sftp-servers.

List of free online SFTP servers

WebSshCheck	Hostname	Login	Note
web check	test.rebex.net:22	demo/password	Includes also SSH, FTP/SSL, FTP, IMAP, POP3 and Time protocols. Read-only.
web check	itcsubmit.wustl.edu:22	-	Only for connection test. No public username/password available.
web check	demo.wftpserver.com:2222	demo-user/demo-user	Includes also FTP, FTPS on different ports.

Task 2:
Download an SFTP client if you don't already have one. I have FileZilla, which is free and easy to use.

Task 3:

Use the details provided to open an SFTP session to the server.

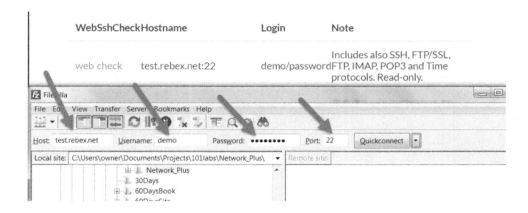

Task 4:

It might take a few seconds for the session to open.

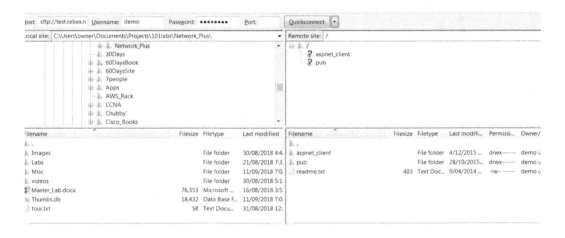

Task 5:

Click on the 'pub/example' folder and find the list of images. This will be found under the right window in FileZilla (if you are using it).

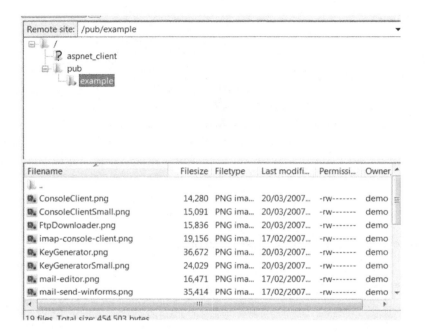

Task 6:

You can drag it over into any folder on your PC, but let's right-click and download. It will go into the folder you have open on the left panel.

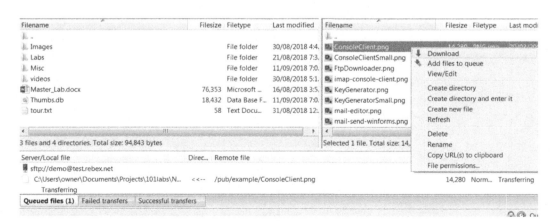

Task 7:

Navigate to your folder and find the file.

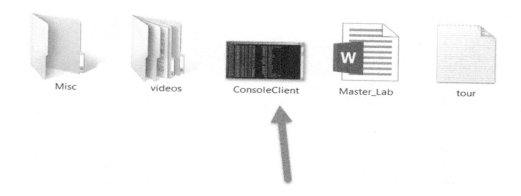

Misc   videos   ConsoleClient   Master_Lab   tour

Task 8:

Open the file.

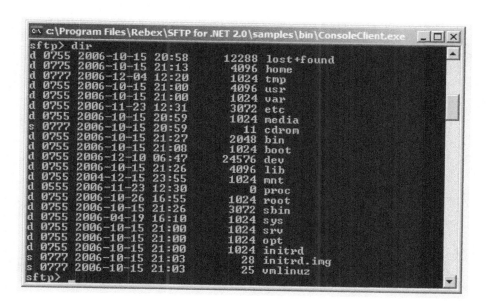

Note:

There is a good chance there'll be a question trying to catch you out, so learn about FTPS and SFTP.

Remote File Access–TFTP

Lab Objective:

Learn how to transfer a router operating system (IOS) using TFTP.

Lab Purpose:

Trivial File Transfer Protocol is useful for transporting small files across a network. It offers no security, so it is usually banned in corporate environments.

Lab Tool:

Packet Tracer

Lab Topology:

Please use the following topology to complete this lab exercise:

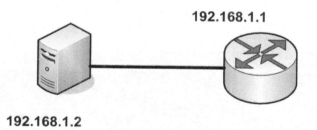

192.168.1.1

192.168.1.2

Lab Walkthrough:

Task 1:

Connect a router to a server using a crossover cable. I used an 1841 model.

Task 2:

Configure an IP address on the Ethernet interface on your router.

```
Router>en
Router#conf t
Enter configuration commands, one per line. End with CNTL/Z.
Router(config)#interface f0/0
```

```
Router(config-if)#ip address 192.168.1.1 255.255.255.0
Router(config-if)#no shut
```

Task 3:

Configure an IP address on your server Ethernet interface. Set the default gateway to the router.

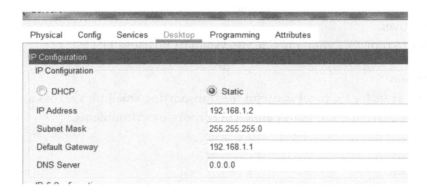

Task 4:

Ping the router from the server.

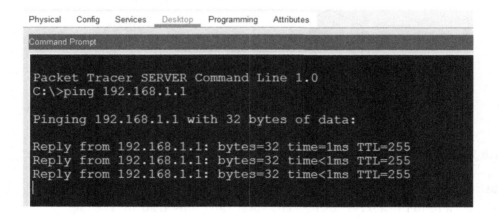

Task 5:

Check which version of Cisco operating system you are running. These systems have a specific naming convention, and their names end in .bin.

```
Router#dir flash
Directory of flash:/
```

```
3 -rw- 33591768 <no date> c1841-advipservicesk9-mz.124-15.T1.bin
2 -rw- 28282 <no date> sigdef-category.xml
1 -rw- 227537 <no date> sigdef-default.xml
```

Task 6:

Cisco Packet Tracer comes pre-loaded with several IOS files, so find one which matches your router model (mine is an 1841 above) and choose one to copy over to your router using TFTP. I chose 'c1841-ipbase-mz.123-14.T7.bin'. If you choose a larger image, then it might fail due to lack of memory space.

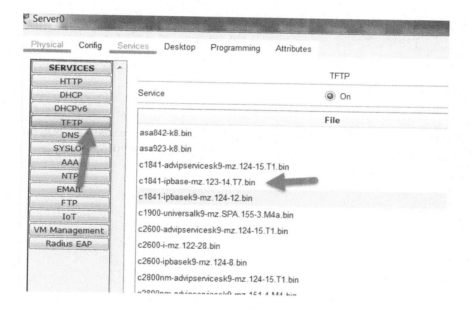

Task 7:

It might be easier to write out the name and put it into Notepad. You can't copy and paste it from the PT server. Then, issue the 'copy tftp: flash:' command on the router and input the other fields as they appear.

```
Router#copy tftp: flash:
Address or name of remote host []? 192.168.1.2
Source filename []? c1841-ipbase-mz.123-14.T7.bin
Destination filename [c1841-ipbase-mz.123-14.T7.bin]?

Accessing tftp://192.168.1.2/c1841-ipbase-mz.123-14.T7.bin...
Loading c1841-ipbase-mz.123-14.T7.bin from 192.168.1.2: !!!!!!!!!!!!!!!
!!!!!!!!!!!!!!!!!!!!!!!!!!!!!!!!!!!!!!!!!!!!!!!!!!!!!!!!!!!!!!!!!!!!!!!!!!
!!!!!!!!!!!!!!!!!!!!!!!!!!!!!!!!!!!!!!!!!!!!!!!!!!!!!!!!!!!!!!!!!!!!!!!!!!
```

```
!!!!!!!!!!!!!!!!!!!!!!!!!!!!!!!!!!!!!!!!!!!!!!!!!!!!!!!!!!!!!!!!!!!!!!!!!!!!!!!!!!!!!!!
!!!!!!!!!!!!!!!!!!!!!!!!!!!!!!!!!!!!!!!!!!!!!!!!!!!
[OK - 13832032 bytes]

13832032 bytes copied in 0.267 secs (3547303 bytes/sec)
```

Task 8:

Check the flash memory on the router to see if your IOS was copied over.

```
Router#dir flash
Directory of flash:/

3 -rw- 33591768 <no date> c1841-advipservicesk9-mz.124-15.T1.bin
4 -rw- 13832032 <no date> c1841-ipbase-mz.123-14.T7.bin
2 -rw- 28282 <no date> sigdef-category.xml
1 -rw- 227537 <no date> sigdef-default.xml
64016384 bytes total (16336765 bytes free)
```

Notes:

Depending on how much memory you have, you can store more than one IOS on a router and choose which one to boot from. You would also use TFTP for disaster recovery if you had no IOS to boot to.

Modem Connections

Lab Objective:

Learn how to connect to a router or switch using a modem.

Lab Purpose:

Along with console connections, modems are an out-of-band connection option for network equipment. 'Out-of-band' refers to a data stream independent of the usual connection stream, such as a DSL or leased line. It is often used for emergency access and is physically connected only when needed for security purposes.

Lab Tool:

Packet Tracer

Lab Topology:

Please use the following topology to complete this lab exercise:

Lab Walkthrough:

Task 1:

Connect a modem card to your PC in PT and to the router. You will need to power them off before doing so. Power both devices back on. You click on the card name and then physically drag the image onto the slot. The modem in the above image is to illustrate the fact that it's installed inside the PC.

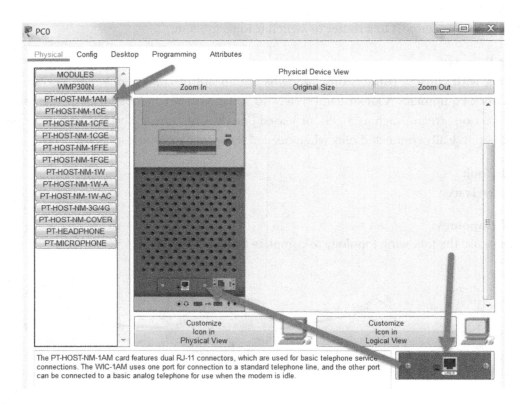

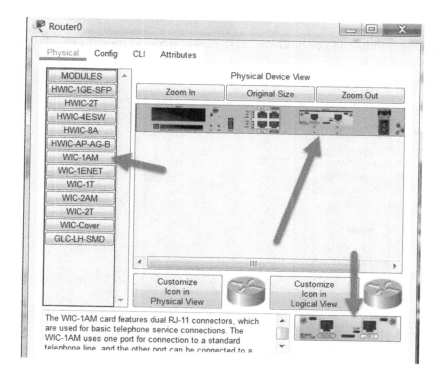

Task 2:

Drag a PT cloud onto the canvas. Connect the PC modem port to port 4, and port 5 to the router modem port. Use a phone cable.

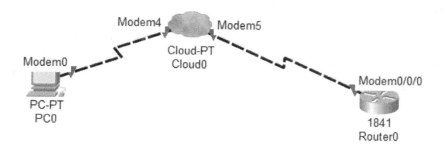

Task 3:

Assign phone number 444 to modem interface 4 and 555 to modem interface 5.

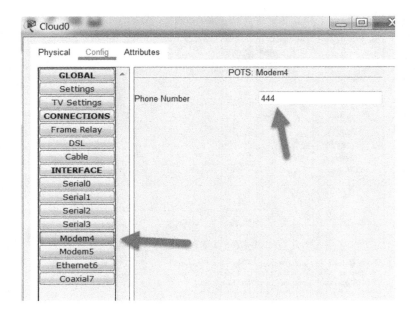

Task 4:

Assign a username and password to the router.

```
Router(config)#username 101labs password hello
```

Task 5:

Assign IP address 192.168.1.1 to the router modem interface.

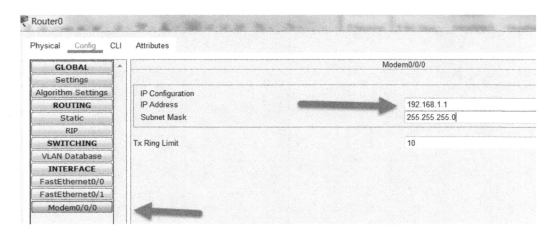

Task 6:

On the PC assign IP address 192.168.1.2 and default gateway 192.168.1.1 to the modem interface.

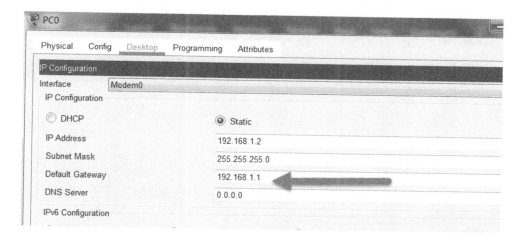

Task 7:

On the PC go to a modem interface (dial-up) and enter the username and password. Put the dial number as 555 and hit 'Dial'.

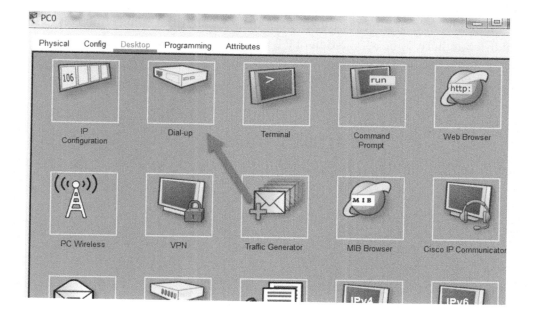

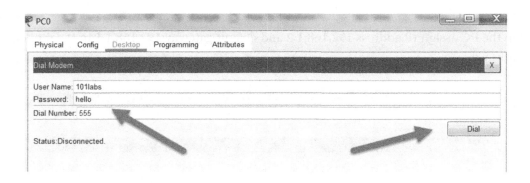

Task 8:

You should now be connected.

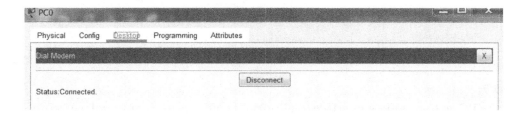

Notes:

You should be able to ping the router from the host after the connection comes up. I couldn't, but this may be a limitation of PT, which is just a network emulator.

LAB 65

Console Connections

Lab Objective:

Learn how to connect to a router or switch using a console cable.

Lab Purpose:

When you first configure a router or switch, there will be no configuration present, so you can't telnet or SSH to it. Also, if there is some sort of disaster or you have forgotten your passwords, you will be able to connect to it only via a console connection.

Lab Tool:

Packet Tracer

Lab Topology:

Please use the following topology to complete this lab exercise:

Lab Walkthrough:

Task 1:

Connect a console cable to a router. When you do this on live equipment, you may need to use a USB connector or some sort of adapter. Check your documentation for details. In Packet Tracer you connect from the PC RS232 port to the router console port.

Task 2:

Click on the 'Terminal' option in the PC desktop settings. Console connections should be 9600 bits per second, 8 data bits, no parity, 1 stop bit, and no flow control. These are usually the default.

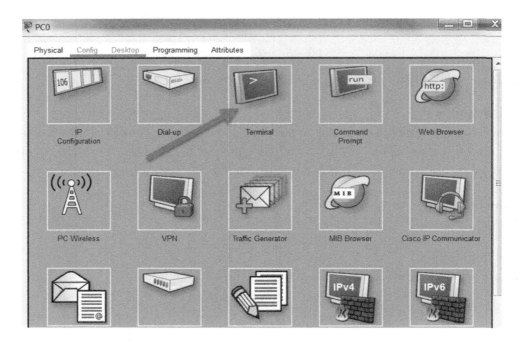

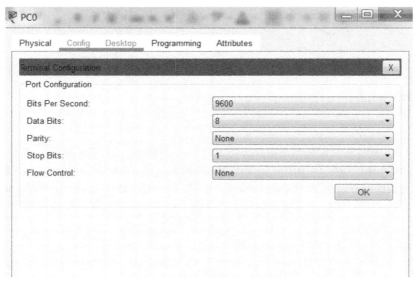

Task 3:

Click 'OK' and start your console session. If you are trying to recover the router or switch due to forgotten passwords, you will need to follow a special procedure. However, this isn't in the syllabus, so don't worry about it for now.

```
PC0

Physical    Config    Desktop    Programming    Attributes

Cisco 1841 (revision 5.0) with 114688K/16384K bytes of memory.
Processor board ID FTX0947Z18E
M860 processor: part number 0, mask 49
2 FastEthernet/IEEE 802.3 interface(s)
191K bytes of NVRAM.
63488K bytes of ATA CompactFlash (Read/Write)
Cisco IOS Software, 1841 Software (C1841-ADVIPSERVICESK9-M), Version 12.4(15)T1,
RELEASE SOFTWARE (fc2)
Technical Support: http://www.cisco.com/techsupport
Copyright (c) 1986-2007 by Cisco Systems, Inc.
Compiled Wed 18-Jul-07 04:52 by pt_team


        --- System Configuration Dialog ---

Would you like to enter the initial configuration dialog? [yes/no]:
% Please answer 'yes' or 'no'.
Would you like to enter the initial configuration dialog? [yes/no]: no


Press RETURN to get started!



Router>enable
Router#
```

Note:

It's very handy to learn how to console to your devices because when you have to do it for real, you may have lost your internet connection and be unable to look up instructions.

4.0 Network Security

LAB 66

Motion Detection

Lab Objective:

Learn how to configure motion detection to activate video surveillance.

Lab Purpose:

Motion detection can use optics, infrared, radio frequencies, or other methods to detect movement. This can trigger alarm systems, but in our case we will trigger a camera to activate. We can record the movement or, with the advent of the IoT, speak to somebody via a speaker (e.g., tell a caller we are busy and can't come to the door).

Lab Tool:

Packet Tracer

Lab Topology:

Please use the following topology to complete this lab exercise:

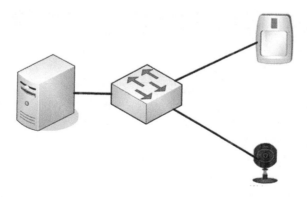

Lab Walkthrough:

Task 1:

Drag a server and switch onto the canvas. Under 'End Devices/Home/Smart City' drag up a webcam and a sensor. Link them all with Ethernet cables to the switch (any interface will do fine).

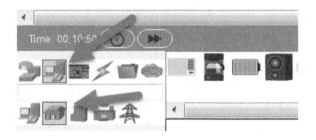

Task 2:

Add IP address 192.168.1.1 to the server configuration.

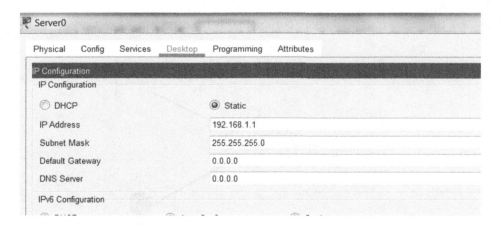

Task 3:

On the server, enable the IoT service.

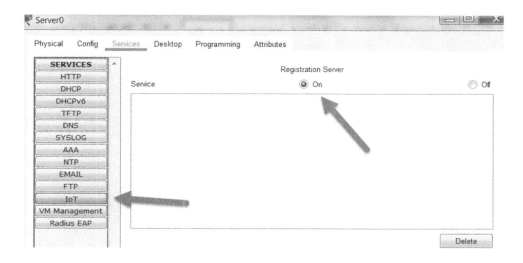

Task 4:

Open a web browser window on the server and enter the IP address 192.168.1.1 in the address bar. Create a new account and configure username '101labs' and password 'hello'.

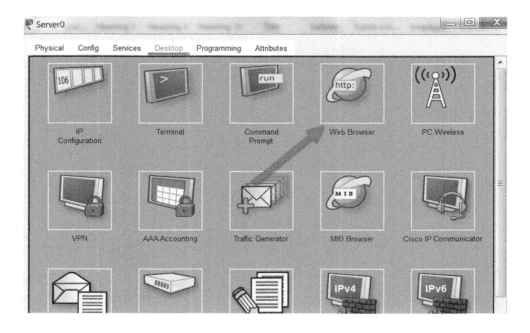

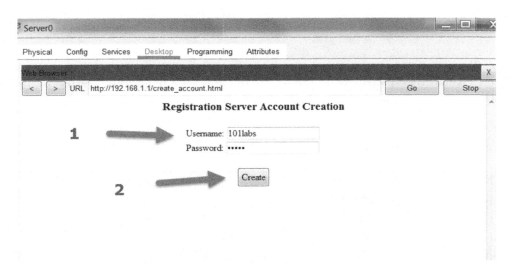

Task 5:

On the motion detector click on 'Settings' and change the name to 'Motion'. On the webcam change the name to 'Webcam'.

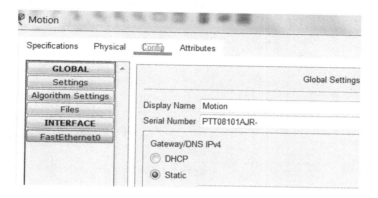

Task 6:

Set the IP address of the motion sensor to 192.168.1.2 and that of the webcam to 192.168.1.3.

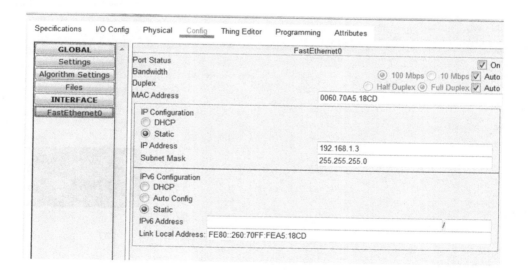

Task 7:

Under 'Settings' for both devices, set the IoT registration server to the server address. Add the username '101labs' and the password 'hello'.

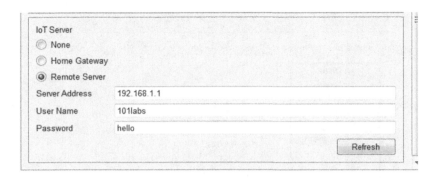

Task 8:

Go back to the server and both devices should be registered. You might have to click on the 'Home' link at the top of the window if it doesn't automatically go there.

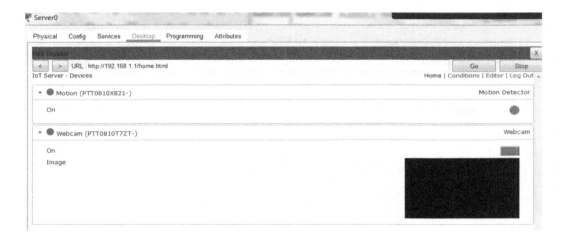

Task 9:

Press 'Conditions' and name the new condition 'webcam on'. Set it as below. If Motion On is true, then set the webcam to on. Then press 'OK' at the bottom.

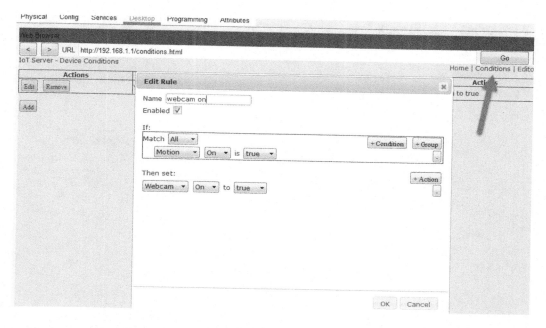

Task 10:

If we tested now, the webcam would come on and stay on, so add another condition. If Motion On is false, then set the webcam status to off.

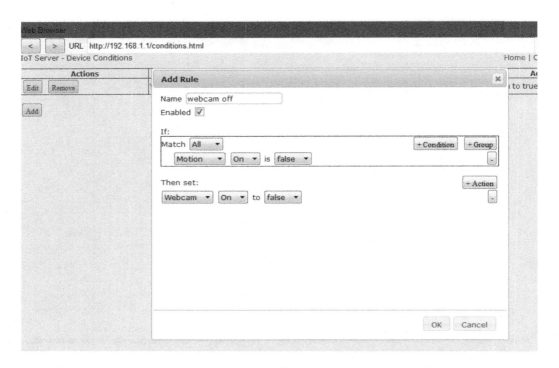

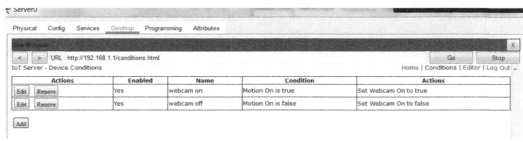

Task 11:

Hold down your Alt key and move your mouse in front of the movement sensor. This should activate the webcam. A red LED should show on the motion detector when it detects movement. Move the window for the server config next to the canvas so you can see both.

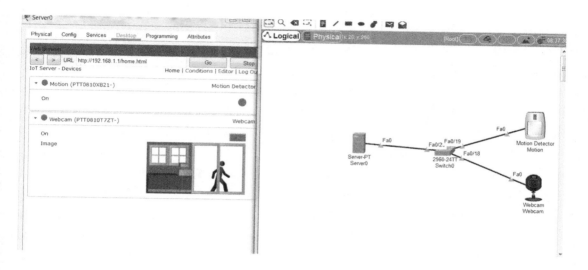

Notes:

There is a huge range of options and devices with IoT in Packet Tracer. You can also use a programming interface called Blockly to program events.

I could get the IoT registration server to work only AFTER the server was connected to the switch and the interfaces came up.

LAB 67

Smart Cards and Locks

Lab Objective:

Learn how to configure a smart card reader to activate a door lock.

Lab Purpose:

Part of the Net+ syllabus is smart cards, IoT, and locks—we put these three things together in a lab. We will configure a smart card reader, smart card, and IoT server. If the card is authorized, we will unlock the door for the holder.

Lab Tool:

Packet Tracer

Lab Topology:

Please use the following topology to complete this lab exercise:

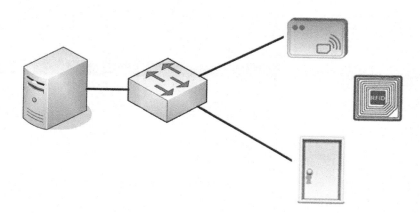

Lab Walkthrough:

Task 1:

Drag a server and switch onto the canvas. Under 'End Devices/Home/Industrial' drag up a door, RFID card reader, and RFID card. Link them all with Ethernet cables to the switch (any interface will do fine). The card has no interface, so don't try to attach it to the switch.

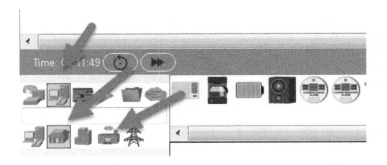

Task 2:

Add IP address 192.168.1.1 to the server configuration.

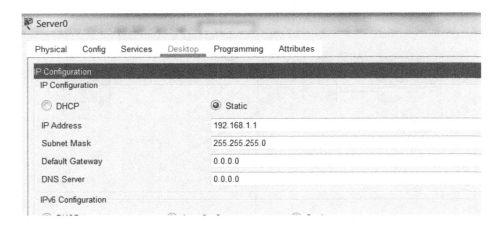

Task 3:

On the server, enable the IoT service.

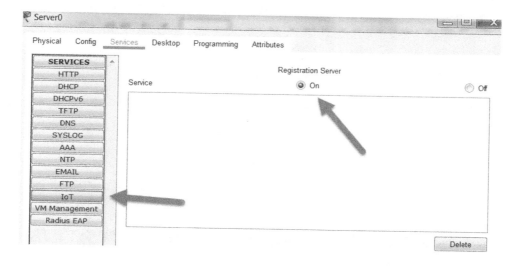

Task 4:

Open a web browser window on the server. Enter the IP address in the URL bar: 192.168.1.1. Create a new account and configure username '101labs' and password 'hello'.

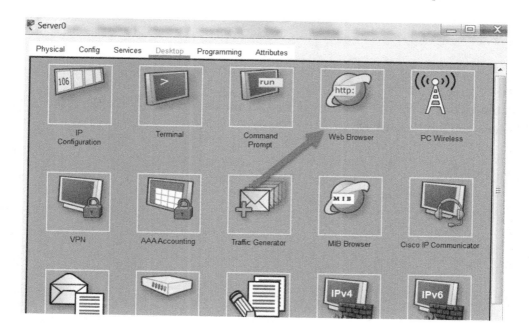

Task 5:

On the motion card click on 'Settings' and set the name to 'Card'. For the reader write 'Reader' and for the door 'Door'.

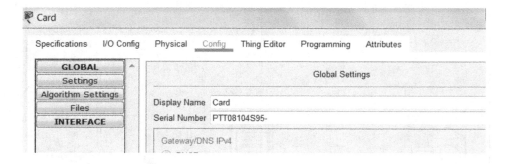

Task 6:

Set the IP address of the door to 192.168.1.2 and that of the card reader to 192.168.1.3.

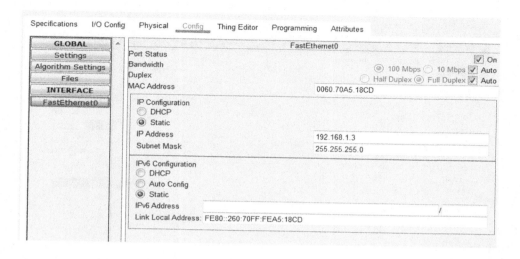

Task 7:

Under 'Settings' for all three devices, set the IoT registration server to the server address 192.168.1.1. Add the username '101labs' and the password 'hello'.

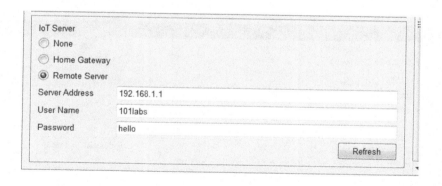

Task 8:

Go back to the server and both the door and reader should be registered.

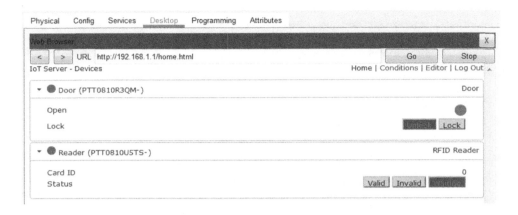

Task 9:

Press 'Conditions' and name the new condition 'Open Door'. Set it as below. If the card ID is 1005, then set the door to unlock.

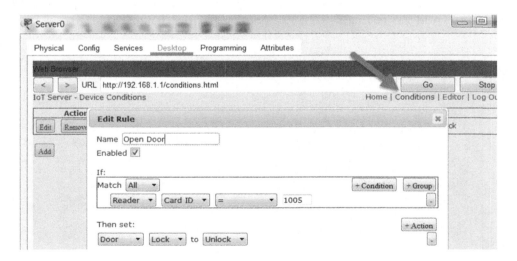

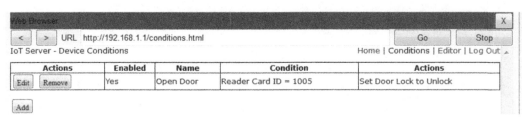

Task 10:

Go to the card attributes and set the card value to 1005 by clicking on the current value and inputting the new one.

	Name	Attribute
1	MTBF	300000
2	cost	250
3	power source	1
4	rack units	2
5	wattage	5

Properties:

	Property	Value
1	ardID	1005

Task 11:

You will need to press the 'Lock' button on the IoT server window (below) if you want to change the lock on the door icon from green to red.

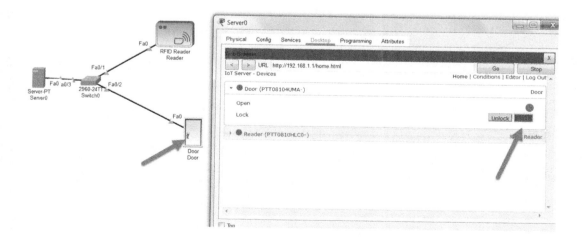

Task 12:

Note that the card ID is 0 and the door is locked. Now drag the card to the reader. You should see the color on the door lock change to green, indicating the door is unlocked.

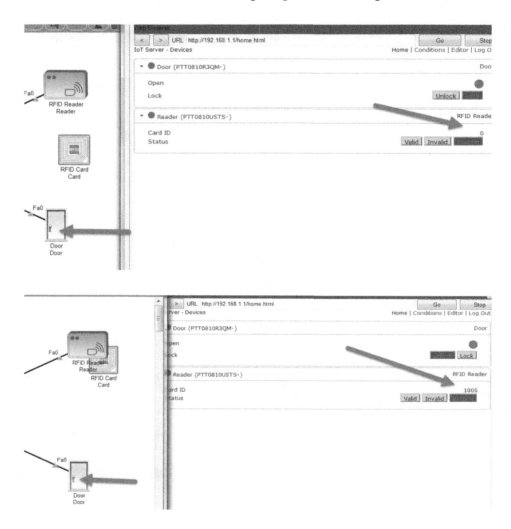

Notes:

There is a huge range of options and devices with IoT in Packet Tracer. You can also use a programming interface called Blockly to program events.

LAB 68

Configuring RADIUS

Lab Objective:
Learn how to configure RADIUS.

Lab Purpose:
As I'm sure you've read in your study guide, AAA can use TACACS+ or RADIUS to control user access to network equipment. In this lab we will configure a RADIUS server to authenticate a user to connect to a router.

Lab Tool:
Packet Tracer

Lab Topology:
Please use the following topology to complete this lab exercise:

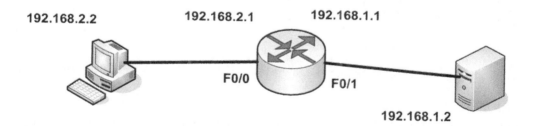

Lab Walkthrough:

Task 1:
Connect a PC to a router F0/0 and F0/1 on the router to a server. You may have different interfaces from mine, so just swap to your relevant interfaces.

Task 2:

Configure the IP address and default gateway on the host as per the diagram.

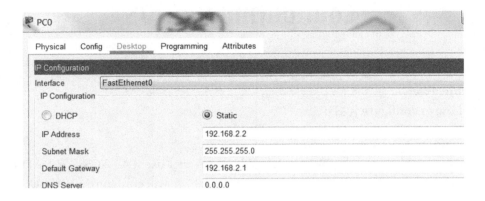

Task 3:

Configure the IP addresses on the router interfaces. Change the hostname to R1, which will be checked by the RADIUS server.

```
Router(config)#int f0/0
Router(config-if)#ip add 192.168.2.1 255.255.255.0
Router(config-if)#no shut
Router(config-if)#int f0/1
Router(config-if)#ip add 192.168.1.1 255.255.255.0
Router(config-if)#no shut
Router(config-if)#exit
Router(config)#hostname R1
Router(config)#enable password hello
```

Task 4:

Make sure you also add an IP address of 192.168.1.2 to the server and a default gateway of 192.168.1.1.

Task 5:

Configure AAA on the server. The client name is R1, the IP is 192.168.1.1, the key is p@ssword (goes in the 'Secret' field), and the server type is RADIUS. After you click 'Add', create a username of '101labs' and a password of 'cisco' under User Setup and click 'Add'.

Task 6:

Add the RADIUS configuration to the router. Create the RADIUS server IP address and the key to be sent. The 'login default—local' line of config tells the router to use any local usernames and passwords if it can't reach the server to authenticate the client.

```
R1(config)#aaa new-model
R1(config)#radius-server host 192.168.1.2 key p@ssword
R1(config)#aaa authentication login default group radius local
R1(config)#line vty 0 15
R1(config-line)#login authentication default
```

Task 7:

Enable debugging for AAA on the router.

```
R1#debug aaa authentication
```

Task 8:

Telnet from the PC to the router. The session will be validated by the RADIUS server. You will see the router prompt appear to show you are connected. Feel free to log in if you wish.

```
Packet Tracer PC Command Line 1.0
C:\>telnet 192.168.1.1
Trying 192.168.1.1 ...Open


User Access Verification

Username: 1011abs
Password:
R1>enable
```

Task 9:

Check the router debug messages.

```
*Aug 29 14:19:24.267: AAA/BIND(4): Bind i/f
*Aug 29 14:19:24.267: AAA/AUTHEN/LOGIN(4): Pick method list 'default'
```

Note:

This is a simple AAA configuration; it can be far more complicated of course!

LAB 69

Configuring TACACS+

Lab Objective:

Learn how to configure TACACS+.

Lab Purpose:

As I'm sure you've read in your study guide, AAA can use TACACS+ or RADIUS to control user access to network equipment. In this lab we will configure a TACACS+ server to authenticate a user to connect to a multilayer switch.

Lab Tool:

Packet Tracer

Lab Topology:

Please use the following topology to complete this lab exercise:

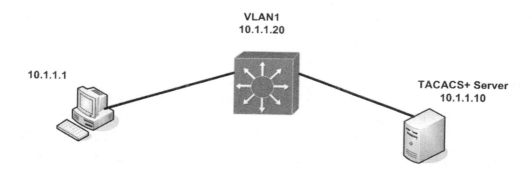

Lab Walkthrough:

Task 1:

Connect a PC to a multilayer switch (such as a 3560) and the switch to a server.

Task 2:

Configure an IP address and default gateway on the host as per the diagram.

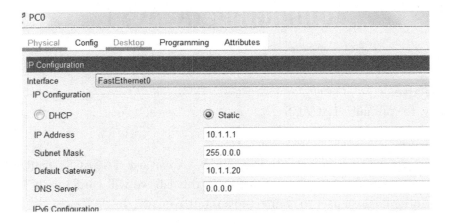

Task 3:

Configure an IP address for VLAN1, where all ports are by default. You must 'no shut' a switched virtual interface (SVI), which is what you create when you apply an IP address to a VLAN.

```
Switch(config)#int vlan 1
Switch(config-if)#ip add 10.1.1.20 255.0.0.0
Switch(config-if)#no shut
Switch(config-if)#exit
```

Task 4:

Configure AAA on the switch. Add a username, password, and enable password. Next, create a TACACS+ group; if the TACACS+ server becomes unreachable, the switch can use its local database for authentication. Set the Telnet lines to use AAA and the method list 'myauth', which we shall create shortly (so ignore any error messages which show up).

```
Swit<<ch(config)#aaa new-model
Switch(config)#username cisco password cisco
Switch(config)#enable password mycisco
Switch(config)#aaa authentication login myauth group tacacs+ local
Switch(config)#line vty 0 15
Switch(config-line)#login authentication myauth
Switch(config-line)#exit
```

Task 5:

Create a key string called 'mykey', which will be known only by the switch and server and will be used to encrypt the session.

```
Switch(config)#tacacs-server host 10.1.1.10 key mykey
```

Task 6:

Add an IP address of 10.1.1.10 to the server Ethernet port.

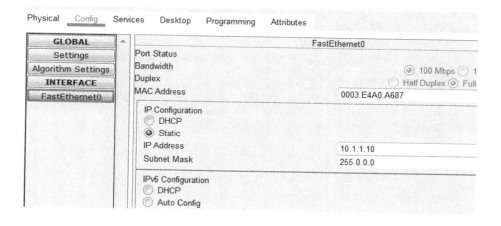

Task 7:

On the server enable AAA. Add the client name 'Switch', the IP address 10.1.1.20, and the key 'mykey', then choose 'Tacacs' as the server type and press 'Add'. Then add the user credentials underneath that of username 'cisco' and password 'cisco' and press 'Add'.

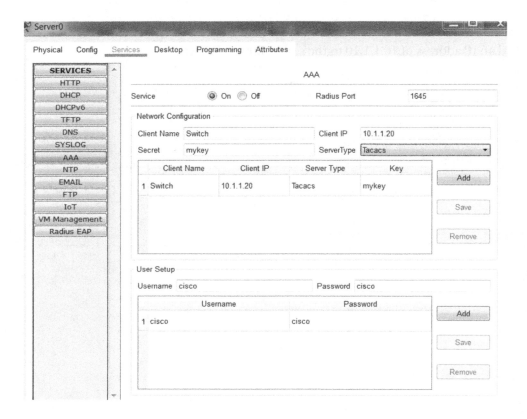

Task 8:

Configure what can be done on the switch once authorized. The user should be allowed to go into exec mode, which is the Switch# prompt. Then use the 'local' command to authorize the user for all sessions.

```
Switch(config)#aaa authorization exec default group tacacs+
Switch(config)#aaa authorization exec default group tacacs+ local
```

Task 9:

Enable debugging for AAA sessions on the switch and then telnet from the PC to the switch. The PC should be authorized by the server and then permitted access.

```
Switch#debug aaa authentication
```

```
Command Prompt

Packet Tracer PC Command Line 1.0
C:\>telnet 10.1.1.20
Trying 10.1.1.20 ...Open


User Access Verification

Username: cisco
Password:
Switch>enable
Password:
Password:
Switch#

[Connection to 10.1.1.20 closed by foreign host]
C:\>
```

Task 10:

Check the debug output on the switch.

```
AAA Authentication debugging is on
Switch#
*Aug 29 13:20:16.253: AAA/BIND(1): Bind i/f

*Aug 29 13:20:16.253: AAA/AUTHEN/LOGIN(1): Pick method list 'myauth'
```

Notes:

This is a simple TACACS+ configuration; it can be far more complicated of course! I recommend you check Cisco documentation for more information on what the commands achieve. This is actually CCNA Security level stuff, so it's pretty tough.

Port Security

Lab Objective:

Learn how to configure port security on a switch.

Lab Purpose:

Port security is a feature used on most networks. At the access switch level it can prevent certain hosts from using the port or a certain number of devices. In this lab we will prevent somebody from plugging in a hub to their network port and adding more devices by permitting only one host to use it at a time.

Lab Tool:

Packet Tracer

Lab Topology:

Please use the following topology to complete this lab exercise:

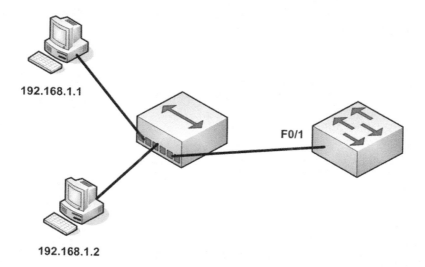

Lab Walkthrough:

Task 1:
Connect a hub to a switch and then two PCs to the hub. It won't matter which ports you use, but connect to F0/1 on the switch from the hub using a crossover cable.

Task 2:
Configure port security on the switch. Permit only one host to use the port. The default setting on the switch will be to shut down the port. You need to set the port to access before applying security settings. Also, check the port security settings.

```
Switch(config)#int f0/1
Switch(config-if)#switchport port-security
Command rejected: FastEthernet0/1 is a dynamic port.
Switch(config-if)#switchport mode access
Switch(config-if)#switchport port-security
Switch(config-if)#switchport port-security ?
aging Port-security aging commands
mac-address Secure mac address
maximum Max secure addresses
violation Security violation mode
<cr>
Switch(config-if)#switchport port-security max 1
Switch(config-if)#end
Switch#show port-security int f0/1
Port Security : Enabled
Port Status : Secure-up
Violation Mode : Shutdown
Aging Time : 0 mins
Aging Type : Absolute
SecureStatic Address Aging : Disabled
Maximum MAC Addresses : 1
Total MAC Addresses : 0
Configured MAC Addresses : 0
Sticky MAC Addresses : 0
Last Source Address:Vlan : 0000.0000.0000:0
Security Violation Count : 0
```

Task 3:

Add the IP addresses to both hosts. Frames may well leave the devices as you add the IP addresses for keepalives. When you add a second IP address, it should trigger the port to shut down. If this doesn't happen, you can ping .1 to .2. Here is the config for PC0:

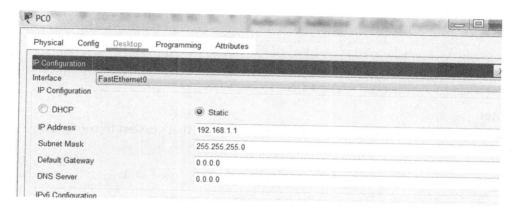

Task 4:

Check the port security status for F0/1. It should have been shut down when it saw a second device trying to send frames through it. You can also check the MAC address seen on the port with the offending PC. Yours will differ from mine of course.

```
Switch#show port-security int f0/1
Port Security : Enabled
Port Status : Secure-shutdown
Violation Mode : Shutdown
Aging Time : 0 mins
Aging Type : Absolute
SecureStatic Address Aging : Disabled
Maximum MAC Addresses : 1
Total MAC Addresses : 0
Configured MAC Addresses : 0
Sticky MAC Addresses : 0
Last Source Address:Vlan : 000A.41E6.B12D:1
Security Violation Count : 1
```

Task 5:

Issue a 'show port-security' command to check the general settings for the port security on the switch.

```
Switch#show port-security
Secure Port MaxSecureAddr CurrentAddr SecurityViolation Security Action
            (Count)       (Count)     (Count)
-----------------------------------------------------------------------
      Fa0/1       1           0                 1        Shutdown
-----------------------------------------------------------------------
```

Note:

The best sort of security for your LAN is often the one that's easiest to configure.

WPA2 with TKIP

Lab Objective:

Learn how to configure WPA2 and TKIP on a wireless access point.

Lab Purpose:

WPA2 has replaced WPA as the preferred security protocol for wireless connections. WPA2 can work with other protocols to offer enhanced security. TKIP-RC4 stream cipher is used with a 128-bit per packet key, meaning each packet has a unique key.

Lab Tool:

Packet Tracer

Lab Topology:

Please use the following topology to complete this lab exercise:

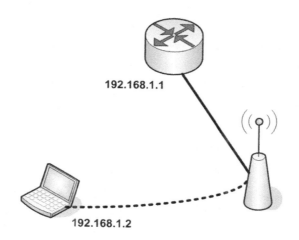

192.168.1.1

192.168.1.2

Lab Walkthrough:

Task 1:

Connect a router to an access point using a crossover cable. Add a laptop and put a wireless card into the side slot (as we have already done in an earlier lab). I used a wireless device with the label 'AP-PT' in Packet Tracer. This might move places as PT is updated over time.

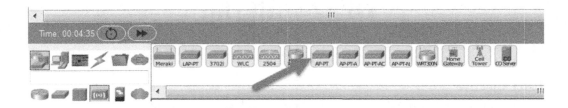

Task 2:

Configure IP address 192.168.1.1 on the router Ethernet interface.

```
Router>en
Router#conf t
Enter configuration commands, one per line. End with CNTL/Z.
Router(config)#int f0/0
Router(config-if)#ip add 192.168.1.1 255.255.255.0
Router(config-if)#no shut
```

Task 3:

Set the security and wireless settings on the access point as follows:

SSID—101labs
Pass Phrase—123456789
Security—WPA2-PSK
Encryption—TKIP

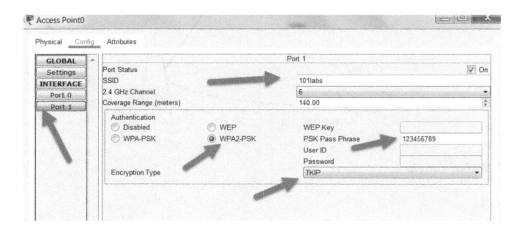

Task 4:

Find the wireless card settings on the laptop. Match the AP settings, but also add the IP address 192.168.1.2.

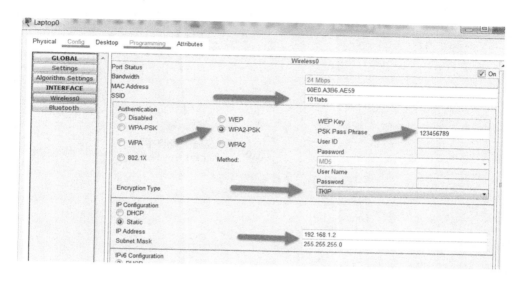

Task 5:

Add a default gateway of 192.168.1.1 on the laptop.

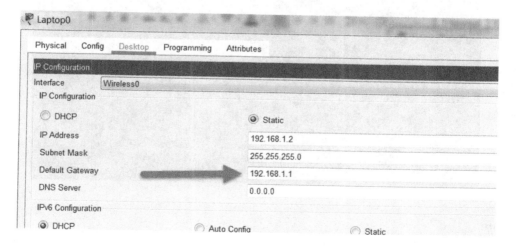

Task 6:

Check the canvas and you should see the wireless connection go live.

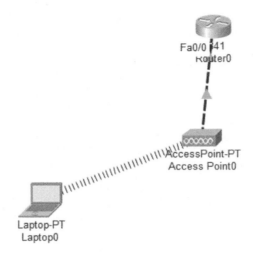

Task 7:

Ping from the laptop to the router.

```
C:\>ping 192.168.1.1

Pinging 192.168.1.1 with 32 bytes of data:

Reply from 192.168.1.1: bytes=32 time=30ms TTL=255
Reply from 192.168.1.1: bytes=32 time=13ms TTL=255
Reply from 192.168.1.1: bytes=32 time=8ms TTL=255
Reply from 192.168.1.1: bytes=32 time=17ms TTL=255

Ping statistics for 192.168.1.1:
    Packets: Sent = 4, Received = 4, Lost = 0 (0% loss),
Approximate round trip times in milli-seconds:
    Minimum = 8ms, Maximum = 30ms, Average = 17ms
```

Note:

WPA2 has been replaced by WPA3, but it will take some time for new devices to incorporate it.

LAB 72

MAC Filtering

Lab Objective:
Learn how to configure MAC address filtering on a switch.

Lab Purpose:
MAC address filtering allows you to configure which addresses can be accepted through a port. This can be achieved through layer 2 access lists, firewalls, or (as in this instance) switch port security settings.

Lab Tool:
Packet Tracer

Lab Topology:
Please use the following topology to complete this lab exercise:

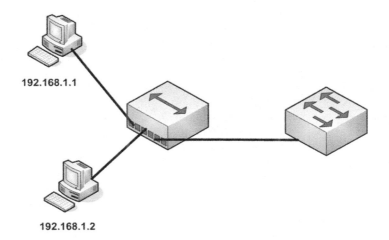

192.168.1.1

192.168.1.2

Lab Walkthrough:

Task 1:
Connect a hub to a switch and then two PCs to the hub. It won't matter which ports you use, but connect to F0/1 on the switch from the hub using a crossover cable.

Task 2:

Configure IP addresses on the hosts as per the diagram. Here is the config on PC0:

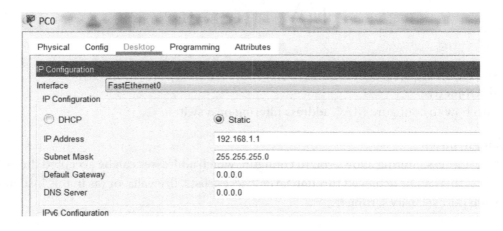

Task 3:

Note the MAC address on PC1. Copy it. Please note that your MAC address will differ from mine.

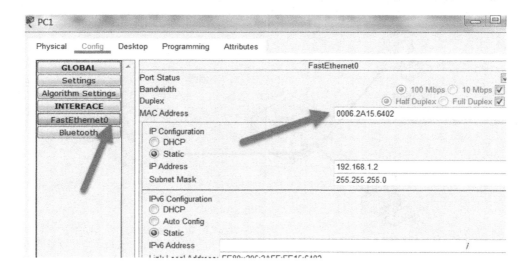

Task 4:

Configure MAC address filtering on the switch. Enter the MAC address of PC1, which will be permitted on the port. If any other MAC address reaches the port, it will shut down.

```
Switch(config)#int f0/1
Switch(config-if)#switchport mode access
Switch(config-if)#switchport port-security
Switch(config-if)#switch port-security mac-address ?
H.H.H 48 bit mac address
sticky Configure dynamic secure addresses as sticky
Switch(config-if)#switch port-security mac-address 0006.2A15.6402
Switch(config-if)#end
```

Task 5:

Check the port security settings on the switch. The configured MAC address won't show, but it will show when you issue a 'show run' command. I've highlighted the most relevant parts of the output for you.

```
Switch#show port-security int f0/1
Port Security : Enabled
Port Status : Secure-up
Violation Mode : Shutdown
Aging Time : 0 mins
Aging Type : Absolute
SecureStatic Address Aging : Disabled
Maximum MAC Addresses : 1
Total MAC Addresses : 1
Configured MAC Addresses : 1
Sticky MAC Addresses : 0
Last Source Address:Vlan : 0000.0000.0000:0
Security Violation Count : 0

Switch#show run
Building configuration...

Current configuration : 1181 bytes
!
version 12.2
!
hostname Switch
!
interface FastEthernet0/1
switchport mode access
switchport port-security
switchport port-security mac-address 0006.2A15.6402
[output truncated]
```

Task 6:

Ping from PC0 to PC1. This will send frames through the switchport via the hub and trigger MAC filtering.

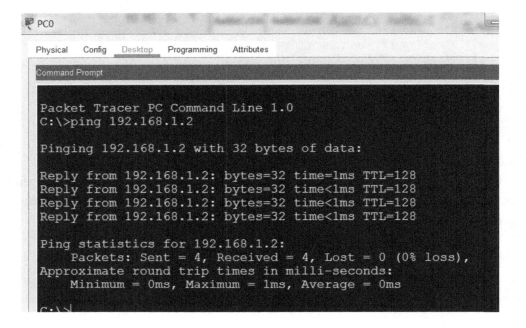

Task 7:

Issue a 'show port-security' command to check the general settings for the port security on the switch. The interface should have gone down.

```
Switch#show port-security int f0/1
Port Security : Enabled
Port Status : Secure-shutdown
Violation Mode : Shutdown
Aging Time : 0 mins
Aging Type : Absolute
SecureStatic Address Aging : Disabled
Maximum MAC Addresses : 1
Total MAC Addresses : 1
Configured MAC Addresses : 1
Sticky MAC Addresses : 0
Last Source Address:Vlan : 0000.0CE0.A38C:1
Security Violation Count : 1
```

Task 8:

Check the MAC address of PC0 to ensure this was the one which triggered the port shutdown.

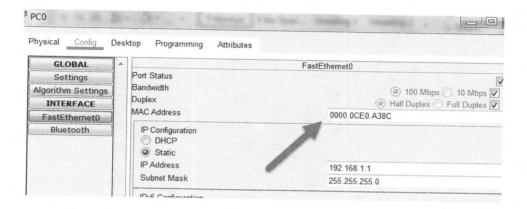

Note:

The only way to recover ports from the security shutdown is to manually 'no shut' them.

File Hashing

Lab Objective:
Learn how to hash a file and then check its integrity.

Lab Purpose:
File hashing is ubiquitous. You find it in PPP authentication and password encryption, and in this example, you use it to prove file integrity. We will create a file and get a hashed value. We will then send the file and the hash to a recipient, which can check the hash matches and the file hasn't been tampered with.

Lab Tool:
Free hashing software installed on Windows VM

Lab Topology:
There are a number of hashing programs out there. I used **https://www.quickhash-gui. org/**, which has versions for most operating systems.

Lab Walkthrough:

Task 1:

Download QuickHash to your virtual PC. Create a short text file and save it to your desktop.

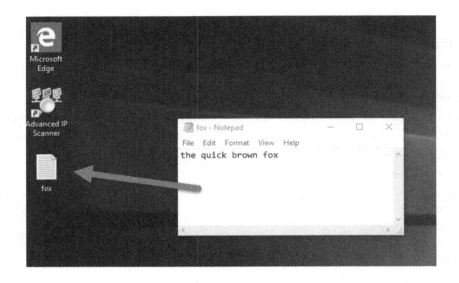

Task 2:

Find your QuickHash installation and open it. It doesn't need to be installed.

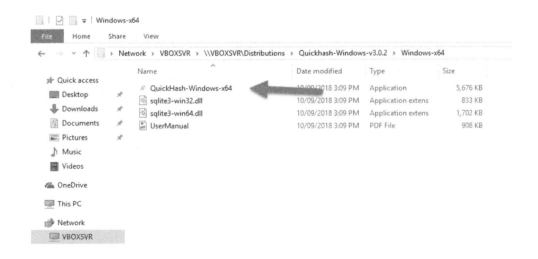

Task 3:

Click on the 'File' tab. You can either open the file you created or drag it into the 'File being hashed...' window.

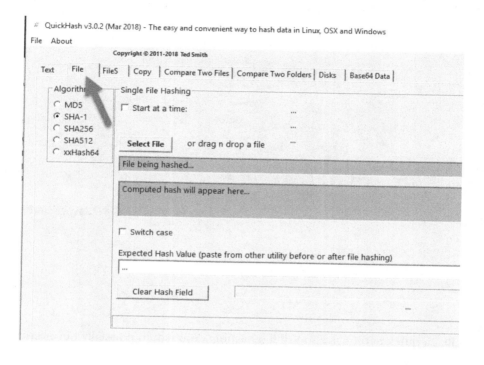

Task 4:

I used SHA1. Copy the hash value and paste it into another Notepad file.

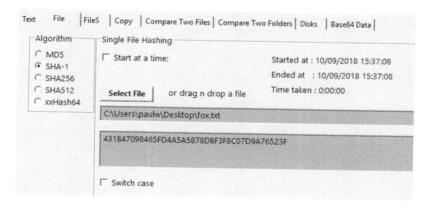

Task 5:

If you have another connected PC networked to this one, you can open the files remotely and use another version of QuickHash to check the hash. I emailed mine to another PC. Check the hash you were sent with the one created.

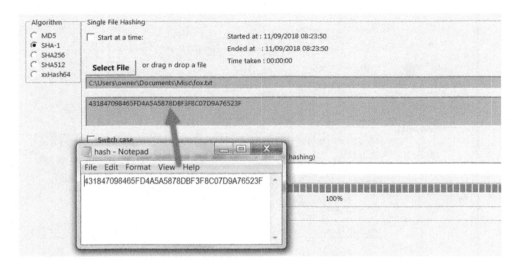

Notes:

This is just a quick demonstration of file hashing. You would normally never email over both files together.

LAB 74

Disabling Unused Services

Lab Objective:
Learn how to disable unused services on a router.

Lab Purpose:
Hackers prefer to find vulnerabilities in services and ports. You will regularly see software updates plugging security holes and notices for your network hardware suggesting you make configuration changes to prevent unauthorized access.

Lab Tool:
Packet Tracer

Lab Topology:
Please use the following topology to complete this lab exercise:

Lab Walkthrough:

Task 1:
Drag two routers onto the canvas and connect them via a crossover cable.

Task 2:
Don't add any IP addresses yet. Change the hostnames and 'no shut' both Ethernet interfaces. Here is the config for Router1:

```
Router(config)#host R1
R1(config)#
R1(config)#int f0/0
R1(config-if)#no shut
```

Task 3:

Now you will see the first vulnerability. Many devices run a layer 2 service which discovers their neighbors. The open standard is LLDP (Link Layer Discovery Protocol), and Cisco devices run their own, known as CDP (Cisco Discovery Protocol). Issue the 'show cdp neighbors' command and then the 'show cdp neighbors detail' command. Another layer 2 device can establish your device type, IOS release, and attached port. You will also see the IP address if one is configured.

```
R0#show cdp neighbors
Capability Codes: R - Router, T - Trans Bridge, B - Source Route Bridge
S - Switch, H - Host, I - IGMP, r - Repeater, P - Phone
Device ID Local Intrfce Holdtme Capability Platform Port ID
R1 Fas 0/0 175 R C1841 Fas 0/0
R0#

R0#show cdp neighbors detail

Device ID: R1
Entry address(es):
Platform: cisco C1841, Capabilities: Router
Interface: FastEthernet0/0, Port ID (outgoing port): FastEthernet0/0
Holdtime: 169

Version :
Cisco IOS Software, 1841 Software (C1841-ADVIPSERVICESK9-M), Version
12.4(15)T1, RELEASE SOFTWARE (fc2)
Technical Support: http://www.cisco.com/techsupport
Copyright (c) 1986-2007 by Cisco Systems, Inc.
Compiled Wed 18-Jul-07 04:52 by pt_team

advertisement version: 2
Duplex: full
```

Task 4:

Add IP address 192.168.1.2 to R1 and then clear the CDP table on R0 (this is the list of devices discovered by CDP). After a short time you will see that the IP address has been learned by R0. This isn't great for your security!

```
R1(config)#int f0/0
R1(config-if)#ip add 192.168.1.2 255.255.255.0
R1(config-if)#end

R0#clear cdp table
R0#show cdp neighbors detail
Device ID: R1
Entry address(es):
IP address : 192.168.1.2
```

```
Platform: cisco C1841, Capabilities: Router
Interface: FastEthernet0/0, Port ID (outgoing port): FastEthernet0/0
Holdtime: 171
```

Task 5:

Disable CDP on R1. You could do this on the interface only or on the entire device. We will disable it on the entire device.

```
R1(config)#no cdp run

R0#clear cdp table
R0#show cdp neighbors
Capability Codes: R - Router, T - Trans Bridge, B - Source Route Bridge
S - Switch, H - Host, I - IGMP, r - Repeater, P - Phone
Device ID Local Intrfce Holdtme Capability Platform Port ID
R0#
```

Task 6:

If you have access to a live router at home or online, you will see far more services enabled. On Packet Tracer we are a little more limited. On R0 check which services you can disable or enable with the 'service ?' command.

```
R0(config)#service ?
dhcp Enable DHCP server and relay agent
nagle Enable Nagle's congestion control algorithm
password-encryption Encrypt system passwords
timestamps Timestamp debug/log messages
```

Task 7:

You can disable any of these services by typing it out but with 'no' in front.

```
R0(config)#no service ?
dhcp Enable DHCP server and relay agent
nagle Enable Nagle's congestion control algorithm
password-encryption Encrypt system passwords
timestamps Timestamp debug/log messages
R0(config)#no service dhcp
```

Task 8:

It's important that you shut any ports you aren't using. We will cover shutting unused ports and changing the native VLAN in other labs. As software is updated, default settings are changed, which is why it's important you keep your software up-to-date. If you issue a 'show run' command on a router, you will see what is on by default (and the fact you disabled DHCP):

```
RO#show run
Building configuration...

Current configuration : 555 bytes
!
version 12.4
no service timestamps log datetime msec
no service timestamps debug datetime msec
no service password-encryption
no service dhcp
```

Task 9:

Lastly, disable any Telnet or SSH access to your device.

```
RO(config)#line vty 0 15
RO(config-line)#transport input none
```

Note:

Every device will have different vulnerabilities, so please do check all release notes.

Disabling Unused Ports

Lab Objective:

Learn how to configure switch ports to prevent unauthorized use.

Lab Purpose:

Any port on your network devices should be locked down to prevent users or hackers from plugging in hosts, hubs, or other devices and causing serious issues or security problems.

Lab Tool:

Packet Tracer

Lab Topology:

Please use the following topology to complete this lab exercise:

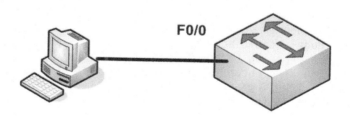

Lab Walkthrough:

Task 1:

Drag a PC and switch onto the canvas. Don't connect them yet.

Task 2:

Issue 'show interface f0/1' and 'show interface f0/1 switchport' commands on the switch.

```
Switch#show interfaces f0/1
FastEthernet0/1 is down, line protocol is down (disabled)
Hardware is Lance, address is 00e0.b048.e601 (bia 00e0.b048.e601)
BW 100000 Kbit, DLY 1000 usec,
[output truncated]
```

```
Switch#show interface f0/1 switchport
Name: Fa0/1
Switchport: Enabled
Administrative Mode: dynamic auto
Operational Mode: down
[output truncated]
```

Task 3:

Plug a PC into f0/1 and watch the interface come up. You will see the link lights go green after about 30 seconds. Also, issue the above two commands again.

PC-PT
PC0

2960-24TT
Switch0

```
Switch#show interface f0/1
FastEthernet0/1 is up, line protocol is up (connected)
Hardware is Lance, address is 00e0.b048.e601 (bia 00e0.b048.e601)
BW 100000 Kbit, DLY 1000 usec,

Switch#show interface f0/1 switchport
Name: Fa0/1
Switchport: Enabled
Administrative Mode: dynamic auto
Operational Mode: static access
Administrative Trunking Encapsulation: dot1q
Operational Trunking Encapsulation: native
Negotiation of Trunking: On
Access Mode VLAN: 1 (default)
Trunking Native Mode VLAN: 1 (default)
[output truncated]
```

Task 4:

Of course, this behavior is not desirable. Administratively shut the interface and then put it into an unused VLAN.

```
Switch(config)#int f0/1
Switch(config-if)#shutdown
%LINK-5-CHANGED: Interface FastEthernet0/1, changed state to
administratively down

%LINEPROTO-5-UPDOWN: Line protocol on Interface FastEthernet0/1,
changed state to down
```

```
Switch(config-if)#switchport mode access
Switch(config-if)#switchport access vlan 888
% Access VLAN does not exist. Creating vlan 888
```

Task 5:

Reissue the show commands again.

```
Switch#show interface f0/1
FastEthernet0/1 is administratively down, line protocol is down
(disabled)
Hardware is Lance, address is 00e0.b048.e601 (bia 00e0.b048.e601)
BW 100000 Kbit, DLY 1000 usec,

Switch#show interface f0/1 switchport
Name: Fa0/1
Switchport: Enabled
Administrative Mode: static access
Operational Mode: down
Administrative Trunking Encapsulation: dot1q
Operational Trunking Encapsulation: native
Negotiation of Trunking: Off
Access Mode VLAN: 888 (VLAN0888)
Trunking Native Mode VLAN: 1 (default)
Voice VLAN: none
```

Note:

You would usually apply the above commands to ALL switch ports and then manually enable those you wish to use.

LAB 76

Changing the Native VLAN

Lab Objective:
Learn how to change the native VLAN.

Lab Purpose:
The native VLAN is simply the default VLAN all ports are in on the switch. Frames in the native VLAN are untagged by default and represent a security vulnerability. It's an important security step to change this default behaviour. Native VLAN numbers must match on both sides of a trunk link.

Lab Tool:
Packet Tracer

Lab Topology:
Please use the following topology to complete this lab exercise:

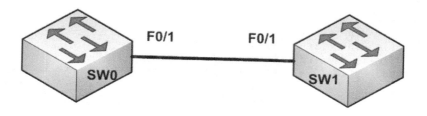

Lab Walkthrough:

Task 1:
Drag two switches onto the canvas and connect them via a crossover cable.

Task 2:
Configure one side as a trunk link and it will create a trunk between the switches.

```
Switch>en
Switch#conf t
Enter configuration commands, one per line. End with CNTL/Z.
Switch(config)#hostname SW0
```

```
SW0(config)#int f0/1
SW0(config-if)#switchport mode trunk

%LINEPROTO-5-UPDOWN: Line protocol on Interface FastEthernet0/1,
changed state to up
```

Task 3:

Check the layer 2 status of the port. Note the fact it is now a trunk and is using VLAN1 as the native VLAN. Check this output on SW1 also. Do you notice any differences with the modes (because it hasn't been hard set to trunk)?

```
SW0#show interface f0/1 switchport
Name: Fa0/1
Switchport: Enabled
Administrative Mode: trunk
Operational Mode: trunk
Administrative Trunking Encapsulation: dot1q
Operational Trunking Encapsulation: dot1q
Negotiation of Trunking: On
Access Mode VLAN: 1 (default)
Trunking Native Mode VLAN: 1 (default)
```

Task 4:

Create VLAN10 and then change the native VLAN. You should see errors right away because Switch1 still uses VLAN1 as the native VLAN.

```
SW0(config)#vlan 10
SW0(config-vlan)#exit
SW0(config)#interface f0/1
SW0(config-if)#switchport trunk native vlan ?
  <1-4094>  VLAN ID of the native VLAN when this port is in trunking
mode
SW0(config-if)#switchport trunk native vlan 10
SW0(config-if)#end
SW0#
%CDP-4-NATIVE_VLAN_MISMATCH: Native VLAN mismatch discovered on
FastEthernet0/1 (10), with Switch FastEthernet0/1 (1).
```

Task 5:

Check the layer 2 configurations on F0/1 for Switch0.

```
SW0#show int f0/1 switchport
Name: Fa0/1
Switchport: Enabled
Administrative Mode: trunk
Operational Mode: trunk
Administrative Trunking Encapsulation: dot1q
```

```
Operational Trunking Encapsulation: dot1q
Negotiation of Trunking: On
Access Mode VLAN: 1 (default)
Trunking Native Mode VLAN: 10 (VLAN0010)
Voice VLAN: none
```

Task 6:

Configure VLAN10 on Switch1 and put F0/1 as using it as the native VLAN.

```
Switch>
Switch>en
Switch#conf t
Switch(config)#hostname SW1
SW1(config)#vlan 10
SW1(config-vlan)#int f0/1
SW1(config-if)#switchport trunk native vlan 10
SPANTREE-2-UNBLOCK_CONSIST_PORT: Unblocking FastEthernet0/1 on
VLAN0010. Port consistency restored.
```

Notes:

This is yet another important security step. You would usually use a high number for the VLAN and one which is unused by hosts. You can also check the native VLAN with the 'show interfaces trunk' command.

```
SW0#show interfaces trunk
Port Mode  Encapsulation Status   Native vlan
Fa0/1 on    802.1q       trunking  1

Port Vlans allowed on trunk
Fa0/1 1-1005

Port Vlans allowed and active in management domain
Fa0/1 1

Port Vlans in spanning tree forwarding state and not pruned
Fa0/1 none
```

LAB 77

Secure Trunk Links

Lab Objective:
Learn how to prevent certain VLANs from crossing a trunk.

Lab Purpose:
This security step isn't actually in the syllabus, but it should be included under 'Common Mitigation Techniques'. You would do this along with the other trunking lab of 'Changing the Native VLAN' to an unused one. This will prevent unwanted traffic from traversing the link, especially if a hacker has found an unused VLAN to exploit.

Lab Tool:
Packet Tracer

Lab Topology:
Please use the following topology to complete this lab exercise:

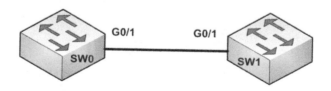

Lab Walkthrough:

Task 1:
Connect two switches using a crossover cable.

Task 2:
Configure interface G0/1 as a trunk; it will bring both sides of the link up because the other end is auto and is therefore waiting for a request to become a trunk. Bear in mind that the default settings vary by switch model, so check the documentation. I'm using a 2960 model.

```
Switch>en
Switch#conf t
```

```
Enter configuration commands, one per line. End with CNTL/Z.
Switch(config)#host SW0
SW0(config)#int g0/1
SW0(config-if)#switchport mode trunk
```

Task 3:

Confirm which interfaces are set to trunk. Note also which VLANs are allowed across the trunk link.

```
SW0#show interfaces trunk
Port  Mode Encapsulation Status Native vlan
Gig0/1 on   802.1q          trunking 1

Port Vlans allowed on trunk
Gig0/1 1-1005

Port Vlans allowed and active in management domain
Gig0/1 1

Port Vlans in spanning tree forwarding state and not pruned
Gig0/1 1
```

Task 4:

Check which VLANs are present already; VLANs 1 and 1002-5 are created by default to support LAN and legacy traffic. I've had to paste in an image of the output to keep the formatting.

```
SW0#show vlan brief

VLAN Name                             Status    Ports
---- -------------------------------- --------- -------------------------------
1    default                          active    Fa0/1, Fa0/2, Fa0/3, Fa0/4
                                                Fa0/5, Fa0/6, Fa0/7, Fa0/8
                                                Fa0/9, Fa0/10, Fa0/11, Fa0/12
                                                Fa0/13, Fa0/14, Fa0/15, Fa0/16
                                                Fa0/17, Fa0/18, Fa0/19, Fa0/20
                                                Fa0/21, Fa0/22, Fa0/23, Fa0/24
                                                Gig0/2
1002 fddi-default                     active
1003 token-ring-default               active
1004 fddinet-default                  active
1005 trnet-default                    active
```

Task 5:

Create VLANs 10, 20, 30, 40, and 50. Higher models of switches allow you to do this with one command, but we'll have to do each individually for now. Then check if they are allowed across the trunk.

```
SW0#conf t
Enter configuration commands, one per line. End with CNTL/Z.
```

```
SW0(config)#vlan 10
SW0(config-vlan)#vlan 20
SW0(config-vlan)#vlan 30
SW0(config-vlan)#vlan 40
SW0(config-vlan)#vlan 50
SW0(config-vlan)#end

SW0#show interfaces trunk
Port Mode Encapsulation Status Native vlan
Gig0/1 on 802.1q          trunking 1

Port Vlans allowed on trunk
Gig0/1 1-1005

Port Vlans allowed and active in management domain
Gig0/1 1,10,20,30,40,50

Port Vlans in spanning tree forwarding state and not pruned
Gig0/1 1,10,20,30,40,50
```

Task 6:

Configure the trunk so as to allow only VLANs 10, 20, 30, and 40. All other VLANs should be blocked.

```
SW0(config)#int g0/1
SW0(config-if)#switchport trunk allowed vlan 10,20,30,40
SW0(config-if)#end
SW0#show interfaces trunk
Port Mode Encapsulation Status Native vlan
Gig0/1 on 802.1q trunking 1

Port Vlans allowed on trunk
Gig0/1 10,20,30,40

Port Vlans allowed and active in management domain
Gig0/1 10,20,30,40

Port Vlans in spanning tree forwarding state and not pruned
Gig0/1 40
```

Task 7:

Now remove VLAN 20 from the list of allowed VLANs. The syntax is somewhat confusing, but this is why network engineers get paid the big bucks. If you get it wrong, you may end up permitting or removing all VLANs from the trunk!

```
SW0(config)#int g0/1
SW0(config-if)#switchport trunk allowed vlan remove 20
SW0(config-if)#end
SW0#
```

```
SW0#show interfaces trunk
Port Mode Encapsulation Status Native vlan
Gig0/1 on 802.1q trunking 1
```

Port Vlans allowed on trunk
Gig0/1 10,30,40

```
Port Vlans allowed and active in management domain
Gig0/1 10,30,40
```

```
Port Vlans in spanning tree forwarding state and not pruned
Gig0/1 none
```

Task 8:

Finally, add VLAN 50 to the list of permitted VLANs on the trunk.

```
SW0(config)#int g0/1
SW0(config-if)#switchport trunk allowed vlan add 50
SW0(config-if)#end
SW0#show interfaces trunk
Port Mode Encapsulation Status Native vlan
Gig0/1 on 802.1q trunking 1
```

Port Vlans allowed on trunk
Gig0/1 10,30,40,50

```
Port Vlans allowed and active in management domain
Gig0/1 10,30,40,50
```

```
Port Vlans in spanning tree forwarding state and not pruned
Gig0/1 50
```

Note:

This is one of many security steps you would take to protect your network.

STP

Lab Objective:

Learn how to configure Spanning Tree Protocol and manually set the root of the spanning tree domain.

Lab Purpose:

The role of STP is to prevent loops on your LAN. It does this by determining a root of the spanning tree domain and then closing off ports which would cause a loop (traffic to continually circle the network without reaching its destination).

IMPORTANT—Your switches will use different MAC addresses from mine, so your root switch may well differ from mine. Just make any adjustments necessary.

Lab Tool:

Packet Tracer

Lab Topology:

Please use the following topology to complete this lab exercise:

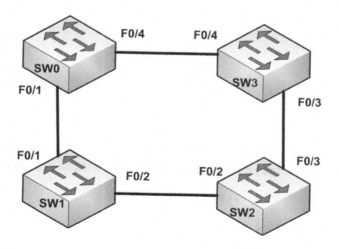

Lab Walkthrough:

Task 1:
Connect four switches using crossover cables as indicated and name them all as per the diagram. You already know how to do this from earlier labs.

Task 2:
When you connect the switches, STP will run, electing a root bridge and creating root and designated ports. In the above topology, one port will be shut in order to prevent a loop from forming. The root bridge will be determined by the device with the lowest bridge ID, which is created from the base MAC address and the bridge priority (which is 32768 by default). There are several commands to choose from, but we will start with 'show span vlan 1'. The root bridge will have all ports as designated, and the root ports will be the ports closest to the root bridge. You can see that the bridge ID is the default value plus the VLAN number.

```
SW0#show span vlan 1
VLAN0001
Spanning tree enabled protocol ieee
Root ID Priority 32769
Address 0000.0C08.1228
Cost 38
Port 1(FastEthernet0/1)
Hello Time 2 sec Max Age 20 sec Forward Delay 15 sec

Bridge ID Priority 32769 (priority 32768 sys-id-ext 1)
Address 000C.8529.CC65
Hello Time 2 sec Max Age 20 sec Forward Delay 15 sec
Aging Time 20

Interface Role Sts Cost Prio.Nbr Type
---------------- ---- --- --------- -----
Fa0/4      Altn BLK 19 128.4 P2p
Fa0/1      Root FWD 19 128.1 P2p
```

Task 3:
From the output in task 2 you can see that this switch isn't the root for VLAN1. One port is blocked, so we should follow the root port direction to the next switch to find the root.

```
SW1#show spanning-tree vlan 1
VLAN0001
Spanning tree enabled protocol ieee
Root ID Priority 32769
Address 0000.0C08.1228
Cost 19
```

```
Port 2(FastEthernet0/2)
Hello Time 2 sec Max Age 20 sec Forward Delay 15 sec

Bridge ID Priority 32769 (priority 32768 sys-id-ext 1)
Address 0001.C9E4.7BA5
Hello Time 2 sec Max Age 20 sec Forward Delay 15 sec
Aging Time 20

Interface Role Sts Cost Prio.Nbr Type
---------------- ---- --- --------- -----
Fa0/2      Root FWD 19 128.2 P2p
Fa0/1      Desg FWD 19 128.1 P2p
```

Task 4:

We still haven't found the root, but we can see that F0/2 is the root on this switch, so let's keep going.

```
SW2#show span vlan 1
VLAN0001
Spanning tree enabled protocol ieee
Root ID Priority 32769
Address 0000.0C08.1228
This bridge is the root
Hello Time 2 sec Max Age 20 sec Forward Delay 15 sec

Bridge ID Priority 32769 (priority 32768 sys-id-ext 1)
Address 0000.0C08.1228
Hello Time 2 sec Max Age 20 sec Forward Delay 15 sec
Aging Time 20

Interface Role Sts Cost Prio.Nbr Type
---------------- ---- --- --------- ----
Fa0/1      Desg FWD 19 128.1 P2p
Fa0/3      Desg FWD 19 128.3 P2p
```

We've found the STP root. It says as much in the above output and you can see that the ports are all designated which will only be the case on the root.

Task 5:

Note the base MAC address for each of your switches and note the lowest. This will confirm that the lowest address has become the STP root. You can see the addresses above, but you can also use the 'show version' command to find the base MAC address, which is allocated to the switch chassis.

```
SW0#show version
Cisco IOS Software, C2960 Software (C2960-LANBASE-M), Version 12.2(25)
FX, RELEASE SOFTWARE (fc1)
```

```
Copyright (c) 1986-2005 by Cisco Systems, Inc.
Compiled Wed 12-Oct-05 22:05 by pt_team

ROM: C2960 Boot Loader (C2960-HBOOT-M) Version 12.2(25r)FX, RELEASE
SOFTWARE (fc4)

System returned to ROM by power-on

Cisco WS-C2960-24TT (RC32300) processor (revision C0) with 21039K bytes
of memory.

24 FastEthernet/IEEE 802.3 interface(s)
2 Gigabit Ethernet/IEEE 802.3 interface(s)

63488K bytes of flash-simulated non-volatile configuration memory.
Base ethernet MAC Address : 000C.8529.CC65
```

SW0—000C.8529.CC65

SW1—0001.C9E4.7BA5

SW2—0000.0C08.1228

SW3—000B.BE99.48D0

Task 6:

You need to choose a different switch to be the STP root. You would usually do this for improved traffic flow or because the switch is a more powerful model or has higher throughput. There are two commands you can choose from; feel free to do the lab twice, choosing a different command each time.

```
SW0(config)#spanning-tree vlan 1 priority ?
  <0-61440>  bridge priority in increments of 4096
SW0(config)# spanning-tree vlan 1 root primary
```

If you set a priority, you need to have it in increments of 4096 AND it must be lower than the other switches' priority.

Task 7:

Check that the switch has become the root. The ports will take around 30 seconds to move from blocking to learning and then be designated.

```
SW0#show spanning-tree vlan 1
VLAN0001
Spanning tree enabled protocol ieee
Root ID Priority 24577
Address 000C.8529.CC65
This bridge is the root
Hello Time 2 sec Max Age 20 sec Forward Delay 15 sec
```

```
Bridge ID Priority 24577 (priority 24576 sys-id-ext 1)
Address 000C.8529.CC65
Hello Time 2 sec Max Age 20 sec Forward Delay 15 sec
Aging Time 20

Interface Role Sts Cost Prio.Nbr Type
---------------- ---- --- ---------
Fa0/4      Desg FWD 19 128.4 P2p
Fa0/1      Desg FWD 19 128.1 P2p
```

Notes:

You would normally never leave your switches to decide which is the root of the STP domain. You would work it out during the design phase.

Configuring BPDU Guard

Lab Objective:
Learn how to configure BPDU Guard on a switch.

Lab Purpose:
BPDU Guard is an important security step to take on your switch. It prevents a person from attaching, by accident or on purpose, another switch to a port and reconfiguring your entire layer 2 topology.

Lab Tool:
Packet Tracer

Lab Topology:
Please use the following topology to complete this lab exercise:

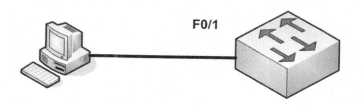

Lab Walkthrough:

Task 1:
Connect a PC to a switch interface using a straight-through cable.

Task 2:
Configure BPDU Guard on the switch interface.

```
Switch(config)#int f0/1
Switch(config-if)#switchport mode access
Switch(config-if)#spanning-tree bpduguard enable
Switch(config-if)#end

Task 3:
```

```
Check the layer 2 configurations for the port.
Switch#show interface f0/1 switchport
Name: Fa0/1
Switchport: Enabled
Administrative Mode: static access
Operational Mode: static access
Administrative Trunking Encapsulation: dot1q
Operational Trunking Encapsulation: native
Negotiation of Trunking: Off
Access Mode VLAN: 1 (default)
Trunking Native Mode VLAN: 1 (default)
Voice VLAN: none
```

Task 4:

Drag another switch onto the canvas and remove the PC. Plug the switch into the port the PC was connected to with a crossover cable. Here is my Packet Tracer canvas:

Task 5:

On the switch you configured check the debug message and then the layer 2 settings.

```
%LINEPROTO-5-UPDOWN: Line protocol on Interface FastEthernet0/1,
changed state to up
%SPANTREE-2-BLOCK_BPDUGUARD: Received BPDU on port FastEthernet0/1 with
BPDU Guard enabled. Disabling port.

Switch#show interface f0/1 switchport
Name: Fa0/1
Switchport: Enabled
Administrative Mode: static access
Operational Mode: down
Administrative Trunking Encapsulation: dot1q
Operational Trunking Encapsulation: native
Negotiation of Trunking: Off
Access Mode VLAN: 1 (default)
Trunking Native Mode VLAN: 1 (default)
Voice VLAN: none
```

Note:

Packet Tracer is somewhat limited with configuration and show commands because it's a simulator, but you've seen enough to be able to configure BPDU Guard!

LAB 80

Configuring Root Guard

Lab Objective:

Learn how to configure Root Guard on a switch.

Lab Purpose:

It's crucial that you manually determine your layer 2 topology. Root Guard prevents a particular port from becoming the root of the STP network. If a superior BPDU is received on the interface, it will be placed into a 'root-inconsistent' state and have to be manually recovered by the network administrator.

Lab Tool:

Packet Tracer

Lab Topology:

Please use the following topology to complete this lab exercise:

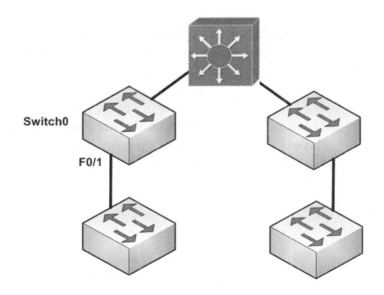

Lab Walkthrough:

Task 1:

Drag one switch onto the canvas. The others in the diagram are for illustration purposes only. Switch0 F0/1 should never become a root port because a far more powerful switch has been set as the root and the closest port to that will be the root port.

Task 2:

Configure Root Guard on the switch interface.

```
Switch(config)#int f0/1
Switch(config-if)#spanning-tree guard root
```

Task 3:

There is no show command to verify the fact you configured Root Guard. On live devices you would issue a 'show run interface f0/1' command, but Packet Tracer doesn't support this command, so here is a 'show run' command displaying only the relevant output.

```
Switch#show run
Building configuration...
Current configuration : 1104 bytes
interface FastEthernet0/1
spanning-tree guard root
```

Task 4:

If you want to test the configuration, you will have to add more switches and then set the STP topology to try to force the port to become the root, but this is well beyond the scope of the syllabus.

Notes:

You may be lucky and have the switch attempt to make that port the root *if* you connect it to another switch. This will all depend on the STP priority. You can add another switch and try the command on both switches to force the error.

```
Switch(config-if)#%SPANTREE-2-ROOTGUARDBLOCK: Port 0/1 tried to become
non-designated in VLAN 1
```

Fa0/1   Fa0/1

2960-24TT   2960-24TT
Switch0   Switch1

LAB 81

DHCP Snooping

Lab Objective:

Learn how to configure DHCP snooping on a switch.

Lab Purpose:

DHCP snooping provides protection from rogue DHCP servers on your network by creating a logical firewall between untrusted hosts and DHCP servers. We will keep this lab very simple, but you may want to create more complex labs of your own with rogue DHCP servers.

Lab Tool:

Packet Tracer

Lab Topology:

Please use the following topology to complete this lab exercise:

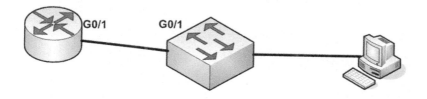

Lab Walkthrough:

Task 1:

Connect a router to a switch and then a PC to the switch as per the topology (all straight-through cables).

Task 2:

Configure interface G0/1 on the router with an IP address and 'no shut' it.

```
Router>en
Router#conf t
Enter configuration commands, one per line. End with CNTL/Z.
```

```
Router(config)#int g0/1
Router(config-if)#ip add 192.168.1.1 255.255.255.0
Router(config-if)#no shut
Router(config-if)#exit
```

Task 3:

Set up the router as a DHCP server allocating hosts from the 192.168.1.0 network. Remember to exclude the router IP address and to set the default router address.

```
Router(config)#ip dhcp pool 101labs
Router(dhcp-config)#network 192.168.1.0 255.255.255.0
Router(dhcp-config)#default-router 192.168.1.1
Router(dhcp-config)#exit
Router(config)#ip dhcp excluded-address 192.168.1.1
```

Task 4:

Configure the host to obtain IP addresses via DHCP. The IP address field should populate very quickly.

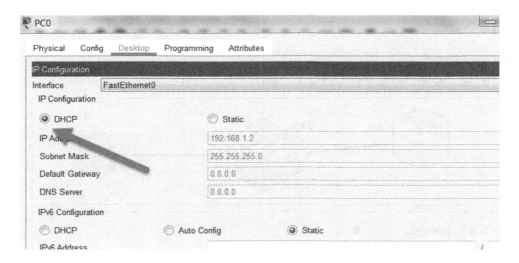

Task 5:

Enable DHCP snooping on the switch. We won't add any trusted ports yet because we want to test that DHCP packets are blocked.

```
Switch>en
Switch#conf t
Enter configuration commands, one per line. End with CNTL/Z.
Switch(config)#ip dhcp snooping
Switch(config)#ip dhcp snooping vlan 1
```

Task 6:

Renew the IP address allocation on the PC with the 'ipconfig /renew' command. If you wish, you can turn on simulation mode and press on the envelope to see the DCHP packet being blocked by the switch.

You will also see that the host has self-allocated an IP address due to the DHCP failure.

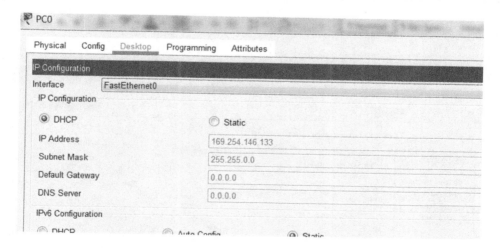

Task 7:

The router is attached to port G0/1 on the switch, so we need to set this port to trust in order for DHCP packets to be permitted. Packet Tracer has some limitations, so we need to add the 'no DHCP option-82 data insertion' command to turn off a security feature.

```
Switch(config)#int g0/1
Switch(config-if)#ip dhcp snooping trust
Switch(config-if)#no ip dhcp snooping information option
Switch(config-if)#end
```

Task 8:

We will request an IP address for the host again. Feel free to also use simulation mode.

```
C:\>ipconfig /renew

    IP Address......................: 192.168.1.2
    Subnet Mask.....................: 255.255.255.0
    Default Gateway.................: 192.168.1.1
    DNS Server......................: 0.0.0.0

C:\>
```

Task 9:

Optionally you can check the DHCP snooping binding table and compare the entry against the host MAC address.

```
Switch#show ip dhcp snooping binding
MacAddress          IpAddress       Lease(sec)   Type            VLAN   Interface
------------------  --------------  ----------   -------------   ----   ------------------
00:02:4A:63:92:85   192.168.1.2     86400        dhcp-snooping   1      FastEthernet0/1
Total number of bindings: 1
```

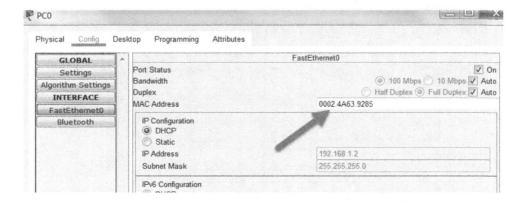

Notes:

DHCP snooping is an important security step you will want to take for your LAN protection.

Packet Tracer seems to allow only limited information to be allocated to hosts via DHCP, so don't worry if your DNS server or other parameters are not allocated.

Restricting Access via Access Lists

Lab Objective:
Learn how to restrict who can access the router by applying an access list.

Lab Purpose:
Access lists can be used to restrict access to networks, ports, and services, such as Telnet. You can apply them to physical ports as well as to virtual lines. This would be ideal if you want a management station to be able to connect to your router or switch only remotely.

Lab Tool:
Packet Tracer

Lab Topology:
Please use the following topology to complete this lab exercise:

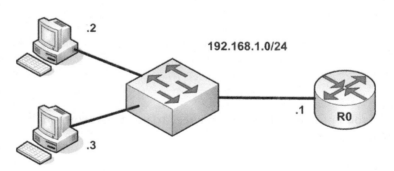

Lab Walkthrough:

Task 1:
Drag two PCs, one switch, and one router onto the canvas. Connect them all with straight-through cables.

Task 2:

Add the IP address on the router as indicated.

```
Router>en
Router#conf t
Enter configuration commands, one per line. End with CNTL/Z.
Router(config)#host R0
R0(config)#int f0/0
R0(config-if)#ip add 192.168.1.1 255.255.255.0
R0(config-if)#no shut
```

Task 3:

Add the IP addresses to both hosts. Here is the config for PC0:

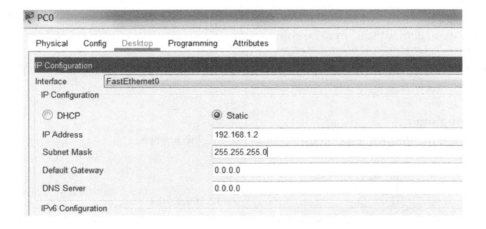

Task 4:

Configure the router for Telnet access. You need to put a password on the Telnet lines in order for them to work.

```
R0(config-if)#exit
R0(config)#line vty 0 15
R0(config-line)#password 101labs
R0(config-line)#login
```

Task 5:

On PC1 open a command prompt window and telnet to the router. You can type 'exit' to quit the session.

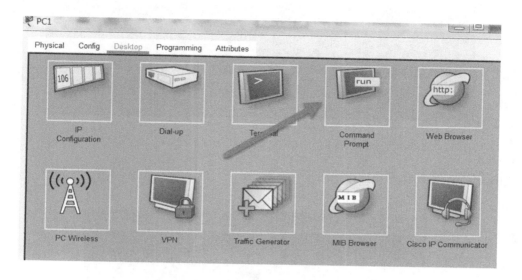

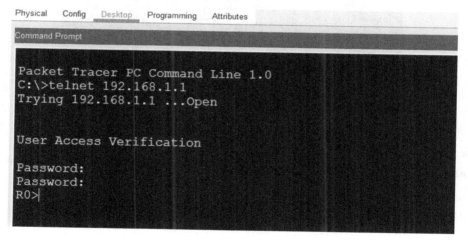

Task 6:

Configure an access list to permit only host 192.168.1.2 to telnet to the router.

```
R0(config)#access-list 1 permit host 192.168.1.2
R0(config)#line vty 0 15
R0(config-line)#access-class 1 in
R0(config-line)#end
R0#
```

Task 7:

Telnet to R0 once again from PC1. Exit the previous session first.

```
R0>exit

[Connection to 192.168.1.1 closed by foreign host]
C:\>telnet 192.168.1.1
Trying 192.168.1.1 ...
% Connection refused by remote host
C:\>
```

Task 8:

Telnet from PC0. It should work.

```
Command Prompt

Packet Tracer PC Command Line 1.0
C:\>telnet 192.168.1.1
Trying 192.168.1.1 ...Open


User Access Verification

Password:
R0>
```

Task 9:

Optionally, check the ACL usage on the router.

```
R0#show ip access-lists 1
Standard IP access list 1
permit host 192.168.1.2 (2 match(es))
```

Note:

Make sure you are familiar with this process because it's a specific syllabus entry.

5.0 Network Troubleshooting

Packet Sniffers

Lab Objective:
Learn how to use the Wireshark packet sniffer.

Lab Purpose:
Most network engineers avoid using packet sniffers because they don't understand them, but with just a couple of hours of effort you can become quite proficient. This lab will give you a basic introduction to Wireshark.

Lab Tool:
Any Windows PC

Lab Topology:
Please use the following topology to complete this lab exercise. I used a virtual Windows 10 PC running inside VirtualBox, but if you are using Windows, you can use your home PC. Just check your firewall settings don't block the test. I installed Wireshark onto my VM, but you can just as easily put it on your home PC and then remove it after your test.

Lab Walkthrough:

Task 1:

Pull up a command prompt by typing 'cmd' into the search box.

Task 2:

At the command prompt issue the 'ipconfig /all' command. Check which interface you are using to get internet access.

```
C:\Users\paulw>ipconfig /all

Windows IP Configuration

    Host Name . . . . . . . . . . . . : DESKTOP-RNLAPQ3
    Primary Dns Suffix  . . . . . . . :
    Node Type . . . . . . . . . . . . : Hybrid
    IP Routing Enabled. . . . . . . . : No
    WINS Proxy Enabled. . . . . . . . : No
    DNS Suffix Search List. . . . . . : localdomain

Ethernet adapter Ethernet:

    Connection-specific DNS Suffix  . : localdomain
    Description . . . . . . . . . . . : Intel(R) PRO/1000 MT Desktop Adapter
    Physical Address. . . . . . . . . : 08-00-27-07-D6-5B
    DHCP Enabled. . . . . . . . . . . : Yes
    Autoconfiguration Enabled . . . . : Yes
    Link-local IPv6 Address . . . . . : fe80::54b2:5b3e:5de2:fb13%6(Preferred)
    IPv4 Address. . . . . . . . . . . : 10.0.2.15(Preferred)
    Subnet Mask . . . . . . . . . . . : 255.255.255.0
    Lease Obtained. . . . . . . . . . : Monday, 3 September 2018 5:46:19 PM
```

Task 3:

Open Wireshark and confirm you are capturing packets (sniffing) on the correct interface. Click on the interface name to open the capture. Your interface name may differ from mine depending on your device and configuration.

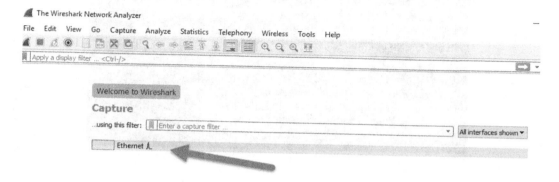

Task 4:

Press the interface name to open Wireshark. There will be some generic traffic already passing on the interface, but we want to send some specific traffic out and check the packet captures. Note that my Ethernet interface is 10.0.2.15.

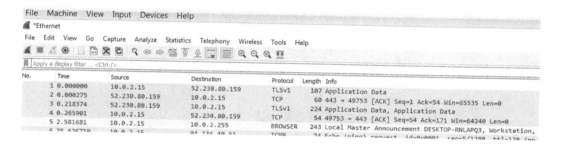

Task 5:

From a command prompt ping 101labs.net.

```
C:\Users\paulw>ping 101labs.net

Pinging 101labs.net [94.136.40.51] with 32 bytes of data:
Request timed out.
Reply from 94.136.40.51: bytes=32 time=371ms TTL=234
Reply from 94.136.40.51: bytes=32 time=386ms TTL=234
Reply from 94.136.40.51: bytes=32 time=370ms TTL=234

Ping statistics for 94.136.40.51:
    Packets: Sent = 4, Received = 3, Lost = 1 (25% loss),
Approximate round trip times in milli-seconds:
    Minimum = 370ms, Maximum = 386ms, Average = 375ms
```

Task 6:

Stop the captures (press the stop button) and then look at the Wireshark capture. You can click on individual packets to check the contents. The packets can be viewed at all OSI layers. Remember that ARP must be used to help our host encapsulate the packet with the address of the next hop. This is before the ping packet is sent. This is why you often see a timeout for the first ping packet.

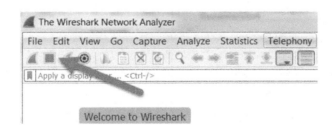

```
ICMP    74 Echo (ping) request  id=0x0001, seq=5/1280, ttl=128 (no response found
ARP     42 Who has 10.0.2.2? Tell 10.0.2.15
ARP     60 10.0.2.2 is at 52:54:00:12:35:02
ICMP    74 Echo (ping) request  id=0x0001, seq=6/1536, ttl=128 (reply in 10)
ICMP    74 Echo (ping) reply    id=0x0001, seq=6/1536, ttl=234 (request in 9)
ICMP    74 Echo (ping) request  id=0x0001, seq=7/1792, ttl=128 (reply in 12)
ICMP    74 Echo (ping) reply    id=0x0001, seq=7/1792, ttl=234 (request in 11)
ICMP    74 Echo (ping) request  id=0x0001, seq=8/2048, ttl=128 (reply in 14)
ICMP    74 Echo (ping) reply    id=0x0001, seq=8/2048, ttl=234 (request in 13)
```

Task 7:

Click on the layer 4 part of the first ICMP packet. Note the source (Src:) and destination (Dst:) addresses.

```
> Frame 9: 74 bytes on wire (592 bits), 74 bytes captured (592 bits) on interface 0
> Ethernet II, Src: PcsCompu_07:d6:5b (08:00:27:07:d6:5b), Dst: RealtekU_12:35:02 (52:54:00:12:35:02)
∨ Internet Protocol Version 4, Src: 10.0.2.15, Dst: 94.136.40.51
    0100 .... = Version: 4
    .... 0101 = Header Length: 20 bytes (5)
  > Differentiated Services Field: 0x00 (DSCP: CS0, ECN: Not-ECT)
    Total Length: 60
    Identification: 0x7b28 (31528)
  > Flags: 0x0000
    Time to live: 128
    Protocol: ICMP (1)
```

Task 8:

Click on the reply packet. Note where it matches the command line output for the first ping.

```
∨ Internet Control Message Protocol
    Type: 0 (Echo (ping) reply)
    Code: 0
    Checksum: 0x5555 [correct]
    [Checksum Status: Good]
    Identifier (BE): 1 (0x0001)
    Identifier (LE): 256 (0x0100)
    Sequence number (BE): 6 (0x0006)
    Sequence number (LE): 1536 (0x0600)
    [Request frame: 9]
    [Response time: 371.846 ms]    ⬅
  ∨ Data (32 bytes)
        Data: 6162636465666768696a6b6c6d6e6f707172737475767761...
        [Length: 32]
```

```
    Total Length: 60
    Identification: 0x05db (1499)
  > Flags: 0x0000
    Time to live: 234    ⬅
    Protocol: ICMP (1)
    Header checksum: 0x381c [validation disabled]
    [Header checksum status: Unverified]
    Source: 94.136.40.51
    Destination: 10.0.2.15
Internet Control Message Protocol
    Type: 0 (Echo (ping) reply)
    Code: 0
    Checksum: 0x5555 [correct]
    [Checksum Status: Good]
    Identifier (BE): 1 (0x0001)
    Identifier (LE): 256 (0x0100)
    Sequence number (BE): 6 (0x0006)
    Sequence number (LE): 1536 (0x0600)
    [Request frame: 9]
    [Response time: 371.846 ms]
```

Task 9:

Finally, find any TCP packet with [RST, ACK] bits. Drill down into the frame until you find them. They are not actually used for ping traffic, but it's important you know where to find them. Don't worry if they are turned on (1) or off (0).

```
  19 45.893032     131.253.33.254     10.0.2.15          TCP       60 443 → 49893 [RST, ACK] Seq=1 Ack=1 Win=65535 Len=0

      [Stream index: 1]
      [TCP Segment Len: 0]
      Sequence number: 1     (relative sequence number)
      [Next sequence number: 1     (relative sequence number)]
      Acknowledgment number: 1     (relative ack number)
      0101 .... = Header Length: 20 bytes (5)
    ∨ Flags: 0x014 (RST, ACK)
         000. .... .... = Reserved: Not set
         ...0 .... .... = Nonce: Not set
         .... 0... .... = Congestion Window Reduced (CWR): Not set
         .... .0.. .... = ECN-Echo: Not set
         .... ..0. .... = Urgent: Not set
         .... ...1 .... = Acknowledgment: Set
         .... .... 0... = Push: Not set
       > .... .... .1.. = Reset: Set
         .... .... ..0. = Syn: Not set
         .... .... ...0 = Fin: Not set
         [TCP Flags: ·······A·R··]
```

Notes:

I strongly recommend you learn Wireshark. It takes only a couple of hours. We have a course at **www.howtonetwork.com** if you want to check it out.

I'm sure you have read about three-way handshakes in your study guide. Feel free to redo this lab, but this time searching for a telnet host. Then check for the [RST, ACK] bits.

Using a WiFi Analyzer

Lab Objective:

Learn how to use a WiFi analyzer.

Lab Purpose:

One of the syllabus requirements is using a WiFi analyzer. This can be used for a site survey for planning the installation of a wireless router or access point or for a security test.

Lab Tool:

Any MAC OS or Windows device with a wireless card. I downloaded NetSpot (free edition) from https://www.netspotapp.com/.

Lab Topology:

Please use your home PC or laptop running Windows or MAC OS. The NetSpot page specifies what it can run on.

Lab Walkthrough:

Task 1:

Download and install NetSpot. It's pretty straightforward.

Task 2:

Open NetSpot and it should start on the DISCOVER page. I live in a quiet village, so you will get far better results if you are in a shopping center or busy street. It's discovered my wireless networks and Roku device.

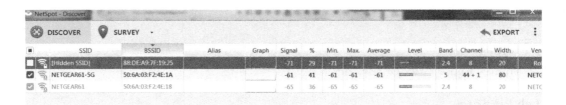

Task 3:

Hover your mouse over each title to get more details. You can see one column indicates the mode, such as 802.11a, b, g, n, etc.

rage	Level	Band	Channel	Width	Vendor	Sec...	Mode	Last seen
71		2.4	8	20	Roku	WP...	n	36 s ago
57		2.4	8	20	NETGEAR	WP...	n	6 s ago
61		5	44 + 1	80	NETGEAR	WP...	n	6 s ago

Task 4:

Double-click one of the devices and you will see a graph indicating signal strength, security changes, channel changes, etc. Click on 'Tabular Data' to see the below details (yours will differ of course).

Time	Signal	Channel	Security mode		
				Summary	
11:47:21 AM	-73	8	WPA2 Personal	Total entries:	**15**
11:46:51 AM	-72	8	WPA2 Personal	Active entries:	**14** ~ 93.3%
11:46:20 AM	-72	8	WPA2 Personal	First seen:	at **11:40:19 AM**
11:45:50 AM	-72	8	WPA2 Personal	Last seen:	at **11:47:21 AM**
11:45:20 AM	-72	8	WPA2 Personal	Max. signal:	-71 dBm
11:44:49 AM	-	-	-		at **11:44:19 AM**
11:44:19 AM	-71	8	WPA2 Personal	Min. signal:	-96 dBm
11:43:48 AM	-71	8	WPA2 Personal		at **11:44:49 AM**
11:43:18 AM	-71	8	WPA2 Personal	Channel was	**never**
11:42:48 AM	-71	8	WPA2 Personal	changed:	
11:42:17 AM	-71	8	WPA2 Personal	Security was	**never**
11:41:47 AM	-71	8	WPA2 Personal	changed:	
11:41:16 AM	-71	8	WPA2 Personal		
11:40:46 AM	-71	8	WPA2 Personal		
11:40:19 AM	-71	8	WPA2 Personal		

Tabs: Signal | Tabular Data | Channels 2.4 GHz | Channels 5 GHz

88:DE:A9:7F:19:25 - [Hidden SSID]

Note:

You will learn more about wireless scanners if you take any wireless networking exam or wireless security exam.

Bandwidth Speed Tester

Lab Objective:

Learn how to check your bandwidth speed with an online testing tool.

Lab Purpose:

Learn how to check your bandwidth speed.

Lab Tool:

Any web browser

Lab Topology:

You can use any device which supports web browsing, or install a speed-testing app on your phone. Bear in mind that you will get different results if you use a wireless connection at home or Ethernet. If you use your phone, you need to turn off either your data or your wireless depending on which you want to check.

Lab Walkthrough:

Task 1:
Pull up **www.speedtest.net** or your favorite speed-testing service.

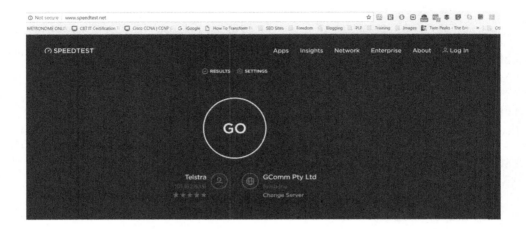

Task 2:
Watch the download speed test take place.

Task 3:

The upload speed test will start automatically.

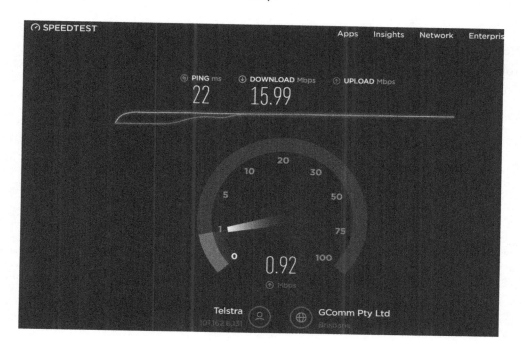

Task 4:

The final speed test results will be displayed.

Task 5:

If you are making configuration changes, then note the results, make the changes, and then run the test again.

Note:

You can purchase specialized WAN testing tools; however, these can prove very expensive.

LAB 86

Ping Command

Lab Objective:

Learn how to use the ping command and its switches.

Lab Purpose:

Ping is short for Packet Internet Groper. It's a TCP/IP service which runs on ICMP and reports on the IP connectivity of network devices. Bear in mind that firewalls and ACLs can block ICMP, so the fact a ping fails may not indicate that the device is down. You would use ping along with traceroute and other tools.

Lab Tool:

Any Windows PC

Lab Topology:

Please use the following topology to complete this lab exercise. I used a virtual Windows 10 PC running inside VirtualBox, but if you are using Windows, you can use your home PC. Just check your firewall settings don't block the test.

Lab Walkthrough:

Task 1:

Pull up a command prompt by typing 'cmd' into the search box.

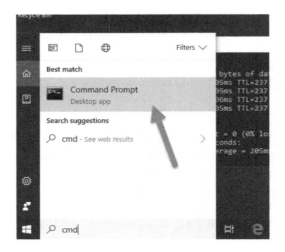

Task 2:

At the command prompt issue the 'ping /?' command. Check your study guide for more information on all the available switches.

```
C:\Users\owner>ping /?

Usage: ping [-t] [-a] [-n count] [-l size] [-f] [-i TTL] [-v TOS]
            [-r count] [-s count] [[-j host-list] | [-k host-list]]
            [-w timeout] [-R] [-S srcaddr] [-4] [-6] target_name

Options:
    -t             Ping the specified host until stopped.
                   To see statistics and continue - type Control-Break;
                   To stop - type Control-C.
    -a             Resolve addresses to hostnames.
    -n count       Number of echo requests to send.
    -l size        Send buffer size.
    -f             Set Don't Fragment flag in packet (IPv4-only).
    -i TTL         Time To Live.
    -v TOS         Type Of Service (IPv4-only. This setting has been deprecated
                   and has no effect on the type of service field in the IP Head
er).
    -r count       Record route for count hops (IPv4-only).
    -s count       Timestamp for count hops (IPv4-only).
    -j host-list   Loose source route along host-list (IPv4-only).
    -k host-list   Strict source route along host-list (IPv4-only).
    -w timeout     Timeout in milliseconds to wait for each reply.
    -R             Use routing header to test reverse route also (IPv6-only).
    -S srcaddr     Source address to use.
    -4             Force using IPv4.
    -6             Force using IPv6.
```

Task 3:

Ping our website, 101labs.net, and note the output. Yours will differ from mine, especially if my site moves hosting companies.

You will see the URL is resolved to an IP address, the ping packet is 32 bytes, the time to live before the packet expires is 235 milliseconds, and the responses vary from 363 to 402 ms. Four ping packets were sent, and all four received a response.

```
C:\Users\owner>ping 101labs.net

Pinging 101labs.net [94.136.40.51] with 32 bytes of data:
Reply from 94.136.40.51: bytes=32 time=364ms TTL=235
Reply from 94.136.40.51: bytes=32 time=402ms TTL=235
Reply from 94.136.40.51: bytes=32 time=364ms TTL=235
Reply from 94.136.40.51: bytes=32 time=363ms TTL=235

Ping statistics for 94.136.40.51:
    Packets: Sent = 4, Received = 4, Lost = 0 (0% loss),
Approximate round trip times in milli-seconds:
    Minimum = 363ms, Maximum = 402ms, Average = 373ms
```

Task 4:

Find the IP address of your home router and issue a ping to repeat until you stop it with the Ctrl and C keys (ping -t). DO NOT try this at work. DO NOT ping a public IP address or you may be accused of a hacking attempt. You can find your home router IP through the admin panel or 'ipconfig /all'.

Your home firewall may block this if you have it so configured.

```
C:\Users\owner>ipconfig /all

Windows IP Configuration

    Host Name . . . . . . . . . . . . : owner-PC
    Primary Dns Suffix  . . . . . . . :
    Node Type . . . . . . . . . . . . : Hybrid
    IP Routing Enabled. . . . . . . . : No
    WINS Proxy Enabled. . . . . . . . : No

Wireless LAN adapter Wireless Network Connection 7:

    Connection-specific DNS Suffix  . :
    Description . . . . . . . . . . . : NETGEAR A6100 WiFi Adapter
    Physical Address. . . . . . . . . : 2C-30-33-A7-8D-9E
    DHCP Enabled. . . . . . . . . . . : Yes
    Autoconfiguration Enabled . . . . : Yes
    IPv4 Address. . . . . . . . . . . : 192.168.0.12(Preferred)
    Subnet Mask . . . . . . . . . . . : 255.255.255.0
    Lease Obtained. . . . . . . . . . : Monday, 3 September 2018 6:55:50 AM
    Lease Expires . . . . . . . . . . : Tuesday, 4 September 2018 6:56:06 AM
    Default Gateway . . . . . . . . . : 192.168.0.1
    DHCP Server . . . . . . . . . . . : 192.168.0.1
    DNS Servers . . . . . . . . . . . : 192.168.0.1
    NetBIOS over Tcpip. . . . . . . . : Enabled
```

```
C:\Users\owner>ping -t 192.168.0.1

Pinging 192.168.0.1 with 32 bytes of data:
Reply from 192.168.0.1: bytes=32 time=3ms TTL=64
Reply from 192.168.0.1: bytes=32 time=3ms TTL=64
Reply from 192.168.0.1: bytes=32 time=3ms TTL=64
Reply from 192.168.0.1: bytes=32 time=3ms TTL=64
Reply from 192.168.0.1: bytes=32 time=1ms TTL=64
Reply from 192.168.0.1: bytes=32 time=1ms TTL=64
Reply from 192.168.0.1: bytes=32 time=3ms TTL=64
Reply from 192.168.0.1: bytes=32 time=2ms TTL=64
Reply from 192.168.0.1: bytes=32 time=3ms TTL=64
Reply from 192.168.0.1: bytes=32 time=1ms TTL=64

Ping statistics for 192.168.0.1:
    Packets: Sent = 10, Received = 10, Lost = 0 (0% loss),
Approximate round trip times in milli-seconds:
    Minimum = 1ms, Maximum = 3ms, Average = 2ms
Control-C
^C
```

Task 5:

Ping 101labs.net again. This time specify five ping packets to be sent (instead of four) and set the packet size to 1500 bytes (instead of the default 32). The command is 'ping -n 5 -l 1500 101labs.net').

```
C:\Users\owner>ping -n 5 -l 1500 101labs.net

Pinging 101labs.net [94.136.40.51] with 1500 bytes of data:
Reply from 94.136.40.51: bytes=1500 time=377ms TTL=235
Reply from 94.136.40.51: bytes=1500 time=376ms TTL=235
Reply from 94.136.40.51: bytes=1500 time=377ms TTL=235
Reply from 94.136.40.51: bytes=1500 time=376ms TTL=235
Reply from 94.136.40.51: bytes=1500 time=377ms TTL=235

Ping statistics for 94.136.40.51:
    Packets: Sent = 5, Received = 5, Lost = 0 (0% loss),
Approximate round trip times in milli-seconds:
    Minimum = 376ms, Maximum = 377ms, Average = 376ms
```

Notes:

Ping is a useful troubleshooting tool, but you will often use it in conjunction with other command line tools to gather information before coming to a conclusion. Many websites and ISPs block ping traffic, so find one on which it works.

LAB 87

Tracert Command

Lab Objective:

Learn how to use the tracert command and its switches.

Lab Purpose:

Tracert is one of many command line tools you can use to troubleshoot network issues. On Cisco and Unix-type devices you would use the 'traceroute' command, but on Windows it's 'tracert'. Bear in mind that firewalls, access lists, and load balancers can all affect the output of the command.

Lab Tool:

Any Windows PC

Lab Topology:

Please use the following topology to complete this lab exercise. I used a virtual Windows 10 PC running inside VirtualBox, but if you are using Windows, you can use your home PC. Just check your firewall settings don't block the test.

Lab Walkthrough:

Task 1:

Pull up a command prompt by typing 'cmd' into the search box.

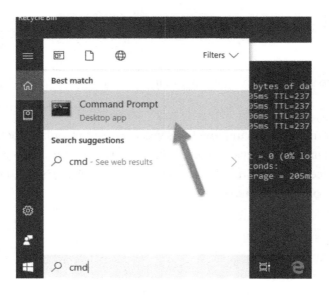

Task 2:

At the command prompt issue the 'tracert /?' command. Check your study guide for more information on all the available switches.

```
C:\Users\paulw>tracert /?

Usage: tracert [-d] [-h maximum_hops] [-j host-list] [-w timeout]
               [-R] [-S srcaddr] [-4] [-6] target_name

Options:
    -d                 Do not resolve addresses to hostnames.
    -h maximum_hops    Maximum number of hops to search for target.
    -j host-list       Loose source route along host-list (IPv4-only).
    -w timeout         Wait timeout milliseconds for each reply.
    -R                 Trace round-trip path (IPv6-only).
    -S srcaddr         Source address to use (IPv6-only).
    -4                 Force using IPv4.
    -6                 Force using IPv6.

C:\Users\paulw>_
```

Task 3:

Issue a 'tracert cisco.com' command. Note that your hops will differ from mine! The output pushed the command off the screen but I entered it at the start.

```
Command Prompt

1    <1 ms     <1 ms     <1 ms   10.0.2.2
2    1851 ms    1 ms      1 ms   www.routerlogin.com [192.168.0.1]
3    22 ms     23 ms     22 ms   172.18.212.11
4    *         23 ms     22 ms   172.18.69.141
5    24 ms     32 ms     25 ms   bundle-ether4.woo-edge902.brisbane.telstra.net [203.50.44.42]
6    29 ms     24 ms     25 ms   bundle-ether6.woo-core1.brisbane.telstra.net [203.50.11.138]
7    35 ms     37 ms    134 ms   bundle-ether20.chw-core10.sydney.telstra.net [203.50.11.180]
8    40 ms     37 ms     38 ms   bundle-ether1.oxf-gw11.sydney.telstra.net [203.50.6.93]
9    *         *         44 ms   bundle-ether1.sydo-core03.sydney.reach.com [203.50.13.98]
10   50 ms     44 ms     44 ms   i-0-1-0-15.sydo-core04.bi.telstraglobal.net [202.84.222.54]
11   *         *        174 ms   i-10604.1wlt-core02.telstraglobal.net [202.84.141.225]
12   *         *        173 ms   i-93.tlot02.bi.telstraglobal.net [202.84.253.86]
13   276 ms    179 ms   172 ms   l3-peer.tlot02.pr.telstraglobal.net [134.159.61.46]
14   *         *        203 ms   ae-4-13.edge5.Dallas3.Level3.net [4.69.208.233]
15   204 ms    211 ms   237 ms   CISCO-SYSTE.edge5.Dallas3.Level3.net [4.59.34.66]
16   204 ms    205 ms   214 ms   rcdn9-cd1-dmzbb-gw1-ten1-1.cisco.com [72.163.0.5]
17   210 ms    221 ms   226 ms   rcdn9-cd1-dmzdcc-gw1-por1.cisco.com [72.163.0.178]
18   211 ms    219 ms   213 ms   rcdn9-16b-dcz05n-gw2-por1.cisco.com [72.163.2.102]
19   240 ms    205 ms   206 ms   redirect-ns.cisco.com [72.163.4.185]

Trace complete.
```

Task 4:

Note which addresses are private (RFC1918). Note when the trace leaves your home network and reaches your ISP (in my case telstra.net).

Note that each hop is tested three times and the output is in milliseconds.

Note any drops, as indicated by an asterisk (*). With three * markers the packet may fail, or an alternative route may be found.

Note the big leap in delay at step 11.

Notes:

Test the various switches available. Also, ping using just an website IP address. Note also that there is a DNS lookup for the IP address associated with the hostname before the tracert command can execute.

nslookup Command

Lab Objective:

Learn how to use the nslookup command and its switches.

Lab Purpose:

Nslookup is short for nameserver lookup. It's a powerful command line tool available on any operating system and used to query DNS domain names or IP address mappings. You would use it to troubleshoot DNS issues on your hosts or server.

Lab Tool:

Any Windows PC

Lab Topology:

Please use the following topology to complete this lab exercise. I used a virtual Windows 10 PC running inside VirtualBox, but if you are using Windows, you can use your home PC. Just check your firewall settings don't block the test.

Lab Walkthrough:

Task 1:

Pull up a command prompt by typing 'cmd' into the search box.

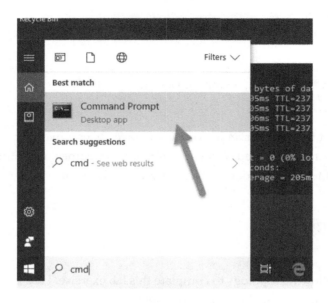

Task 2:

At the command prompt issue the 'nslookup /?' command. Check your study guide for more information on all the available switches.

```
C:\Users\owner>nslookup /?
Usage:
    nslookup [-opt ...]            # interactive mode using default server
    nslookup [-opt ...] - server   # interactive mode using 'server'
    nslookup [-opt ...] host       # just look up 'host' using default server
    nslookup [-opt ...] host server # just look up 'host' using 'server'

C:\Users\owner>
```

Task 3:

Issue an nslookup for IP address 72.163.4.185. Notice that my home router 192.168.0.1) is providing the entry. This is a reverse lookup—i.e., finding which website is associated with which IP address.

```
C:\Users\owner>nslookup 72.163.4.185
Server:    www.routerlogin.com
Address:   192.168.0.1

Name:      redirect-ns.cisco.com
Address:   72.163.4.185
```

Task 4:

We have discovered which website is associated with the above IP address. Now, let's determine which mail servers are present for that domain with the 'nslookup -querytype=mx cisco.com' command. If your output is 'Non-authoritative answer', it means the response came from a cached entry and not the authoritative server for that domain.

```
C:\Users\owner>nslookup -querytype=mx cisco.com
Server:    www.routerlogin.com
Address:   192.168.0.1

Non-authoritative answer:
cisco.com        MX preference = 30, mail exchanger = aer-mx-01.cisco.com
cisco.com        MX preference = 20, mail exchanger = rcdn-mx-01.cisco.com
cisco.com        MX preference = 10, mail exchanger = alln-mx-01.cisco.com

cisco.com        nameserver = ns1.cisco.com
cisco.com        nameserver = ns3.cisco.com
cisco.com        nameserver = ns2.cisco.com
alln-mx-01.cisco.com    internet address = 173.37.147.230
rcdn-mx-01.cisco.com    internet address = 72.163.7.166
aer-mx-01.cisco.com     internet address = 173.38.212.150
ns1.cisco.com    internet address = 72.163.5.201
ns2.cisco.com    internet address = 64.102.255.44
ns3.cisco.com    internet address = 173.37.146.41
alln-mx-01.cisco.com    AAAA IPv6 address = 2001:420:1201:6::ad25:93e6
aer-mx-01.cisco.com     AAAA IPv6 address = 2001:420:4621::ad26:d496
ns1.cisco.com    AAAA IPv6 address = 2001:420:1101:6::a
ns2.cisco.com    AAAA IPv6 address = 2001:420:2041:5000::a
ns3.cisco.com    AAAA IPv6 address = 2001:420:1201:7::a
```

Task 5:

Query one of the Google DNS servers to do the same lookup. The Google DNS servers (free to use for anybody) are 8.8.8.8 and 8.8.4.4. This time I've also been provided with the IPv6 address.

```
C:\Users\owner>nslookup cisco.com 8.8.8.8
Server:  google-public-dns-a.google.com
Address:  8.8.8.8

Non-authoritative answer:
Name:    cisco.com
Addresses:  2001:420:1101:1::185
            72.163.4.185
```

Note:

There are many other options inside nslookup, including a verbose debugging facility and a command line tool.

IPConfig Command

Lab Objective:

Learn how to use the ipconfig command and its switches.

Lab Purpose:

Ipconfig is short for IP configuration. It's a Windows command designed to display current TCP/IP network configurations, but it can also be used to modify your DNS and DHCP settings.

Lab Tool:

Any Windows PC

Lab Topology:

Please use the following topology to complete this lab exercise. I used a virtual Windows 10 PC running inside VirtualBox, but if you are using Windows, you can use your home PC. Just check your firewall settings don't block the test.

Lab Walkthrough:

Task 1:

Pull up a command prompt by typing 'cmd' into the search box.

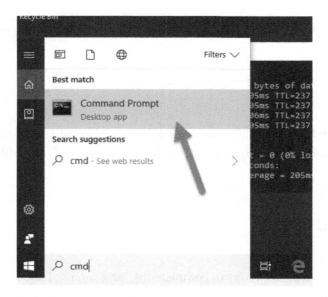

Task 2:

At the command prompt issue the 'ipconfig /?' command. Check your study guide for more information on all the available switches.

```
C:\Users\owner>ipconfig /?

USAGE:
    ipconfig [/allcompartments] [/? | /all |
                                 /renew [adapter] | /release [adapter] |
                                 /renew6 [adapter] | /release6 [adapter] |
                                 /flushdns | /displaydns | /registerdns |
                                 /showclassid adapter |
                                 /setclassid adapter [classid] |
                                 /showclassid6 adapter |
                                 /setclassid6 adapter [classid] ]

where
    adapter             Connection name
                        (wildcard characters × and ? allowed, see examples)

    Options:
       /?               Display this help message
       /all             Display full configuration information.
       /release         Release the IPv4 address for the specified adapter.
       /release6        Release the IPv6 address for the specified adapter.
       /renew           Renew the IPv4 address for the specified adapter.
       /renew6          Renew the IPv6 address for the specified adapter.
       /flushdns        Purges the DNS Resolver cache.
       /registerdns     Refreshes all DHCP leases and re-registers DNS names
       /displaydns      Display the contents of the DNS Resolver Cache.
       /showclassid     Displays all the dhcp class IDs allowed for adapter.
       /setclassid      Modifies the dhcp class id.
       /showclassid6    Displays all the IPv6 DHCP class IDs allowed for adapter

       /setclassid6     Modifies the IPv6 DHCP class id.

The default is to display only the IP address, subnet mask and
default gateway for each adapter bound to TCP/IP.

For Release and Renew, if no adapter name is specified, then the IP address
leases for all adapters bound to TCP/IP will be released or renewed.

For Setclassid and Setclassid6, if no ClassId is specified, then the ClassId is
removed.

Examples:
    > ipconfig                     ... Show information
    > ipconfig /all                ... Show detailed information
    > ipconfig /renew              ... renew all adapters
    > ipconfig /renew EL*          ... renew any connection that has its
                                       name starting with EL
    > ipconfig /release ×Con×      ... release all matching connections,
                                       eg. "Local Area Connection 1" or
                                           "Local Area Connection 2"
    > ipconfig /allcompartments    ... Show information about all
                                       compartments
    > ipconfig /allcompartments /all ... Show detailed information about all
                                         compartments
```

Task 3:

You can start with a very basic output which will print your IP address, subnet mask, and default gateway for all your network adapters. Of course my output will differ from yours. You can see I'm running some virtualization software on my PC, and interestingly, my Ethernet adapter is disconnected (I'm using wireless). This command will give you some important information to start with. You now know your default gateway and IP address.

```
C:\Users\owner>ipconfig

Windows IP Configuration


Wireless LAN adapter Wireless Network Connection 7:

   Connection-specific DNS Suffix  . :
   IPv4 Address. . . . . . . . . . . : 192.168.0.12
   Subnet Mask . . . . . . . . . . . : 255.255.255.0
   Default Gateway . . . . . . . . . : 192.168.0.1

Ethernet adapter Local Area Connection:

   Media State . . . . . . . . . . . : Media disconnected
   Connection-specific DNS Suffix  . :

Ethernet adapter VMware Network Adapter VMnet1:

   Connection-specific DNS Suffix  . : localdomain
   Link-local IPv6 Address . . . . . : fe80::7112:cbf6:b8f2:6984%14
   IPv4 Address. . . . . . . . . . . : 192.168.157.1
   Subnet Mask . . . . . . . . . . . : 255.255.255.0
   Default Gateway . . . . . . . . . :

Ethernet adapter VirtualBox Host-Only Network:

   Connection-specific DNS Suffix  . :
   Link-local IPv6 Address . . . . . : fe80::ed19:aa94:941:2e2e%28
   IPv4 Address. . . . . . . . . . . : 192.168.56.1
   Subnet Mask . . . . . . . . . . . : 255.255.255.0
   Default Gateway . . . . . . . . . :
```

Task 4:

Issue the 'ipconfig /all' command. You can see far more information printed, including the MAC address, lease details, DNS server, etc. This command generates far more detail you would use to troubleshoot issues.

```
C:\Users\owner>ipconfig /all

Windows IP Configuration

    Host Name . . . . . . . . . . . . : owner-PC
    Primary Dns Suffix  . . . . . . . :
    Node Type . . . . . . . . . . . . : Hybrid
    IP Routing Enabled. . . . . . . . : No
    WINS Proxy Enabled. . . . . . . . : No

Wireless LAN adapter Wireless Network Connection 7:

    Connection-specific DNS Suffix  . :
    Description . . . . . . . . . . . : NETGEAR A6100 WiFi Adapter
    Physical Address. . . . . . . . . : 2C-30-33-A7-8D-9E
    DHCP Enabled. . . . . . . . . . . : Yes
    Autoconfiguration Enabled . . . . : Yes
    IPv4 Address. . . . . . . . . . . : 192.168.0.12(Preferred)
    Subnet Mask . . . . . . . . . . . : 255.255.255.0
    Lease Obtained. . . . . . . . . . : Saturday, 1 September 2018 9:25:14 AM
    Lease Expires . . . . . . . . . . : Sunday, 2 September 2018 9:25:14 AM
    Default Gateway . . . . . . . . . : 192.168.0.1
    DHCP Server . . . . . . . . . . . : 192.168.0.1
    DNS Servers . . . . . . . . . . . : 192.168.0.1
    NetBIOS over Tcpip. . . . . . . . : Enabled
```

Task 5:

Release and renew your IP address using the 'ipconfig /release' and 'ipconfig /renew' commands. I've cropped some of the output to save space. I've been allocated the same IP address. The results of 'ipconfig /renew' are shown below.

```
C:\Users\owner>ipconfig /renew

Windows IP Configuration

No operation can be performed on Local Area Connection while it has its media di
sconnected.

Wireless LAN adapter Wireless Network Connection 7:

    Connection-specific DNS Suffix  . :
    IPv4 Address. . . . . . . . . . . : 192.168.0.12
    Subnet Mask . . . . . . . . . . . : 255.255.255.0
    Default Gateway . . . . . . . . . : 192.168.0.1
```

Task 6:

Issue the 'ipconfig /displaydns' command. It will print the contents of the DNS client resolver cache, which includes your local host file and any queries resolved recently by your computer. The list could be pretty long, so I cropped my output. If you are on a virtual machine, you will need to ping a few websites first or visit some websites!

You can research the output on your own time, I'm sure.

```
C:\Users\owner> ipconfig /displaydns

Windows IP Configuration

    0.docs.google.com
    ----------------------------------------
    Record Name . . . . . : 0.docs.google.com
    Record Type . . . . . : 5
    Time To Live  . . . . : 185
    Data Length . . . . . : 8
    Section . . . . . . . : Answer
    CNAME Record  . . . . : browserchannel-sites.1.google.com


    sa.bbc.co.uk
    ----------------------------------------
    Record Name . . . . . : sa.bbc.co.uk
    Record Type . . . . . : 5
    Time To Live  . . . . : 9
    Data Length . . . . . : 8
    Section . . . . . . . : Answer
    CNAME Record  . . . . : bbc01.sitestat.com


    www.google-analytics.com
    ----------------------------------------
    Record Name . . . . . : www.google-analytics.com
    Record Type . . . . . : 5
    Time To Live  . . . . : 143
    Data Length . . . . . : 8
    Section . . . . . . . : Answer
    CNAME Record  . . . . : www-google-analytics.1.google.com
```

Task 7:

You can clear your DNS cache with the 'ipconfig /flushdns' command. (Avoid doing this if you are at work, please!) After that, check your DNS cache. Mine has only one entry left (out of around 30).

```
C:\Users\owner>ipconfig /flushdns

Windows IP Configuration

Successfully flushed the DNS Resolver Cache.

C:\Users\owner>ipconfig /displaydns

Windows IP Configuration

    play.google.com
    ----------------------------------------
    Record Name . . . . . : play.google.com
    Record Type . . . . . : 1
    Time To Live  . . . . : 266
    Data Length . . . . . : 4
    Section . . . . . . . : Answer
    A (Host) Record . . . : 216.58.200.110
```

Note:

If you suspect your host has issues with connectivity, then 'ipconfig' is your go-to command.

LAB 90

iptables Command

Lab Objective:

Learn about the iptables command and some of its switches.

Lab Purpose:

Most Linux distributions ship with various firewall tools. One such firewall tool is iptables, which can match packets crossing the network interface against a set of rules to decide whether to permit or deny them.

Lab Tool:

Ubuntu VM

Lab Topology:

Please use the following topology to complete this lab exercise. I used a virtual Ubuntu PC running inside VirtualBox. You will need to run all commands as an administrator or prefix them with 'sudo'.

Lab Walkthrough:

Task 1:

Pull up a terminal by typing 'terminal' into the search box.

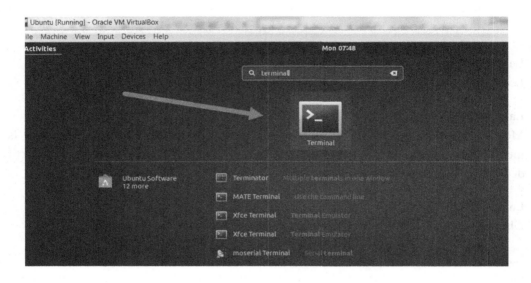

Task 2:

At the command prompt issue the 'sudo iptables --help' command. Check your documentation for more information on all the available switches. You will clearly see here that there are a large number of parameters.

```
paul@paul-VirtualBox:~$ iptables --help
iptables v1.6.1

Usage: iptables -[ACD] chain rule-specification [options]
       iptables -I chain [rulenum] rule-specification [options]
       iptables -R chain rulenum rule-specification [options]
       iptables -D chain rulenum [options]
       iptables -[LS] [chain [rulenum]] [options]
       iptables -[FZ] [chain] [options]
       iptables -[NX] chain
       iptables -E old-chain-name new-chain-name
       iptables -P chain target [options]
       iptables -h (print this help information)

Commands:
Either long or short options are allowed.
  --append    -A chain              Append to chain
  --check     -C chain              Check for the existence of a rule
  --delete    -D chain              Delete matching rule from chain
  --delete    -D chain rulenum
                                    Delete rule rulenum (1 = first) from chain
  --insert    -I chain [rulenum]
                                    Insert in chain as rulenum (default 1=first)
  --replace   -R chain rulenum
                                    Replace rule rulenum (1 = first) in chain
  --list      -L [chain [rulenum]]
                                    List the rules in a chain or all chains
  --list-rules -S [chain [rulenum]]
                                    Print the rules in a chain or all chains
  --flush     -F [chain]            Delete all rules in  chain or all chains
  --zero      -Z [chain [rulenum]]
                                    Zero counters in chain or all chains
  --new       -N chain             Create a new user-defined chain
  --delete-chain
              -X [chain]            Delete a user-defined chain
  --policy    -P chain target      Change policy on chain to target
```

Task 3:

We will issue one configuration command to get some hands-on practice. The command is 'sudo iptables -A INPUT -m conntrack --ctstate ESTABLISHED,RELATED -j ACCEPT'.

'A INPUT' means that the rule will be added to the end of the chain of the current rules on the INPUT chain. '-m conntrack' refers to a set of modules providing extra capabilities. '--ctstate' refers to matching packets that are associated with an established connection—in this case an ESTABLISHED connection examining RELATED packets. '-j ACCEPT' means the packets will be permitted.

```
ties    Terminal                                    Mon 08:56
                                            paul@paul-VirtualBox: ~

  File Edit View Search Terminal Help
  paul@paul-VirtualBox:~$ sudo iptables -A INPUT -m conntrack --ctstate ESTABLISHED,RELATED -j ACCEPT
  [sudo] password for paul:
```

Task 4:

We can check the current iptables configuration with the 'sudo iptables -L' command. You must use an uppercase L for the switch.

```
paul@paul-VirtualBox:~$ sudo iptables -L
Chain INPUT (policy ACCEPT)
target     prot opt source            destination
ACCEPT     all  --  anywhere          anywhere               ctstate RELATED,ESTABLISHED

Chain FORWARD (policy ACCEPT)
target     prot opt source            destination

Chain OUTPUT (policy ACCEPT)
```

Task 5:

Next we will permit SSH traffic with the 'sudo iptables -A INPUT -p tcp --dport 22 -j ACCEPT' command. '-p tcp' matches TCP packets, and '-dport' I'm sure you will already have worked out is the destination port.

```
paul@paul-VirtualBox:~$ sudo iptables -A INPUT -p tcp --dport 22 -j ACCEPT
```

Task 6:

Check the iptables again.

```
paul@paul-VirtualBox:~$ sudo iptables -L
Chain INPUT (policy ACCEPT)
target     prot opt source               destination
ACCEPT     all  --  anywhere             anywhere             ctstate RELATED,ESTABLISHED
ACCEPT     tcp  --  anywhere             anywhere             tcp dpt:ssh

Chain FORWARD (policy ACCEPT)
target     prot opt source               destination

Chain OUTPUT (policy ACCEPT)
target     prot opt source               destination
paul@paul-VirtualBox:~$
```

Task 7:

Finally we need to clear the iptables with the 'sudo iptables -F' command and then check the tables again.

```
paul@paul-VirtualBox:~$ sudo iptables -F
paul@paul-VirtualBox:~$ sudo iptables -L
Chain INPUT (policy ACCEPT)
target     prot opt source               destination

Chain FORWARD (policy ACCEPT)
target     prot opt source               destination

Chain OUTPUT (policy ACCEPT)
target     prot opt source               destination
paul@paul-VirtualBox:~$
```

Notes:

To filter IPv6 packets use the 'ip6tables' command.

LAB 91

netstat Command

Lab Objective:
Learn how to use the netstat command and its switches.

Lab Purpose:
Netstat is short for network statistics. It's another command line tool and is used to display network connections for TCP, routing tables, and various network interface statistics. It is available on Linux, Solaris, Windows, and BSD. You would typically use it to troubleshoot network issues, determine traffic details, and measure performance.

Lab Tool:
Any Windows PC

Lab Topology:
Please use the following topology to complete this lab exercise. I used a virtual Windows 10 PC running inside VirtualBox, but if you are using Windows, you can use your home PC. Just check your firewall settings don't block the test.

Lab Walkthrough:

Task 1:

Pull up a command prompt by typing 'cmd' into the search box.

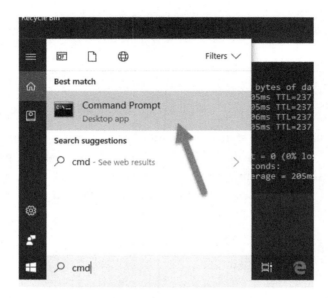

Task 2:

At the command prompt issue the 'netstat /?' command. Check your study guide for more information on all the available switches.

```
C:\Users\owner>netstat /?

Displays protocol statistics and current TCP/IP network connections.

NETSTAT [-a] [-b] [-e] [-f] [-n] [-o] [-p proto] [-r] [-s] [-t] [interval]

    -a            Displays all connections and listening ports.
    -b            Displays the executable involved in creating each connection or
                  listening port. In some cases well-known executables host
                  multiple independent components, and in these cases the
                  sequence of components involved in creating the connection
                  or listening port is displayed. In this case the executable
                  name is in [] at the bottom, on top is the component it called,
                  and so forth until TCP/IP was reached. Note that this option
                  can be time-consuming and will fail unless you have sufficient
                  permissions.
    -e            Displays Ethernet statistics. This may be combined with the -s
                  option.
    -f            Displays Fully Qualified Domain Names (FQDN) for foreign
                  addresses.
    -n            Displays addresses and port numbers in numerical form.
    -o            Displays the owning process ID associated with each connection.
    -p proto      Shows connections for the protocol specified by proto; proto
                  may be any of: TCP, UDP, TCPv6, or UDPv6.  If used with the -s
                  option to display per-protocol statistics, proto may be any of:
                  IP, IPv6, ICMP, ICMPv6, TCP, TCPv6, UDP, or UDPv6.
    -r            Displays the routing table.
    -s            Displays per-protocol statistics.  By default, statistics are
                  shown for IP, IPv6, ICMP, ICMPv6, TCP, TCPv6, UDP, and UDPv6;
                  the -p option may be used to specify a subset of the default.
    -t            Displays the current connection offload state.
    interval      Redisplays selected statistics, pausing interval seconds
                  between each display.  Press CTRL+C to stop redisplaying
                  statistics.  If omitted, netstat will print the current
                  configuration information once.
```

Task 3:

Issue a 'netstat -a' command in order to print a list of the current TCP connections on your machine. The list may grow as you look at the output. You will be able to see if the connection is established and listening, and see the port used.

```
C:\Users\owner>netstat -a

Active Connections

  Proto  Local Address          Foreign Address        State
  TCP    0.0.0.0:135            owner-PC:0             LISTENING
  TCP    0.0.0.0:445            owner-PC:0             LISTENING
  TCP    0.0.0.0:623            owner-PC:0             LISTENING
  TCP    0.0.0.0:902            owner-PC:0             LISTENING
  TCP    0.0.0.0:912            owner-PC:0             LISTENING
  TCP    0.0.0.0:16992          owner-PC:0             LISTENING
  TCP    0.0.0.0:27275          owner-PC:0             LISTENING
  TCP    0.0.0.0:49152          owner-PC:0             LISTENING
  TCP    0.0.0.0:49153          owner-PC:0             LISTENING
  TCP    0.0.0.0:49154          owner-PC:0             LISTENING
  TCP    0.0.0.0:49161          owner-PC:0             LISTENING
  TCP    0.0.0.0:49162          owner-PC:0             LISTENING
  TCP    0.0.0.0:49177          owner-PC:0             LISTENING
  TCP    127.0.0.1:5354         owner-PC:0             LISTENING
  TCP    127.0.0.1:5354         owner-PC:49155         ESTABLISHED
  TCP    127.0.0.1:5354         owner-PC:49156         ESTABLISHED
  TCP    127.0.0.1:5939         owner-PC:0             LISTENING
  TCP    127.0.0.1:12110        owner-PC:0             LISTENING
  TCP    127.0.0.1:12119        owner-PC:0             LISTENING
  TCP    127.0.0.1:12143        owner-PC:0             LISTENING
  TCP    127.0.0.1:12563        owner-PC:0             LISTENING
  TCP    127.0.0.1:12993        owner-PC:0             LISTENING
  TCP    127.0.0.1:12995        owner-PC:0             LISTENING
  TCP    127.0.0.1:27015        owner-PC:0             LISTENING
  TCP    127.0.0.1:27275        owner-PC:0             LISTENING
  TCP    127.0.0.1:49155        owner-PC:5354          ESTABLISHED
  TCP    127.0.0.1:49156        owner-PC:5354          ESTABLISHED
  TCP    127.0.0.1:62013        owner-PC:0             LISTENING
  TCP    127.0.0.1:62522        owner-PC:0             LISTENING
  TCP    127.0.0.1:65000        owner-PC:0             LISTENING
  TCP    192.168.0.12:139       owner-PC:0             LISTENING
  TCP    192.168.0.12:52840     ti-in-f188:https      ESTABLISHED
  TCP    192.168.0.12:52846     a23-206-242-40:http   ESTABLISHED
```

Task 4:

Check the current routing table of the PC with the 'netstat -r' command (you can also use the 'routeprint' command on Windows). I've regularly asked for this output from server engineers when they try to blame the network team for routing issues! You would get more interesting output from a live network server, but I'm working on a home PC for these labs.

```
C:\Users\owner>route print
===========================================================================
Interface List
 24...2c 30 33 a7 8d 9e ......NETGEAR A6100 WiFi Adapter
 11...60 a4 4c 41 33 77 ......Realtek PCIe GBE Family Controller
 14...00 50 56 c0 00 01 ......VMware Virtual Ethernet Adapter for VMnet1
 15...00 50 56 c0 00 08 ......VMware Virtual Ethernet Adapter for VMnet8
 28...0a 00 27 00 00 1c ......VirtualBox Host-Only Ethernet Adapter
  1...........................Software Loopback Interface 1
 12...00 00 00 00 00 00 00 e0 Teredo Tunneling Pseudo-Interface
 27...00 00 00 00 00 00 00 e0 Microsoft ISATAP Adapter #2
 29...00 00 00 00 00 00 00 e0 Microsoft ISATAP Adapter #3
 30...00 00 00 00 00 00 00 e0 Microsoft ISATAP Adapter #4
===========================================================================

IPv4 Route Table
===========================================================================
Active Routes:
Network Destination        Netmask          Gateway       Interface  Metric
          0.0.0.0          0.0.0.0      192.168.0.1    192.168.0.12     25
        127.0.0.0        255.0.0.0         On-link        127.0.0.1    306
        127.0.0.1  255.255.255.255         On-link        127.0.0.1    306
  127.255.255.255  255.255.255.255         On-link        127.0.0.1    306
      192.168.0.0    255.255.255.0         On-link     192.168.0.12    281
     192.168.0.12  255.255.255.255         On-link     192.168.0.12    281
    192.168.0.255  255.255.255.255         On-link     192.168.0.12    281
     192.168.56.0    255.255.255.0         On-link     192.168.56.1    266
     192.168.56.1  255.255.255.255         On-link     192.168.56.1    266
   192.168.56.255  255.255.255.255         On-link     192.168.56.1    266
    192.168.119.0    255.255.255.0         On-link    192.168.119.1    276
    192.168.119.1  255.255.255.255         On-link    192.168.119.1    276
  192.168.119.255  255.255.255.255         On-link    192.168.119.1    276
    192.168.157.0    255.255.255.0         On-link    192.168.157.1    276
    192.168.157.1  255.255.255.255         On-link    192.168.157.1    276
  192.168.157.255  255.255.255.255         On-link    192.168.157.1    276
        224.0.0.0        240.0.0.0         On-link        127.0.0.1    306
        224.0.0.0        240.0.0.0         On-link     192.168.56.1    266
        224.0.0.0        240.0.0.0         On-link    192.168.157.1    276
```

Task 5:

Check for any Ethernet issues with the 'netstat -e' command. This will print details of bytes and packets sent/received.

```
C:\Users\owner>netstat -e
Interface Statistics

                           Received            Sent

Bytes                    2132029888      1307391308
Unicast packets            14004148         7924282
Non-unicast packets           13568           39469
Discards                          0               0
Errors                            0               0
Unknown protocols                 0
```

Task 6:

Issue a 'netstat -s' command to check for statistics on TCP, UDP, ICPM, and IP. I've cropped the output below to save space.

```
C:\Users\owner>netstat -s

IPv4 Statistics

    Packets Received                    = 1832134
    Received Header Errors              = 0
    Received Address Errors             = 19
    Datagrams Forwarded                 = 0
    Unknown Protocols Received          = 0
    Received Packets Discarded          = 4703
    Received Packets Delivered          = 1852136
    Output Requests                     = 1082388
    Routing Discards                    = 0
    Discarded Output Packets            = 3365
    Output Packet No Route              = 104
    Reassembly Required                 = 0
    Reassembly Successful               = 0
    Reassembly Failures                 = 0
    Datagrams Successfully Fragmented   = 0
    Datagrams Failing Fragmentation     = 0
    Fragments Created                   = 0
```

Task 7:

Combine the s and p switches into output printing statistics for UDP only.

```
C:\Users\owner>netstat -sp udp

UDP Statistics for IPv4

    Datagrams Received    = 75859
    No Ports              = 4789
    Receive Errors        = 65577
    Datagrams Sent        = 50279

Active Connections

  Proto  Local Address         Foreign Address        State
```

Note:

There are many other options inside netstat, including wildcards and grouping multiple switches.

tcpdump Command

Lab Objective:

Learn how to use the tcpdump command and its switches.

Lab Purpose:

Tcpdump is the gold standard of network analysis tools. Using it to its full capabilities requires a thorough understanding of TCP/IP. It comes with a variety of filters and switches which reduce the level of output displayed. Never use this tool on a live network unless you know what you are doing and have permission. This lab is a short dip into this very powerful tool.

Lab Tool:

Ubuntu or most other Linux distributions

Lab Topology:

Please use the following topology to complete this lab exercise. I used a virtual Ubuntu machine running inside VirtualBox.

Lab Walkthrough:

Task 1:

Pull up a command prompt. You have several options here (feel free to google them if you are unfamiliar with Linux/Unix/Ubuntu). I used the search facility and typed 'terminal' to bring up the icon.

Task 2:

You may well have to run the 'tcpdump' command as 'sudo tcpdump', which runs the command with advanced user privileges.

Task 3:

Issue a 'sudo tcpdump -i any' command. This will listen on all available interfaces to determine if there is any traffic. You can quit the output anytime by pressing the Ctrl button and the C key.

```
paul@paul-VirtualBox:~$ sudo tcpdump -i any
tcpdump: verbose output suppressed, use -v or -vv for full protocol decode
listening on any, link-type LINUX_SLL (Linux cooked), capture size 262144 bytes
13:56:58.134206 IP6 paul-VirtualBox.mdns > ff02::fb.mdns: 0 [2q] PTR (QM)? _ipps._tcp.local. PTR (QM)? _ipp._tcp.local. (45)
13:56:58.137096 IP localhost.43859 > localhost.domain: 42037+ PTR? b.f.0.0.0.0.0.0.0.0.0.0.0.0.0.0.0.0.0.0.0.0.0.0.0.0.0.0.0.2.0.f.f.ip6.
arpa. (90)
13:56:58.137760 IP paul-VirtualBox.51800 > www.routerlogin.com.domain: 23481+ [1au] PTR? b.f.0.0.0.0.0.0.0.0.0.0.0.0.0.0.0.0.0.0.0.0.0.
0.0.0.0.0.2.0.f.f.ip6.arpa. (101)
13:56:58.242175 IP www.routerlogin.com.domain > paul-VirtualBox.51800: 23481 NXDomain 0/1/1 (165)
13:56:58.242985 IP paul-VirtualBox.51800 > www.routerlogin.com.domain: 23481+ PTR? b.f.0.0.0.0.0.0.0.0.0.0.0.0.0.0.0.0.0.0.0.0.0.0.
0.0.2.0.f.f.ip6.arpa. (90)
13:56:58.345457 IP www.routerlogin.com.domain > paul-VirtualBox.51800: 23481 NXDomain 0/1/0 (154)
13:56:58.347252 IP localhost.34926 > localhost.domain: 14037+ PTR? 53.0.0.127.in-addr.arpa. (41)
13:57:10.497951 IP paul-VirtualBox.36220 > dashboard.snapcraft.io.https: Flags [P.], seq 302369703:302369734, ack 190702123, win 65320,
length 31
13:57:10.498137 IP localhost.47074 > localhost.domain: 61327+ PTR? 18.92.189.91.in-addr.arpa. (43)
13:57:10.498201 IP dashboard.snapcraft.io.https > paul-VirtualBox.36220: Flags [.], ack 31, win 65535, length 0
13:57:10.498348 IP paul-VirtualBox.57601 > www.routerlogin.com.domain: 30250+ PTR? 18.92.189.91.in-addr.arpa. (43)
13:57:10.498439 IP paul-VirtualBox.36220 > dashboard.snapcraft.io.https: Flags [R.], seq 31, ack 1, win 65320, length 0
13:57:11.007220 IP www.routerlogin.com.domain > paul-VirtualBox.57601: 30250 1/0/0 PTR dashboard.snapcraft.io. (79)
13:57:14.129048 IP api.snapcraft.io.https > paul-VirtualBox.46270: Flags [P.], seq 190280302:190280333, ack 2157301440, win 65535, leng
th 31
```

Task 4:

The 'sudo tcpdump -D' command will list all your available interfaces. The output may look a little strange because I'm using a virtual machine, so there is no physical interface. My Ethernet interface name is listed in 1. below.

```
paul@paul-VirtualBox:~$ sudo tcpdump -D
1.enp0s3 [Up, Running]
2.any (Pseudo-device that captures on all interfaces) [Up, Running]
3.lo [Up, Running, Loopback]
4.nflog (Linux netfilter log (NFLOG) interface)
5.nfqueue (Linux netfilter queue (NFQUEUE) interface)
6.usbmon1 (USB bus number 1)
```

Task 5:

You can configure tcpdump to print only for a specific interface with the 'sudo tcpdump -i enp0s3' command (if enp0s3 is your interface name).

```
paul@paul-VirtualBox:~$ sudo tcpdump -i enp0s3
tcpdump: verbose output suppressed, use -v or -vv for full protocol decode
listening on enp0s3, link-type EN10MB (Ethernet), capture size 262144 bytes
14:35:39.981544 IP paul-VirtualBox > redirect-ns.cisco.com: ICMP echo request, id 1983, seq 816, length 64
14:35:40.187595 IP redirect-ns.cisco.com > paul-VirtualBox: ICMP echo reply, id 1983, seq 816, length 64
14:35:40.982150 IP paul-VirtualBox > redirect-ns.cisco.com: ICMP echo request, id 1983, seq 817, length 64
14:35:41.985694 ARP, Request who-has _gateway tell paul-VirtualBox, length 28
14:35:41.985868 IP paul-VirtualBox > redirect-ns.cisco.com: ICMP echo request, id 1983, seq 818, length 64
14:35:41.985932 ARP, Reply _gateway is-at 52:54:00:12:35:02 (oui Unknown), length 46
14:35:41.986493 IP paul-VirtualBox.41451 > www.routerlogin.com.domain: 51088+ [1au] PTR? 2.2.0.10.in-addr.arpa. (50)
14:35:42.102936 IP www.routerlogin.com.domain > paul-VirtualBox.41451: 51088 NXDomain* 0/1/1 (109)
14:35:42.103205 IP paul-VirtualBox.41451 > www.routerlogin.com.domain: 51088+ PTR? 2.2.0.10.in-addr.arpa. (39)
14:35:42.204575 IP redirect-ns.cisco.com > paul-VirtualBox: ICMP echo reply, id 1983, seq 818, length 64
14:35:42.205842 IP paul-VirtualBox.45553 > www.routerlogin.com.domain: 54876+ [1au] PTR? 1.0.168.192.in-addr.arpa. (53)
14:35:42.243792 IP www.routerlogin.com.domain > paul-VirtualBox.45553: 54876- 1/0/0 PTR www.routerlogin.com. (75)
14:35:42.244127 IP paul-VirtualBox.45553 > www.routerlogin.com.domain: 53677+ [1au] PTR? 1.0.168.192.in-addr.arpa. (53)
14:35:47.989804 IP paul-VirtualBox > redirect-ns.cisco.com: ICMP echo request, id 1983, seq 824, length 64
^C
14 packets captured
72 packets received by filter
58 packets dropped by kernel
```

Task 6:

Monitor ICMP traffic with the 'sudo tcpdump icmp' command. Then open another command line window.

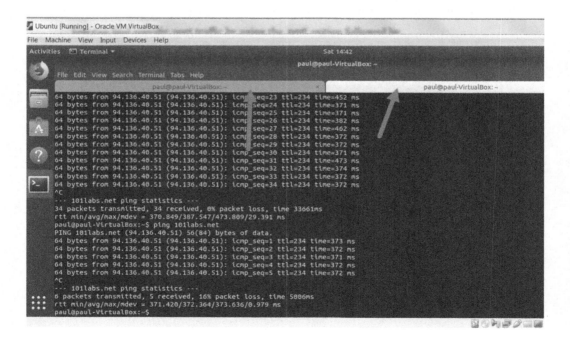

And ping a website, such as 101labs.net or cisco.com. After a few seconds press Ctrl and C to stop the packets.

```
paul@paul-VirtualBox:~$ ping 101labs.net
PING 101labs.net (94.136.40.51) 56(84) bytes of data.
64 bytes from 94.136.40.51 (94.136.40.51): icmp_seq=1 ttl=234 time=373 ms
64 bytes from 94.136.40.51 (94.136.40.51): icmp_seq=2 ttl=234 time=372 ms
64 bytes from 94.136.40.51 (94.136.40.51): icmp_seq=3 ttl=234 time=371 ms
64 bytes from 94.136.40.51 (94.136.40.51): icmp_seq=4 ttl=234 time=372 ms
64 bytes from 94.136.40.51 (94.136.40.51): icmp_seq=5 ttl=234 time=372 ms
^C
--- 101labs.net ping statistics ---
6 packets transmitted, 5 received, 16% packet loss, time 5006ms
rtt min/avg/max/mdev = 371.420/372.364/373.636/0.979 ms
paul@paul-VirtualBox:~$
```

Task 7:

Check the capture and compare against the ping window. As you know from your study guide, ping uses echo request and echo reply. The outgoing and incoming packets have sequence (seq) numbers which will match 1-1, 2-2, etc.

```
paul@paul-VirtualBox:~$ sudo tcpdump icmp
tcpdump: verbose output suppressed, use -v or -vv for full protocol decode
listening on enp0s3, link-type EN10MB (Ethernet), capture size 262144 bytes
14:42:10.354729 IP paul-VirtualBox > 94.136.40.51: ICMP echo request, id 2093, seq 1, length 64
14:42:10.728350 IP 94.136.40.51 > paul-VirtualBox: ICMP echo reply, id 2093, seq 1, length 64
14:42:11.355745 IP paul-VirtualBox > 94.136.40.51: ICMP echo request, id 2093, seq 2, length 64
14:42:11.728085 IP 94.136.40.51 > paul-VirtualBox: ICMP echo reply, id 2093, seq 2, length 64
14:42:12.357351 IP paul-VirtualBox > 94.136.40.51: ICMP echo request, id 2093, seq 3, length 64
14:42:12.728746 IP 94.136.40.51 > paul-VirtualBox: ICMP echo reply, id 2093, seq 3, length 64
14:42:13.358889 IP paul-VirtualBox > 94.136.40.51: ICMP echo request, id 2093, seq 4, length 64
14:42:13.731052 IP 94.136.40.51 > paul-VirtualBox: ICMP echo reply, id 2093, seq 4, length 64
14:42:14.359967 IP paul-VirtualBox > 94.136.40.51: ICMP echo request, id 2093, seq 5, length 64
14:42:14.732153 IP 94.136.40.51 > paul-VirtualBox: ICMP echo reply, id 2093, seq 5, length 64
14:42:15.361134 IP paul-VirtualBox > 94.136.40.51: ICMP echo request, id 2093, seq 6, length 64
14:42:15.731898 IP 94.136.40.51 > paul-VirtualBox: ICMP echo reply, id 2093, seq 6, length 64
```

Notes:

It would take an experienced network engineer several weeks to get a deep understanding of this command line tool, which is why many of us use packet capture programs, such as Wireshark. Here is a sample command stack for tcpdump to capture only TCP FIN flags:

```
# tcpdump 'tcp[13] & 1!=0'
# tcpdump 'tcp[tcpflags] == tcp-fin'
Above command acknowledgment - https://danielmiessler.com/study/
tcpdump/
```

nmap Command

Lab Objective:
Learn how to use the nmap command and its switches.

Lab Purpose:
Nmap is short for network mapper. It is a free and open-source security scanner which (among many other things) can discover hosts and services on a network and build a map from this information. It can spoof, masking its true identity and find vulnerabilities on a host or entire network.

Lab Tool:
Ubuntu running in VirtualBox

Lab Topology:
Please use the following topology to complete this lab exercise. I used a virtual Ubuntu PC running inside VirtualBox, but if you are using Windows, you can use your home PC. Just check your firewall settings don't block the test. For VirtualBox I had to set all my network adapters to 'Bridged' so they can communicate and connect to my home router and devices.

You can download Nmap from **nmap.org**.

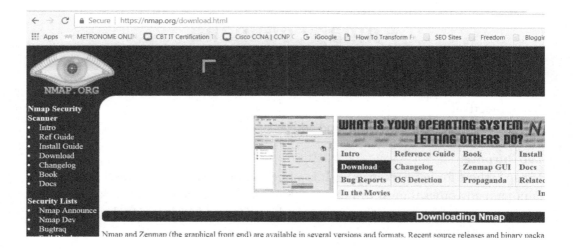

Lab Walkthrough:

Task 1:

Pull up a command prompt by typing 'terminal' into the search box (if you are using Ubuntu).

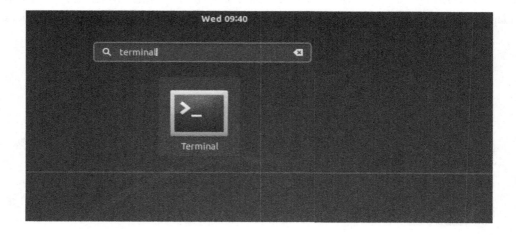

Task 2:

At the command prompt issue the 'nmap' command. Check your study guide for more information on all the available switches. For Ubuntu it may not be installed, so you will be prompted to download it via the 'sudo apt install nmap' command.

```
paul@paul-VirtualBox:~$ nmap

Command 'nmap' not found, but can be installed with:

sudo apt install nmap
```

Task 3:

Issue an 'nmap' command again and examine the various switches and options available.

```
paul@paul-VirtualBox:~$ nmap
Nmap 7.60 ( https://nmap.org )
Usage: nmap [Scan Type(s)] [Options] {target specification}
TARGET SPECIFICATION:
  Can pass hostnames, IP addresses, networks, etc.
  Ex: scanme.nmap.org, microsoft.com/24, 192.168.0.1; 10.0.0-255.1-254
  -iL <inputfilename>: Input from list of hosts/networks
  -iR <num hosts>: Choose random targets
  --exclude <host1[,host2][,host3],...>: Exclude hosts/networks
  --excludefile <exclude_file>: Exclude list from file
HOST DISCOVERY:
  -sL: List Scan - simply list targets to scan
  -sn: Ping Scan - disable port scan
  -Pn: Treat all hosts as online -- skip host discovery
  -PS/PA/PU/PY[portlist]: TCP SYN/ACK, UDP or SCTP discovery to given ports
  -PE/PP/PM: ICMP echo, timestamp, and netmask request discovery probes
  -PO[protocol list]: IP Protocol Ping
  -n/-R: Never do DNS resolution/Always resolve [default: sometimes]
  --dns-servers <serv1[,serv2],...>: Specify custom DNS servers
  --system-dns: Use OS's DNS resolver
  --traceroute: Trace hop path to each host
SCAN TECHNIQUES:
  -sS/sT/sA/sW/sM: TCP SYN/Connect()/ACK/Window/Maimon scans
  -sU: UDP Scan
```

Task 4:

I'm running this in VirtualBox, so I've activated a Windows 10 PC because I want to scan my virtual network for any devices. If you are using this on your home PC, then you should be able to use that and find any devices using it. DO NOT use this tool on a privately owned network.

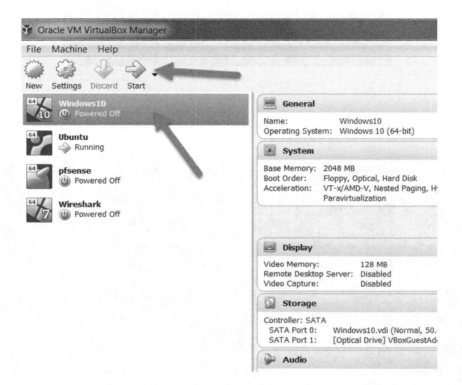

Task 5:

There are so many options, but run a test using 'nmap -sn -v', which is a ping scan and verbose output. I'll scan my home network range; yours may well differ, so input your own range. I've already noted down the IP addresses of my machines so I know which is which.

```
paul@paul-VirtualBox:~$ nmap -sn -v 192.168.0.0/24

Starting Nmap 7.60 ( https://nmap.org ) at 2018-09-05 10:28 AEST
Initiating Ping Scan at 10:28
Scanning 256 hosts [2 ports/host]
Completed Ping Scan at 10:28, 3.10s elapsed (256 total hosts)
Initiating Parallel DNS resolution of 256 hosts. at 10:28
Completed Parallel DNS resolution of 256 hosts. at 10:29, 13.00s elapsed
Nmap scan report for 192.168.0.0 [host down]
Nmap scan report for 192.168.0.1 [host down]
Nmap scan report for 192.168.0.2 [host down]
Nmap scan report for 192.168.0.3 [host down]
Nmap scan report for 192.168.0.4 [host down]
Nmap scan report for 192.168.0.5 [host down]
Nmap scan report for 192.168.0.6 [host down]
Nmap scan report for 192.168.0.7 [host down]
Nmap scan report for 192.168.0.8 [host down]
Nmap scan report for 192.168.0.9 [host down]
Nmap scan report for 192.168.0.10 [host down]      My Home PC
Nmap scan report for 192.168.0.11 [host down]
Nmap scan report for 192.168.0.12
Host is up (0.0016s latency).
Nmap scan report for paul-VirtualBox (192.168.0.13)
Host is up (0.00071s latency).                       Ubuntu
Nmap scan report for 192.168.0.14                    VM
Host is up (0.0014s latency).        Windows
Nmap scan report for 192.168.0.15 [host down]  VM
```

Task 6:

Issue another 'nmap' command. This time we want to determine the OS running on the machines (-O), probe the open ports (-sV), and treat all the hosts as being up (-Pn). You may need to run this command as 'sudo' if you are using Ubuntu, so it's 'sudo nmap -Pn -O -sV 192.168.1.14', which is my home Windows PC.

```
paul@paul-VirtualBox:~$ sudo nmap -Pn -O -sV 192.168.0.14
[sudo] password for paul:

Starting Nmap 7.60 ( https://nmap.org ) at 2018-09-05 10:42 AEST
Nmap scan report for 192.168.0.14
Host is up (0.00038s latency).
Not shown: 997 closed ports
PORT     STATE SERVICE      VERSION
135/tcp open  msrpc        Microsoft Windows RPC
139/tcp open  netbios-ssn  Microsoft Windows netbios-ssn
445/tcp open  microsoft-ds?
MAC Address: 08:00:27:07:D6:5B (Oracle VirtualBox virtual NIC)
No exact OS matches for host (If you know what OS is running on it, see https://n
).
TCP/IP fingerprint:
OS:SCAN(V=7.60%E=4%D=9/5%OT=135%CT=1%CU=34385%PV=Y%DS=1%DC=D%G=Y%M=080027%T
OS:M=5B8F26BE%P=x86_64-pc-linux-gnu)SEQ(SP=104%GCD=1%ISR=10B%TI=I%CI=I%TS=U
OS:)SEQ(SP=104%GCD=1%ISR=10B%TI=I%CI=I%II=I%SS=S%TS=U)SEQ(SP=104%GCD=1%ISR=
OS:10B%TI=I%II=I%SS=S%TS=U)OPS(O1=M5B4NW8NNS%O2=M5B4NW8NNS%O3=M5B4NW8%O4=M5
OS:B4NW8NNS%O5=M5B4NW8NNS%O6=M5B4NNS)WIN(W1=FFFF%W2=FFFF%W3=FFFF%W4=FFFF%W5
OS:=FFFF%W6=FF70)ECN(R=Y%DF=Y%T=80%W=FFFF%O=M5B4NW8NNS%CC=N%Q=)T1(R=Y%DF=Y%
OS:T=80%S=O%A=S+%F=AS%RD=0%Q=)T2(R=Y%DF=Y%T=80%W=0%S=Z%A=S%F=AR%O=%RD=0%Q=)
OS:T3(R=Y%DF=Y%T=80%W=0%S=Z%A=O%F=AR%O=%RD=0%Q=)T4(R=Y%DF=Y%T=80%W=0%S=A%A=
OS:O%F=R%O=%RD=0%Q=)T5(R=Y%DF=Y%T=80%W=0%S=Z%A=S+%F=AR%O=%RD=0%Q=)T6(R=Y%DF
OS:=Y%T=80%W=0%S=A%A=O%F=R%O=%RD=0%Q=)T7(R=Y%DF=Y%T=80%W=0%S=Z%A=S+%F=AR%O=
OS:%RD=0%Q=)U1(R=Y%DF=N%T=80%IPL=164%UN=0%RIPL=G%RID=G%RIPCK=G%RUCK=G%RUD=G
```

```
Network Distance: 1 hop
Service Info: OS: Windows; CPE: cpe:/o:microsoft:windows

OS and Service detection performed. Please report any incorrect results at https:/
t/ .
Nmap done: 1 IP address (1 host up) scanned in 73.46 seconds
```

Task 7:

The Nmap project has provided an online site for you to scan, which overcomes the illegality of scanning a privately held server. You can find it at scanme.nmap.org. They request fair use, so no 100 attacks per day or brute force attacks, please! We will stick to -A, which is OS detection, version, script scan, and traceroute.

The site was usually unavailable when I tried this and when it finally worked, it wouldn't return the OS details so here is a screenshot courtesy of Nmap.

```
31337
# nmap -A scanme.nmap.org

Starting Nmap 6.00 ( http://nmap.org ) at 2012-05-17 12:16 PDT
Nmap scan report for scanme.nmap.org (74.207.244.221)
Host is up (0.00031s latency).
Not shown: 997 closed ports
PORT      STATE SERVICE      VERSION
22/tcp    open  ssh          OpenSSH 5.3p1 Debian 3ubuntu7 (protocol 2.0)
| ssh-hostkey: 1024 8d:60:f1:7c:ca:b7:3d:0a:d6:67:54:9d:69:d9:b9:dd (DSA)
|_2048 79:f8:09:ac:d4:e2:32:42:10:49:d3:bd:20:82:85:ec (RSA)
80/tcp    open  http         Apache httpd 2.2.14 ((Ubuntu))
|_http-title: Go ahead and ScanMe!
9929/tcp  open  nping-echo   Nping echo
Device type: general purpose
Running: Linux 2.6.X|3.X
OS CPE: cpe:/o:linux:kernel:2.6 cpe:/o:linux:kernel:3
OS details: Linux 2.6.32 - 2.6.39, Linux 2.6.38 - 3.0
Network Distance: 2 hops
Service Info: OS: Linux; CPE: cpe:/o:linux:kernel

TRACEROUTE (using port 21/tcp)
HOP RTT      ADDRESS
1   0.45 ms  184.105.143.85
2   0.41 ms  scanme.nmap.org (74.207.244.221)

OS and Service detection performed. Please report any incorrect results a
Nmap done: 1 IP address (1 host up) scanned in 8.81 seconds
#
```

Source - https://nmap.org/6/

Task 8:

If you prefer to use a GUI with Nmap, you can use Zenmap, which can be downloaded from nmap.org/zenmap. It does the same thing but is user-friendly.

Notes:

It would take a few weeks to learn all the features of this command. This is a gentle introduction.

dig Command

Lab Objective:
Learn how to use the dig command and some of its switches.

Lab Purpose:
Dig is short for domain information groper. It's a Unix command line tool used to query DNS name servers. It comes with a large number of options and switches you can use, and it varies according to the platform (e.g., Red Hat, Ubuntu, etc.), so check your documentation.

Lab Tool:
Ubuntu VM

Lab Topology:
Please use the following topology to complete this lab exercise. I used a virtual Ubuntu PC running inside VirtualBox, but if you are using Windows, you can use your home PC. Just check your firewall settings don't block the test.

Lab Walkthrough:

Task 1:

Pull up a terminal by typing 'terminal' into the search box.

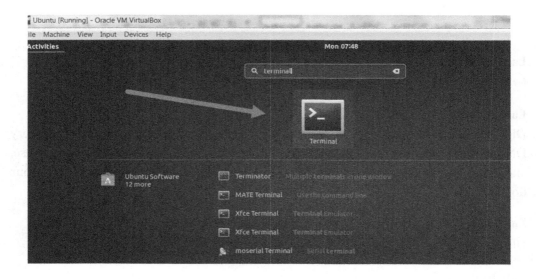

Task 2:

At the command prompt issue the 'dig' command. Check your documentation for more information on all the available switches. Ubuntu doesn't display any after the question mark.

```
paul@paul-VirtualBox:~$ dig ?

; <<>> DiG 9.11.3-1ubuntu1.1-Ubuntu <<>> ?
;; global options: +cmd
;; Got answer:
;; ->>HEADER<<- opcode: QUERY, status: SERVFAIL, id: 19009
;; flags: qr rd ra; QUERY: 1, ANSWER: 0, AUTHORITY: 0, ADDITIONAL: 1

;; OPT PSEUDOSECTION:
; EDNS: version: 0, flags:; udp: 65494
;; QUESTION SECTION:
;?.                             IN      A

;; Query time: 0 msec
;; SERVER: 127.0.0.53#53(127.0.0.53)
;; WHEN: Mon Sep 03 07:50:08 AEST 2018
;; MSG SIZE  rcvd: 30
```

Task 3:

Issue a 'dig cisco.com' command. By default an A record search will be executed.

```
paul@paul-VirtualBox:~$ dig cisco.com

; <<>> DiG 9.11.3-1ubuntu1.1-Ubuntu <<>> cisco.com
;; global options: +cmd
;; Got answer:
;; ->>HEADER<<- opcode: QUERY, status: NOERROR, id: 11046
;; flags: qr rd ra; QUERY: 1, ANSWER: 1, AUTHORITY: 0, ADDITIONAL: 1

;; OPT PSEUDOSECTION:
; EDNS: version: 0, flags:; udp: 65494
;; QUESTION SECTION:
;cisco.com.                     IN     A

;; ANSWER SECTION:
cisco.com.              3145    IN     A        72.163.4.185

;; Query time: 39 msec
;; SERVER: 127.0.0.53#53(127.0.0.53)
;; WHEN: Mon Sep 03 07:51:15 AEST 2018
;; MSG SIZE  rcvd: 54
```

We got one answer: 3145 is the time to live (TTL) before the DNS server rechecks the entry. 'IN' indicates a standard internet class, A record is the standard record type, and 72.163.4.185 is the IP address the domain name resolves to.

Task 4:

We can use one of the many switches available. Let's use the mx switch to query the mail servers.

```
paul@paul-VirtualBox:~$ dig cisco.com mx

; <<>> DiG 9.11.3-1ubuntu1.1-Ubuntu <<>> cisco.com mx
;; global options: +cmd
;; Got answer:
;; ->>HEADER<<- opcode: QUERY, status: NOERROR, id: 30038
;; flags: qr rd ra; QUERY: 1, ANSWER: 3, AUTHORITY: 0, ADDITIONAL: 1

;; OPT PSEUDOSECTION:
; EDNS: version: 0, flags:; udp: 65494
;; QUESTION SECTION:
;cisco.com.                     IN     MX

;; ANSWER SECTION:
cisco.com.              1800    IN     MX      20 rcdn-mx-01.cisco.com.
cisco.com.              1800    IN     MX      10 alln-mx-01.cisco.com.
cisco.com.              1800    IN     MX      30 aer-mx-01.cisco.com.

;; Query time: 361 msec
;; SERVER: 127.0.0.53#53(127.0.0.53)
;; WHEN: Mon Sep 03 08:01:32 AEST 2018
;; MSG SIZE  rcvd: 118
```

Task 5:

The 'ANY' switch will return all information record types. Many users have had very few results here, so don't worry if the same happens to you.

```
paul@paul-VirtualBox:~$ dig dig cisco.com ANY

; <<>> DiG 9.11.3-1ubuntu1.1-Ubuntu <<>> cisco.com ANY
;; global options: +cmd
;; Got answer:
;; ->>HEADER<<- opcode: QUERY, status: NOERROR, id: 54997
;; flags: qr rd ra; QUERY: 1, ANSWER: 17, AUTHORITY: 0, ADDITIONAL: 1

;; OPT PSEUDOSECTION:
; EDNS: version: 0, flags:; udp: 65494
;; QUESTION SECTION:
;cisco.com.                      IN      ANY

;; ANSWER SECTION:
cisco.com.              1800    IN      SOA     ns1.cisco.com. postmaster.cisco.com. 18213019 7200 1800 864000 1800
cisco.com.              1800    IN      NS      ns1.cisco.com.
cisco.com.              1800    IN      NS      ns3.cisco.com.
cisco.com.              1800    IN      NS      ns2.cisco.com.
cisco.com.              1800    IN      MX      30 aer-mx-01.cisco.com.
cisco.com.              1800    IN      MX      10 alln-mx-01.cisco.com.
cisco.com.              1800    IN      MX      20 rcdn-mx-01.cisco.com.
cisco.com.              2544    IN      AAAA    2001:420:1101:1::185
cisco.com.              2418    IN      A       72.163.4.185
cisco.com.              3600    IN      TXT     "google-site-verification=K2w--6oeqrFjHfYtTsYyd2tFw7OQd6g5HJDC9UAI8Jk"
cisco.com.              3600    IN      TXT     "v=spf1 redirect=spfa._spf.cisco.com"
cisco.com.              3600    IN      TXT     "docusign=95052c5f-a421-4594-9227-02ad2d86dfbe"
cisco.com.              3600    IN      TXT     "zpSH7Ye/seyY61hH8+Rq5Kb+ZJ9hDa+qeFBaD/6sPAAg+2POkGdP0byHb1pFVK9uZgYF2AIosUSZq4MB17oy
dQ=="
cisco.com.              3600    IN      TXT     "docusign=5e18de8e-36d0-4a8e-8e88-b7803423fa2f"
cisco.com.              3600    IN      TXT     "926723159-3188410"
cisco.com.              3600    IN      TXT     "MS=ms35724259"
cisco.com.              3600    IN      TXT     "facebook-domain-verification=qr2nigspzrpa96j1nd9criovuuwino"
```

Task 6:

You can drill down to use the AAAA record if you wish with the 'dig -t AAAA' command, where 't' is short for 'type'.

```
paul@paul-VirtualBox:~$ dig cisco.com -t AAAA

; <<>> DiG 9.11.3-1ubuntu1.1-Ubuntu <<>> cisco.com -t AAAA
;; global options: +cmd
;; Got answer:
;; ->>HEADER<<- opcode: QUERY, status: NOERROR, id: 48606
;; flags: qr rd ra; QUERY: 1, ANSWER: 1, AUTHORITY: 0, ADDITIONAL: 1

;; OPT PSEUDOSECTION:
; EDNS: version: 0, flags:; udp: 65494
;; QUESTION SECTION:
;cisco.com.                      IN      AAAA

;; ANSWER SECTION:
cisco.com.              2432    IN      AAAA    2001:420:1101:1::185

;; Query time: 0 msec
;; SERVER: 127.0.0.53#53(127.0.0.53)
;; WHEN: Mon Sep 03 08:05:14 AEST 2018
;; MSG SIZE  rcvd: 66
```

Task 7:

Finally, you can do a reverse lookup with the -x switch and the IP address.

```
paul@paul-VirtualBox:~$ dig -x 72.163.4.185

; <<>> DiG 9.11.3-1ubuntu1.1-Ubuntu <<>> -x 72.163.4.185
;; global options: +cmd
;; Got answer:
;; ->>HEADER<<- opcode: QUERY, status: NOERROR, id: 41586
;; flags: qr rd ra; QUERY: 1, ANSWER: 1, AUTHORITY: 0, ADDITIONAL: 1

;; OPT PSEUDOSECTION:
; EDNS: version: 0, flags:; udp: 65494
;; QUESTION SECTION:
;185.4.163.72.in-addr.arpa.        IN       PTR

;; ANSWER SECTION:
185.4.163.72.in-addr.arpa. 1800 IN       PTR       redirect-ns.cisco.com.

;; Query time: 623 msec
;; SERVER: 127.0.0.53#53(127.0.0.53)
;; WHEN: Mon Sep 03 08:07:02 AEST 2018
;; MSG SIZE  rcvd: 89
```

Note:

There are many other options for this command, so feel free to research further.

Troubleshooting Speed and Duplex Issues

Lab Objective:

Learn how to troubleshoot and solve speed and duplex issues.

Lab Purpose:

Most network installation engineers will tell you that devices should never be left to auto-configure speed and duplex settings. It can often cause issues, especially when you mix equipment from different vendors.

Lab Tool:

Packet Tracer

Lab Topology:

Please use the following topology to complete this lab exercise:

Lab Walkthrough:

Task 1:

Drag a PC and router onto the canvas and connect them using a crossover cable. I used an 1841 model router.

Task 2:

In order to simulate issues, set the PC to half duplex 10 Mbps. Set the IP address to 192.168.1.2 and the gateway to 192.168.1.1.

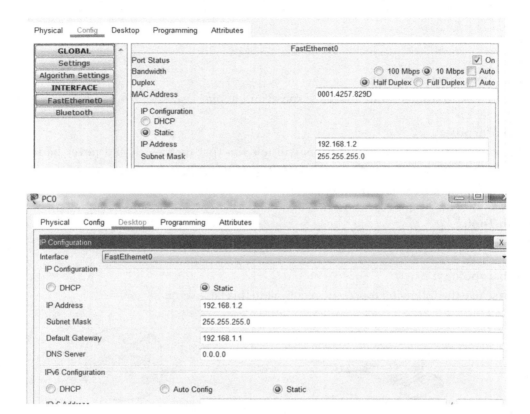

Task 3:

Check the interface settings on the router interface F0/0. The interface will work with either 10 Mpbs or half-duplex devices. Mine is already up from a previous lab, but yours may be down until task 4.

```
Router#show int f0/0
FastEthernet0/0 is up, line protocol is up (connected)
Hardware is Lance, address is 000d.bd83.a601 (bia 000d.bd83.a601)
MTU 1500 bytes, BW 100000 Kbit, DLY 1000 usec,
reliability 255/255, txload 1/255, rxload 1/255
Encapsulation ARPA, loopback not set
Full-duplex, 100Mb/s, media type is RJ45
```

Task 4:

Set the router F0/0 interface to 192.168.1.1, the speed to 100 Mpbs, and the duplex to full. 'No shut' it.

```
Router#config t
Router(config)#interface FastEthernet0/0
Router(config-if)#ip address 192.168.1.1 255.255.255.0
Router(config-if)#no shut
Router(config-if)#speed 100
Router(config-if)#duplex full
Router(config-if)#end
```

Task 5:

Ping the router interface from the PC. It will fail. You would usually see router interface resets and errors, but we are a bit limited on Packet Tracer. The interface will be down on the router due to the fact that keepalives fail.

```
C:\>ping 192.168.1.1

Pinging 192.168.1.1 with 32 bytes of data:

Request timed out.
Request timed out.
Request timed out.
Request timed out.

Ping statistics for 192.168.1.1:
    Packets: Sent = 4, Received = 0, Lost = 4 (100% loss),
```

```
Router#show interfaces f0/0
FastEthernet0/0 is up, line protocol is down (disabled)
Hardware is Lance, address is 000d.bd83.a601 (bia 000d.bd83.a601)
```

Task 6:

Set the PC interface to full duplex and 100 Mbps. Devices are usually set to auto-detect even though when you check, you see them working at 100/full.

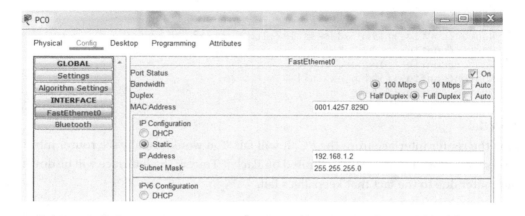

Task 7:

Ping from the PC to the router.

```
C:\>ping 192.168.1.1

Pinging 192.168.1.1 with 32 bytes of data:

Reply from 192.168.1.1: bytes=32 time<1ms TTL=255
Reply from 192.168.1.1: bytes=32 time<1ms TTL=255
Reply from 192.168.1.1: bytes=32 time<1ms TTL=255
Reply from 192.168.1.1: bytes=32 time=1ms TTL=255

Ping statistics for 192.168.1.1:
    Packets: Sent = 4, Received = 4, Lost = 0 (0% loss),
Approximate round trip times in milli-seconds:
    Minimum = 0ms, Maximum = 1ms, Average = 0ms
```

Note:

The only way to really see errors and interface resets is to do this on live equipment.

LAB 96

VLAN Mismatch

Lab Objective:

Learn how to troubleshoot a VLAN mismatch.

Lab Purpose:

Troubleshooting VLAN mismatches features in the exam syllabus. You will really only see these on trunk links, which must have the same native VLAN configured on either side. The only other VLAN mismatch you might encounter is hosts in the same VLAN being in different subnets, which isn't permitted.

Lab Tool:

Packet Tracer

Lab Topology:

Please use the following topology to complete this lab exercise:

Lab Walkthrough:

Task 1:

Drag two switches onto the canvas and connect them with a crossover cable. I used interface G0/1 in this lab, but you can use any interface.

Task 2:

Set the interface to trunk and set the native VLAN to 10.

```
Switch#config t
Switch(config)#host SW0
SW0(config)#int g0/1
SW0(config-if)#switchport mode trunk
```

```
SW0(config-if)#switchport trunk native vlan 10
SW0(config-if)#end
```

Task 3:

Cisco Discovery Protocol (CDP) will begin to generate error messages, which will be printed on your console session.

```
%CDP-4-NATIVE_VLAN_MISMATCH: Native VLAN mismatch discovered on
GigabitEthernet0/1 (10), with Switch GigabitEthernet0/1 (1).
```

Task 4:

Two commands will tell you what the native VLAN on the trunk is. Issue both of the below commands.

```
SW0#show interfaces trunk
Port    Mode Encapsulation Status Native vlan
Gig0/1 on    802.1q           trunking 10

Port Vlans allowed on trunk
Gig0/1 1-1005

Port Vlans allowed and active in management domain
Gig0/1 1

Port Vlans in spanning tree forwarding state and not pruned

Gig0/1 1

SW0#show interfaces g0/1 switchport
Name: Gig0/1
Switchport: Enabled
Administrative Mode: trunk
Operational Mode: trunk
Administrative Trunking Encapsulation: dot1q
Operational Trunking Encapsulation: dot1q
Negotiation of Trunking: On
Access Mode VLAN: 1 (default)
Trunking Native Mode VLAN: 10 (Inactive)
Voice VLAN: none
```

Task 5:

As the administrator you would know what the correct native VLAN should be. You would then configure SW1 G0/1 to use the same native VLAN (after checking the configuration by issuing one of the previous two commands first).

```
Switch>en
Switch#conf t
```

```
Enter configuration commands, one per line. End with CNTL/Z.
Switch(config)#host SW1
%CDP-4-NATIVE_VLAN_MISMATCH: Native VLAN mismatch discovered on
GigabitEthernet0/1 (1), with SW0 GigabitEthernet0/1 (10).
SW1(config)#int g0/1
SW1(config-if)#switchport trunk native vlan 10
SW1(config-if)#end
```

Note:

As mentioned earlier in this guide, you would usually set your native VLAN to a high number and ensure it was unused by hosts.

Incorrect Netmask

Lab Objective:

Learn how to fix an incorrect subnet mask configuration.

Lab Purpose:

Generally speaking, if you put an incorrect subnet mask on an interface, other hosts in the same subnet will be able to reach it. Your trouble begins if you add routing protocols or try to summarize the network to advertise out of an interface. In this lab we'll cover one of the most common mistakes I found when I was teaching Cisco courses, but it could happen with any vendor equipment.

Lab Tool:

Packet Tracer

Lab Topology:

Please use the following topology to complete this lab exercise:

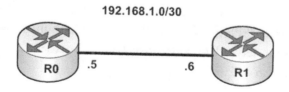

Lab Walkthrough:

Task 1:

Drag two routers onto the canvas. Connect them with a crossover cable.

Task 2:

Add the IP address on the routers as indicated. Here is the config for R0. R1 will be host 192.168.1.6.

```
Router>en
Router#conf t
```

```
Enter configuration commands, one per line. End with CNTL/Z.
Router(config)#hostname R0
R0(config)#int f0/0
R0(config-if)#ip add 192.168.1.5 255.255.255.252
R0(config-if)#no shut
R0(config-if)#exit
```

Task 3:

Configure OSPF on both routers.

```
R0(config)#router ospf 1
R0(config-router)#network 192.168.1.0 0.0.0.3 area 0
R0(config-router)#end

R1(config)#router ospf 1
R1(config-router)#network 192.168.1.0 0.0.0.3 area 0
```

Task 4:

Check that OSPF is working by issuing the 'show ip ospf neighbor' command.

```
R1#show ip ospf neighbor
```

Task 5:

No neighbor is present. You can begin troubleshooting OSPF, debugging packets, and checking for bugs, but the mistake is more fundamental than that. Some protocols (such as EIGRP) will forgive such mistakes, but OSPF will do exactly what you tell it to.

You use a wildcard mask with OSPF to specify the subnet you want to advertise. Subnet 192.168.1.0 0.0.0.3 tells OSPF to advertise the 192.168.1.0 subnet, which includes hosts 192.168.1.1 and .2. Your network features hosts from subnet 1921.168.1.4, which includes the two hosts (only) of .5 and .6.

Task 6:

Fix your OSPF configuration. Best practice is to remove the subnet you don't need to advertise.

```
R0(config)#router ospf 1
R0(config-router)#no network 192.168.1.0 0.0.0.3 area 0
R0(config-router)#network 192.168.1.4 0.0.0.3 area 0
R0(config-router)#end

R1(config)#router ospf 1
R1(config-router)#no network 192.168.1.0 0.0.0.3 area 0
R1(config-router)#network 192.168.1.4 0.0.0.3 area 0
R1(config-router)#end
```

```
00:24:47: %OSPF-5-ADJCHG: Process 1, Nbr 192.168.1.5 on FastEthernet0/0
from LOADING to FULL, Loading Done
```

Task 7:

Check for OSPF neighbors again.

```
R1#show ip ospf neighbor
Neighbor ID Pri State Dead Time Address Interface
192.168.1.5 1 FULL/DR 00:00:36 192.168.1.5 FastEthernet0/0
```

Notes:

Around 50% of my students make this mistake. If you made it on a live network, you could be in big trouble, so it's best to learn the lesson now.

I know this isn't strictly an incorrect netmask lab. Feel free to set up a home lab and try to use an incorrect netmask. I tried in Packet Tracer, but it kept fixing the mistake automatically on hosts!

Duplicate MAC Address

Lab Objective:

Learn how to troubleshoot duplicate MAC addresses.

Lab Purpose:

You will have read in your study guide I'm sure that every MAC address should be unique. Each vendor is given a unique code (OUI) which comprises half of the MAC address, and it allocates the other half. Duplicate MAC address issues can arise if you buy cheap equipment from disreputable vendors or due to a configuration issue.

Packets need a MAC address in order to encapsulate a frame properly. Switches build a table of MAC addresses to ports. If the same MAC address is allocated to multiple ports, then either frame will be dropped or misdirected. Constant table rewrites on a switch may lead to its crashing.

Lab Tool:

Packet Tracer

Lab Topology:

Please use the following topology to complete this lab exercise:

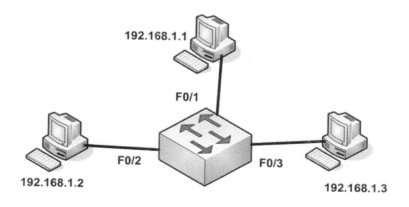

Lab Walkthrough:

Task 1:
Drag three desktops. Connect them all with straight-through cables.

Task 2:
Add the IP addresses on the PCs as indicated. Here is the process for PC0:

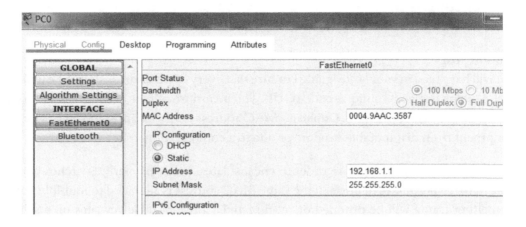

Task 3:
Copy-and-paste the MAC address from PC0 to PC1. Yours will differ from mine of course.

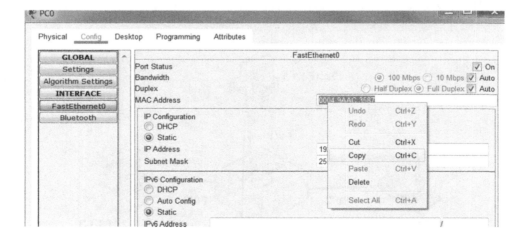

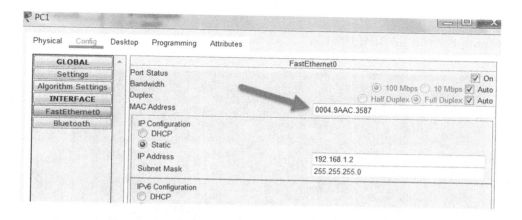

Task 4:

Ping from 192.168.1.1 to .3.

```
C:\>ping 192.168.1.3

Pinging 192.168.1.3 with 32 bytes of data:

Reply from 192.168.1.3: bytes=32 time=1ms TTL=128
Reply from 192.168.1.3: bytes=32 time<1ms TTL=128
Reply from 192.168.1.3: bytes=32 time<1ms TTL=128
Reply from 192.168.1.3: bytes=32 time<1ms TTL=128

Ping statistics for 192.168.1.3:
    Packets: Sent = 4, Received = 4, Lost = 0 (0% loss),
Approximate round trip times in milli-seconds:
    Minimum = 0ms, Maximum = 1ms, Average = 0ms
```

Task 5:

Now check the MAC table on the switch. You will see the 3587 MAC address is associated with F0/1.

```
Switch#show mac-address-table
Mac Address Table
-------------------------------------------

Vlan Mac Address    Type      Ports
---- -----------    --------  -----

1    0004.9aac.3587 DYNAMIC   Fa0/1
1    00d0.ba48.a838 DYNAMIC   Fa0/3
```

Task 6:

Now ping 192.168.1.3 from 192.168.1.2.

```
C:\>ping 192.168.1.3

Pinging 192.168.1.3 with 32 bytes of data:

Reply from 192.168.1.3: bytes=32 time<1ms TTL=128
Reply from 192.168.1.3: bytes=32 time=1ms TTL=128
Reply from 192.168.1.3: bytes=32 time<1ms TTL=128
Reply from 192.168.1.3: bytes=32 time<1ms TTL=128

Ping statistics for 192.168.1.3:
    Packets: Sent = 4, Received = 4, Lost = 0 (0% loss),
Approximate round trip times in milli-seconds:
    Minimum = 0ms, Maximum = 1ms, Average = 0ms
```

Task 7:

Check the MAC table on the switch again.

```
Switch#show mac-address-table
Mac Address Table
---------------------------------------------

Vlan Mac Address Type Ports
---- ----------- -------- -----

1  0004.9aac.3587 DYNAMIC Fa0/2
1  00d0.ba48.a838 DYNAMIC Fa0/3
```

Task 8:

You can repeat this lab but with a sniffer attached to the switch (see next lab). You can capture ARP an ICMP to see the two different IP addresses claiming the same source MAC. You may need to clear the switch MAC table with the command 'clear mac-address-table'.

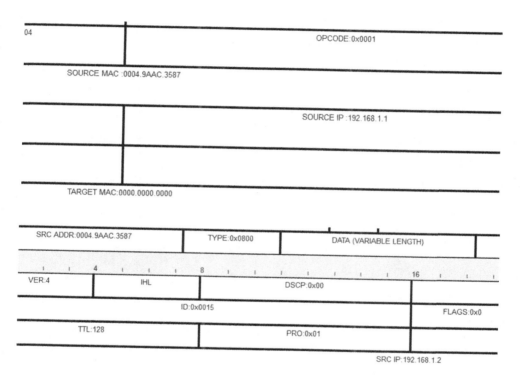

Note:

If you see multiple MAC addresses associated with one port, it usually indicates a trunk interface connected to another switch (or possibly a hub).

LAB 99

Rogue DHCP Server

Lab Objective:

Learn how to troubleshoot a rogue DHCP server operating on your LAN.

Lab Purpose:

We covered DHCP snooping earlier; however, you may well need to troubleshoot a rogue DHCP server on your network before you enable it. This issue can arise when a host machine downloads a virus and begins to allocate IP addresses in an attempt to disrupt your network or spread the virus.

Lab Tool:

Packet Tracer

Lab Topology:

Please use the following topology to complete this lab exercise:

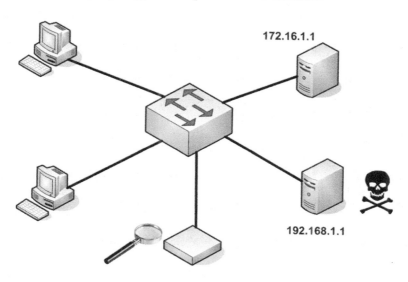

Lab Walkthrough:

Task 1:

Drag a switch, two PCs, two servers, and a sniffer onto the canvas. You can plug them into any ports on the switch with straight-through cables. I usually prefer to use Cisco 2960 switches.

Task 2:

Set the Ethernet interface on the rogue server to 192.168.1.1 and that on the good server to 172.16.1.1.

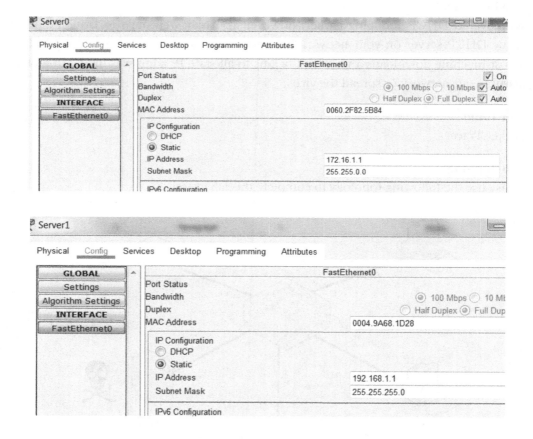

Task 3:

Allocate the DHCP good server pool from the 172.16.0.0 network.

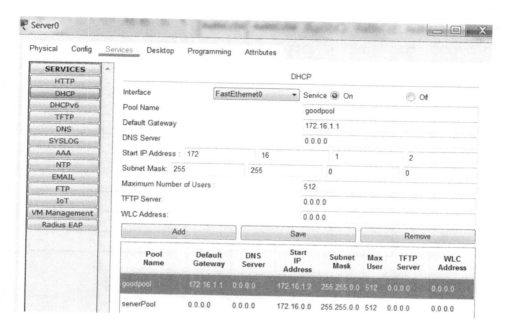

The rogue server should allocate addresses from the 192.168.1.0 pool.

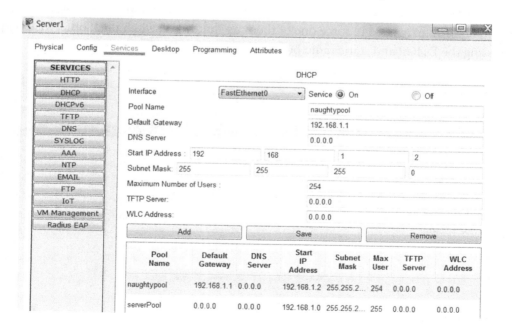

Task 4:

Enable the sniffer to track only DHCP packets.

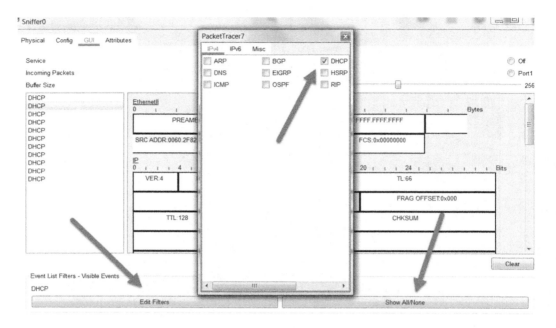

Task 5:

Enable PC0 to obtain addresses via DHCP. It's the luck of the draw which DHCP server responds. You may need to force one of them by shutting a switch port; otherwise keep pressing the DHCP and static radio buttons.

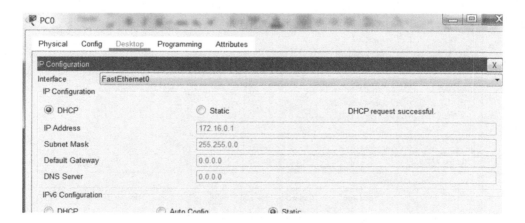

Task 6:

Configure PC1 to obtain an IP address via DHCP. This time I was allocated an address from the rogue server pool.

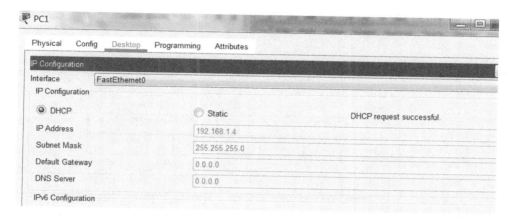

Task 7:

Check through the sniffer captures. Note the source IP and MAC addresses of the allocating servers. The good DHCP server's IP is 172.16.1.1 and the MAC address is 0060.2F82.5B84. As the administrator you would already have a record of this.

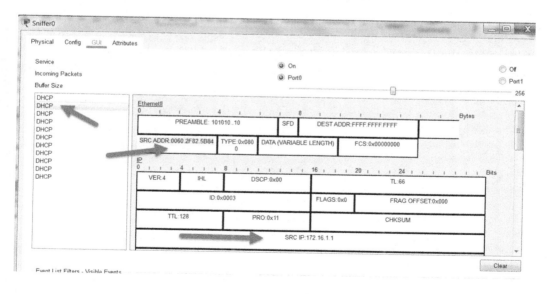

Task 8:

Check the packets sent for PC1. You will see the rogue DHCP IP address is 192.168.1.1 and the MAC address is 0004.9A68.1D28.

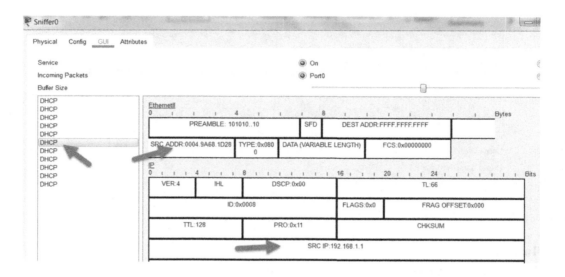

Notes:

Armed with this knowledge you can enable any number of security measures to resolve this issue.

It looks like the Packet Tracer default pool allocated addresses, but don't worry about that—it's more important to see where the packets were sourced from. You could instead, edit the pool PT adds.

Exhausted DHCP Scope

Lab Objective:

Learn how to troubleshoot exhausted DHCP scopes.

Lab Purpose:

As you know from your study guide, DHCP servers allocate groups of IP addresses to hosts. If you have misconfigured your server or your network is over capacity, you can exhaust the pool of available addresses. Users will complain they can't access the network, and you will see hosts self-configuring IP addresses with APIPA addresses (169.254.x.x).

Your options are to increase the address pool size, reduce the lease time, or decrease the number of devices using the pool.

Lab Tool:

Packet Tracer

Lab Topology:

Please use the following topology to complete this lab exercise:

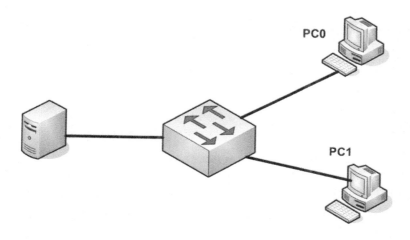

Lab Walkthrough:

Task 1:

Drag a switch, a server, and two hosts onto the canvas. Connect them to any ports on the switch with straight-through cables.

Task 2:

Set the IP address on the server to 192.168.1.1.

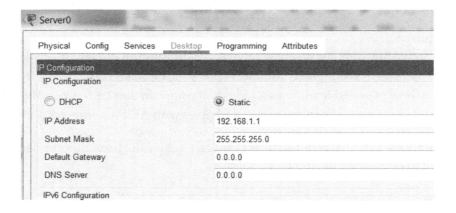

Task 3:

Configure the existing DHCP pool. Turn DHCP service on, start IP address 192.168.1.2, and the maximum number of users will be 1. Remember to click on 'Save'.

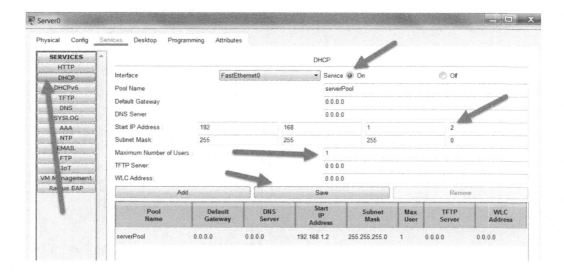

Task 4:

On PC0, set the IP address to be allocated via DHCP.

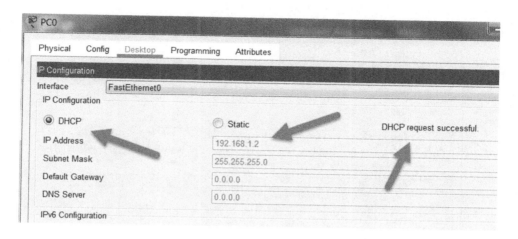

Task 5:

Now do the same on PC1. The DHCP request should fail, and the host will self-configure.

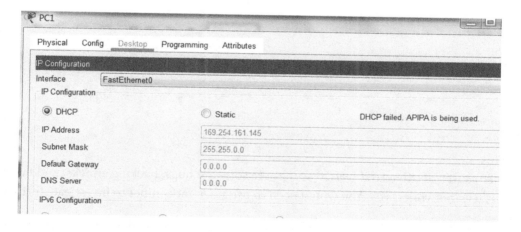

Task 6:

Optionally, turn on simulation mode. You can click on any frame sourced from the DHCP server and see that the pool was exhausted.

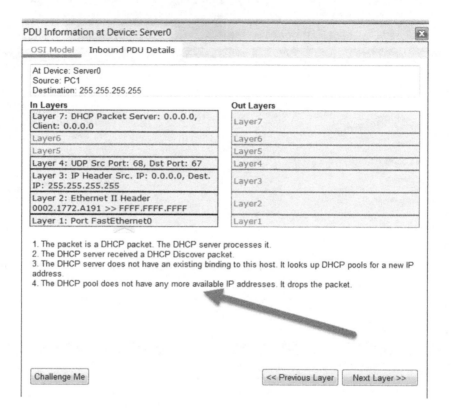

Notes:

Other causes of exhausted DHCP scopes are software bugs, hacking attacks, and faulty interfaces/network cards. You would need to use a network sniffer to investigate further.

Packet Tracer has its own DHCP scope it autoconfigures. You might want to remove that to avoid its interfering with your lab results.

LAB 101

Unresponsive DHCP Service

Lab Objective:
Learn how to troubleshoot an unresponsive DHCP service.

Lab Purpose:
Troubleshooting unresponsive services is an exam syllabus topic. This could cover many types of issues, but I thought we could lab up one I see cropping up quite often with junior network engineers. If the DHCP server resides on a different subnet to the hosts, the broadcasts will be blocked by the router. We'll cover how to get around this by configuring the router to forward the broadcasts for an IP address into a unicast message.

Lab Tool:
Packet Tracer

Lab Topology:
Please use the following topology to complete this lab exercise:

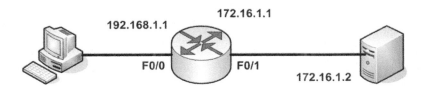

Lab Walkthrough:

Task 1:
Drag a PC, router, and server onto the canvas. To save time and space we will use only one host and no switches. Use crossover cables to connect the devices.

Task 2:

Set the PC-facing interface to 192.168.1.1 and the server-facing interface to 172.16.1.1.

```
Router>en
Router#conf t
Enter configuration commands, one per line. End with CNTL/Z.
Router(config)#int f0/0
Router(config-if)#ip add 192.168.1.1 255.255.255.0
Router(config-if)#no shut
Router(config-if)#int f0/1
Router(config-if)#ip add 172.16.1.1 255.255.0.0
Router(config-if)#no shut
```

Task 3:

Set the server IP address to 172.16.1.2 and the default gateway to the router IP address.

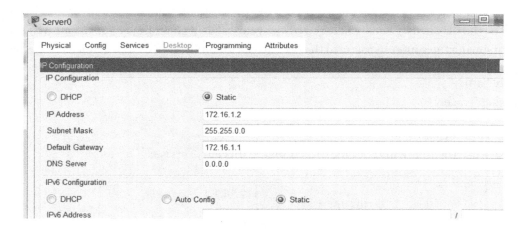

Task 4:

Ping the router from the server to check IP connectivity.

```
C:\>ping 172.16.1.1

Pinging 172.16.1.1 with 32 bytes of data:

Reply from 172.16.1.1: bytes=32 time=1ms TTL=255
Reply from 172.16.1.1: bytes=32 time<1ms TTL=255
Reply from 172.16.1.1: bytes=32 time<1ms TTL=255
Reply from 172.16.1.1: bytes=32 time<1ms TTL=255

Ping statistics for 172.16.1.1:
    Packets: Sent = 4, Received = 4, Lost = 0 (0% loss),
Approximate round trip times in milli-seconds:
    Minimum = 0ms, Maximum = 1ms, Average = 0ms
```

Task 5:

Create a DHCP pool of addresses on the server. Enable DHCP and click 'Add' when done.

Pool—192.168.1.0
Start Address—192.168.1.2
Default Gateway—192.168.1.1

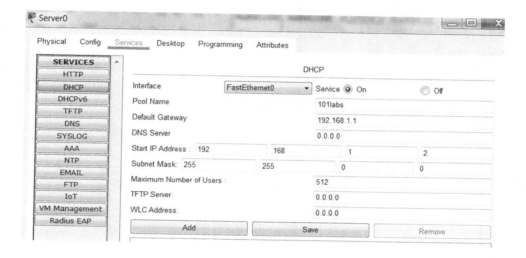

Task 6:

Optionally, enable simulation mode and click to see any DHCP packets.

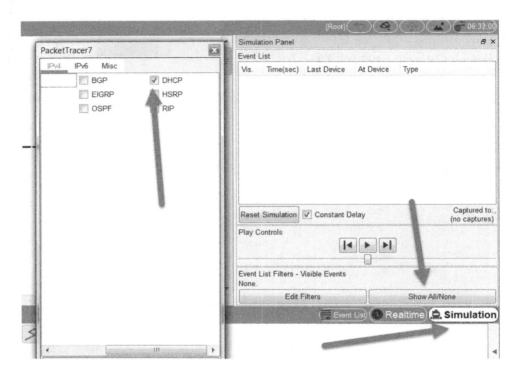

Task 7:

Click on DHCP for PC0. You should see the packet blocked at the router because it does not forward broadcast packets by default.

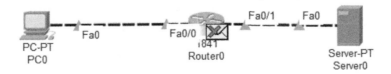

Task 8:

Configure the router to forward DHCP requests to the DHCP server as unicast packets.

```
Router(config)#int f0/0
Router(config-if)#ip helper-address 172.16.1.2
```

Task 9:

Press 'Static' and then 'DHCP' again on the PC to reset the DHCP request. The packet will now be forwarded by the router, and the DHCP address will be allocated.

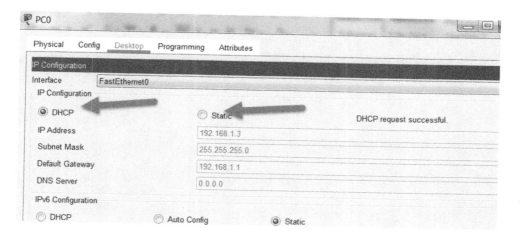

Note:

It's good to know the theory about routers blocking broadcasts, but you also need to know how to fix the problems caused by this default behavior.

Made in the USA
Coppell, TX
08 April 2024

31059213R00299